SINGLE JOURNEY ONLY

Also by Ursula Owen

EDITED VOLUMES

There are Kermodians: A Liber Amicorum For
Frank Kermode with Anthony Holden (1999)
Fathers: Reflections by Daughters (1994)
Whose Cities? with Mark Fisher (1992)

SINGLE
JOURNEY
ONLY

A Memoir

URSULA OWEN

SALT

CROMER

PUBLISHED BY SALT PUBLISHING 2019

2 4 6 8 10 9 7 5 3 1

First published in Great Britain in 2019 by
Salt Publishing Ltd
12 Norwich Road, Cromer, Norfolk NR27 0AX United Kingdom

www.saltpublishing.com

Salt Publishing Limited Reg. No. 5293401

A CIP catalogue record for this book is available from the British Library

ISBN 978 1 78463 187 1 (Paperback edition)
ISBN 978 1 78463 188 8 (Electronic edition)

Typeset in Neacademia by Salt Publishing

Printed and bound in Great Britain by Clays Ltd, Elcograf S.p.A

To my wonderful gang of girls
Kadi, Charlee, Kate with Maya, Tally, Leonie

'Every migration, irrespective of its cause, nature and scale, leads to conflicts. Self-interest and xenophobia are anthropological constants: they are older than all known societies. To avoid bloodbaths and to make possible even a minimum of exchange between different clans, tribes and ethnic groups, ancient societies invented the rituals of hospitality. These provisions, however, do not abrogate the status of a stranger. Quite the reverse: they fix it. The guest is sacred, but he must not stay.'

HANS MAGNUS ENZENSBERGER

'The sense of limitless freedom that I, as a woman, sometimes feel is that of a new kind of being. Because I simply could not have existed, as I am, in any other preceding time or place'

ANGELA CARTER

FIRST JOURNEY

I T'S A CLOUDY March day in 1937. A young woman in her late twenties, dark hair and brown eyes, boards a plane to Berlin at Croydon airport, south of London. The woman is carrying her six-week-old baby. The baby too has brown eyes and a tuft of black hair. My mother later tells me that before the plane reaches Berlin Templehof I start yelling. I am hungry. No German woman at that time may breastfeed her child in public, *das tut man nicht*.

My mother feels intense relief at getting to Berlin, the prospect of being met by my father, being able at last to feed me. As she walks down the steps of the plane and on to the runway with me in her arms, a fellow passenger, English, distinguished-looking with silver hair and elegant grey suit, turns to her and lifts his arm in a mock Nazi salute. 'Goodbye, Madam and baby', he says. And he is gone.

An understandable mistake, my mother always said. 'He

thought I was a Nazi sympathiser, returning to the Fatherland to support my Fuhrer.' And after all, it was 1937 and who but a Nazi sympathiser would be going to Germany with a baby at such a time?

✿

For the first eighteen months of my life Berlin is my home. I don't return there until I'm forty-four, when I've fallen in love with Bill, a man who is completely English – not an un-English gene in him – and he has fallen in love with Central Europe and understands it, culturally and politically, better than I do. I begin to take an interest in the German part of myself, something I've avoided up to now.

In the winter of 1981, Bill takes me to Berlin. I love it immediately; it's full of drama and I discover the subversive vitality Berliners are famous for. It's also full of reminders of the Nazi past. As we wander around the Tiergarten in the biting cold – across the little bridges over the small lakes, through the birch tree woods, down the tree-lined avenues into the open meadows. I imagine how it might have been if this was where I had grown up. We travel on the S-Bahn to Dahlem, the suburb where I lived with my parents and brother for those first eighteen months. I walk down Königin-Luise-Straße and it looks very familiar. There's a watery sun in the sky and it's very cold. I hear German all around me and it sounds like the language I belong to. I have heard it all my life. We reach the place where our house was. I knew that it was no longer there – bombed in 1944. There's a nondescript one-storey building in its place. I walk up the side of it and Bill takes a photograph of me. I begin to weep and I can't stop. I'm thinking about how envious I have so often felt when people are able to claim the place, the house, the territory that they come from. Now I feel overwhelmed by a sense of loss. The past feels like home. I feel an urge to reclaim it, but I don't know how.

2

DISLOCATIONS

IN FEBRUARY 1933, a month after Hitler became Chancellor, my mother, Fips, discovered she was pregnant. My parents were people who planned ahead; they found uncertainty and disorder difficult. A perspicacious friend of the family suggested they must prepare for the worst: Hitler's intentions towards Jews, he said, were clear and malign. My mother should go to England to have her child, giving the baby British citizenship, which would make emigration easier if that time were to come. So, my brother Peter was born, a forceps delivery, on a cold November day in Leeds, where my mother's aunt Flora – part of a branch of the family that had left Germany a generation earlier – had settled. Fips returned to Germany two weeks later.

By the time of Peter's birth, the Nazi Party had already done the groundwork for its brutal regime; the establishment of the first concentration camp, Dachau, the formation of the Gestapo, the beginnings of forced sterilization. My parents had as yet no definite plans to leave Germany. For the time being my father Werner was able to continue his work. He was a chemical engineer in the Jewish family firm, Gesellschaft für Electrometallurgie, GfE – an international company dealing with non-ferrous metals and providing alloys for the German rearmament effort.

But for others in the family, life was deteriorating. By 1933, Werner's sister, sweet round-faced Ilse, three years younger than him, had been prevented from completing her medical studies. In 1935, Hans Sachs, my paternal grandfather was 'retired', for explicitly racial reasons, as director of cancer research in Heidelberg.

At home in Dahlem, Peter, now aged three, repeatedly refused to give the Heil Hitler salute at kindergarten, making my mother increasingly anxious. She herself was regularly defiant. She continued to go into boycotted Jewish shops and at my father's office outing to the 1936 Olympic Games, she refused to raise her arm in salute, shaming the woman next to her into lowering hers. This at a time when Nazi propaganda had manipulated mass opinion and paralysed opponents, when constitutional rights had been suspended, when public humiliation of Jews was commonplace in streets and schools and when living in fear of denunciation or the doorbell ringing at an unusual hour was part of daily life for Jews.

Then Werner accidentally ran his car into an SS officer on a motorbike. He was lucky. The officer rang him that night to say he'd prefer my father not to report the accident as his insurance was out of date. Another reminder that something could happen to them at any time.

At the end of 1936, my mother went to England, this time to

Oxford, again to give birth, where Ilse had settled that year in a community of refugees and sympathetic academics. Peter stayed with my grandparents in Heidelberg. I was born in the Radcliffe Infirmary on January 21 1937, a week later than expected. My father came for the birth but had to hurry back to Germany for work.

It was an easy birth and my mother had family and friends around her. She told me later she loved the hospital staff and felt well looked after, only briefly alarmed when they whisked me off to open up a closed tear duct, returning me to her with a huge bandage round my head. She felt relief at being away from the stresses of life in Germany. It was a happy time for her and she stayed for six more weeks.

Dahlem, to where my mother and I were returning on that March day in 1937, is a prosperous suburb of Berlin, wide tree-lined streets with large villas near woods and lakes. I have a persistent memory of being wheeled in my pram, past the post office, down Königin-Luise-Straße. We lived in a large apartment at number 30. Apparently I cried at night, having got used to night feeds in the Oxford hospital and my parents put me 'in a room in the farthest corner of the flat, where we couldn't hear you' – something of the strictness of a Truby King regime, though I'm sure they knew nothing about him. After a week, my father said, I stopped crying. I have later memories of my mother singing my brother and I to sleep with her light tuneful voice – 'Ah du kleine Augustin', 'GU ten Abend, Guten Nacht'.

We are a family of amateur photographers, my bookshelves full of albums from Fips' and Werner's adolescence onwards. There are photos from the late thirties of the family walking in the

With grandfather Hans and Peter, 1938

woods in nearby Grunewald, Werner in his plus fours, Fips with a patterned scarf round her head, Peter speeding down hills on a sledge in winter, he and I happily sitting on our grandparents' laps in Heidelberg and Frankfurt, or with bucket and spade on a trip to Zoppot, the seaside town on the Baltic Sea where we stayed with my mother's aunt. For some events there are no photos, only stories; none, for instance, of Dahlem's St.-Annen-Kirche where my parents went regularly to hear the Protestant Pastor Niemöller, famous for his opposition to the Nazis, flanked by two Gestapo officers as he gave his sermons. After he was arrested in 1937 and for each day of his eight years in concentration camp, the congregation at Dahlem came together for prayers twice a day.

In 1937, the 'unholy weight of the Nazi machine', as my father described it, descended on Jewish industry and by the end of that year the Jewish management of GfE began organizing a compulsory sale to the most sympathetic 'Aryan' owners they could find.

In 1938 there were new anti-Semitic edicts coming out every few weeks. In March, all Jewish passports were confiscated. After 'endless tedious discussions' GfE was taken over and renamed Reichswerke Hermann Göring, the deal being that the senior staff, including my father and his two cousins, were given permission to emigrate.

The Nazi's infamous Berlin police president, Graf von Helldorff, had to be persuaded to release passports for Werner and his cousins and their families. This involved shouting and bullying which my father described to me in graphic detail. Their colleague, Kurt Dithmer, prepared to go to any lengths to help his Jewish friends get out, faced Helldorff three times before passports were finally issued. Even then, Helldorff decided to keep my father's cousin Ernst temporarily as a hostage in Germany to see how the others 'behaved abroad.' There was no question of compensation, though the new managers were friends of the family and handed back GfE when the war was over.

In July 1938, my mother visited her widowed father Henry in his apartment in Frankfurt. He was old and unwell and she'd decided not to tell him she was leaving Germany – 'though I'm sure he knew,' she said. He died in September that year.

In late July, Fips and Werner left Germany for good. They

left without Peter and me. We stayed with Hans and Lotte, my father's parents, in Heidelberg, where they were still living in middle class comfort, though Hans had by this time lost his job. Like many of their generation, they were still hoping that the 'nonsense' of political extremism would pass, though their hopes were fading. Peter was four and I was eighteen months old.

Much later I questioned my parents about this – why did you go without us? How could you have taken the risk? They replied, vaguely and rather defensively, that they wanted to settle down first, to bring my brother and me over when they'd found somewhere to live.

There is an alternative explanation: given the awful negotiations with the Nazis and having handed over the company, it could be that my father feared that the Nazis had no further use for him, that he and my mother might be arrested as they left. He had signed a certificate, issued by a Nazi office in Berlin, in which he, my mother and my brother and I, resigned from the Jewish Synagogue community and the Jewish religion. I can only imagine what level of fear had induced him to do that.

And it's even harder for me to imagine how they dealt with the contradictions they were living with: on the one hand the fear of the knock on the door in the night; on the other, the insistence, often half conscious, that life goes on, that decisions are made as if these terrors did not exist.

Before they left my parents made sure that Peter and I had each been assigned an exit visa – an official document with a photograph, stamped with a Nazi eagle and the words 'Single

Journey Only.' American Express in Heidelberg provided the £4 12s 6d which despite the gratis stamp, had to be paid.

They sent their books, the crockery, the silver cutlery and crystal glasses, their grand piano, the linen and furniture they'd accumulated over their married life, ahead to England, where it arrived safely a few weeks later. They left Germany with ten Reich marks in cash, worth less than a pound – all they were allowed. When they went through German customs, the official, seeing the large J on their passports, hurried them through without looking at their suitcases, while the SS officer behind them was made to open everything for examination. They were, relatively speaking, fortunate.

A few weeks after they arrived in England, Neville Chamberlain announced that he was to meet Hitler in Berchtesgaden in September, an attempt to keep the peace over the issue of the Sudetenland. My parents, already alarmed at the increasing talk of war, decided to send for us.

In mid-September Hans and Lotte made the arrangements for our journey. Peter and I, he clutching his favourite clockwork rabbit, were taken by an Aryan maid across the Dutch border on the Rheingold train, where my father was waiting to meet us. My grandfather, pipe in hand, came to the border, but, having no exit visa, could not cross over with us.

The three of us caught a plane in Amsterdam, landing in Croydon airport, where my mother and her cousin Dorrie were waiting for us. I'd been sick on the journey and Peter had been playing on the luggage racks; we were tired and scruffy and dishevelled. My mother later told us that Dorrie turned to her in amazement and asked 'Are *these* your children?'

For years I heard this story of our leaving and accepted the way it was told – as unproblematic, routine. My parents usually talked about their experiences in Nazi Germany with the minimum of drama and self-pity. It was years before their fears became apparent to me. Two years before he died, I asked my father whether he'd been frightened at the possibility that the arrangements to get Peter and me out of Germany might have gone wrong. He said yes with uncharacteristic vehemence.

3

LESSONS IN ASSIMILATION

I COME FROM a long line of assimilators. For my family, as for me, being Jewish has been a social, cultural and even psychological inheritance but not a religious one. There was no identification with the idea of a Jewish homeland in Palestine. I don't remember any talk of Israel among my parents or their friends. The story goes that when a question arose about possible emigration to Palestine, my grandfather Hans said that he 'preferred to remain an individual.' Our family never went to synagogue and never celebrated Jewish holidays or festivals. The first time I went to a Seder was in my sixties, with my granddaughter, in the house of friends. I wish I'd taken more part in Jewish life as a child, but there was none available.

But in the 1930s, Jewishness for my family became an inescapable identity. They identified with being part of a persecuted group and took pride in it. When, in the 1990s, twelve branches of the family were together making a property claim over a plot in Berlin, German legal advisers suggested a form of words which indicated the family had emigrated 'on account of their faith'; several of us asked for this to be deleted and replaced with words making clear that their emigration was the result of racial persecution.

My parents were born in Frankfurt in the first decade of the twentieth century, into prosperous Jewish families already highly assimilated into bourgeois German life. My grandparents remained identified with a Germany they thought of as their generation's best.

In the photograph albums I inherit I see my grandparents Hans and Lotte, whose world in the twenties and early thirties was continental Europe, carrying their Baedeker guides, my grandfather in well-cut suits, my grandmother wearing stylish long dresses with lace collars, her thick black hair parted in the middle. There they

Left to right, my father Werner, my aunt Ilse, grandmother
Lotte, grandfather Hans on holiday in Flims, 1928

are, stepping on to trains in Switzerland, sitting on deckchairs on Italian steamers, their handsome brass-bound monogrammed cabin trunks painted across the ends with the imperial German colours, red, white and black, so that they could be easily recognized. They look completely at home and settled, with enough freedom and money to enjoy their comfortable bourgeois life.

There is an ongoing scholarly debate about the virtues and vices of Jewish assimilation into pre-war Germany in particular. Since 1945, assimilation has, it seems to me, been judged more and more harshly, as a way of succumbing to the dominant culture. It is ethnic identity which is seen as desirable, the route to personal satisfaction.

The double identification – Jewish and German – was so much part of my upbringing that I was surprised to discover in my teens that, in the eyes of some Jews, the desire to assimilate is seen as shameful. This sense of shame was particularly aimed at German Jews. Recently a friend told me that when he was working as a graduate in Princeton in 2006, the word 'assimilation' was as hateful in some circles as the word 'nigger'.

I took assimilation for granted. No one particularly made arguments for it. It was just part of our lives.

What was it I was taking for granted? With hindsight and ideally, it seemed like this: you learn the language, keep what's good from your own culture and take what's good for you from other cultures, use familiarity and unfamiliarity to make sense of your world, live with others who are like you and not like you, in places which may not be yours, create a new world for yourself out of other worlds as well as your own, assimilate.

I thought of myself as Jewish and German. I was brought up in a household more German than Jewish in its habits and culture, though it was often hard to distinguish the two. Then, as a child growing up in England, I wanted to be English, to belong to Englishness. I struggled to be at ease with seemingly contradictory desires and identities – which is perhaps not saying more than that I was a person who wanted badly to belong. I, like everyone in my generation – siblings, cousins, second cousins – married out.

વ્ઝ

Assimilation was certainly part of my great grandfather Elias Sachs's thinking. Born in 1829 in Kattowitz, when it was still a village, he started his young adult life shovelling horse manure into carts, which was delivered to the Eisenhütte (iron works) where it was used as fuel. He rose from poverty to great affluence, a successful self-made man of the German industrial revolution, becoming one of the richest men in Prussia. Known in the family as the 'coal king', he acquired several mines in Upper Silesia, set up an iron and steel works and established the first bank in Kattowitz. He became a bürger of the city, which grew rapidly.

At the age of forty-one he married Flora, a woman twenty years younger than him and promptly retired. This early retirement was a mistake. He failed to find enough outlets for his energies and concentrated on the upbringing of his five children. My petite and fierce grandmother, Lotte, his daughter-in-law, always articulate and highly expressive, remembered him as difficult and domineering, forcing his own ambitions on to his children. In 1973, when

Morton Schatzman's book *Soul Murder: Persecution in the Family*,
the study of a man who dominates his sons to the point of driving
them mad, came out, she told me, seething with indignation 'This
was exactly the upbringing of your grandfather and his brothers.'
She was proud of the fact that her husband Hans, the eldest child
and a high achiever, somehow managed to deal with his father's
unbearably controlling behaviour.

Elias wanted to equip Hans with the 'cultural capital' needed
to create the assimilationist dream he shared with many Jews of
his generation. Towards the end of the 19th century it became
possible for Jews to be more active in German culture and society.
Some historians would say that this was the result of Jews aspiring to be Germans, with little help and sometimes considerable
hostility, from Germans. The historian Fritz Stern believes there
was something more – a Jewish-German symbiosis where German
Jews had merged elements of German and Jewish culture into a
unique new one. Whatever the reality, it was almost certainly not
the symbiosis my great grandfather dreamed of.

Born in 1877, my grandfather Hans went to schools where
Jewish children were either a majority or a substantial minority.
Quiet and shy, he was a good pupil and flourished, went to university in Berlin and later Frankfurt. Already there was no possibility,
as a Jew, of a career in surgery and he had to go into the new
medical sciences – he chose bacteriology and serology – the only
ones which promised serious professional opportunities for Jews.

Hans defined himself as a public scientist. He believed in ex-
perimental medical science, in the logic of laboratory work as a
way of trying to contain the scourges of the time – diphtheria,

syphilis, typhus. Together with colleagues, he developed the Sachs-Georgi reaction, the first diagnostic test for syphilis – something my grandmother in her later years delighted in telling anyone who'd listen.

No one would have described my grandmother as shy. There are endless gold-edged sepia photographs of her as a child showing a pretty girl gazing directly and confidently at the camera. She was the eldest child of doting parents, both with strong liberal tendencies. Though her parents divorced, she talked to us of a happy childhood, how close she was to her sisters and especially to her brother Kurt. She made friends easily, though she could be opinionated and bossy – characteristics that stayed with her all her life. Deeply interested in her children's and grandchildren's lives, she never held back from sharp or disapproving comments if she felt they were appropriate.

Lotte met my grandfather Hans when she was still a schoolgirl in Berlin. From the start there was strong attraction between them. Lotte knew her own mind and, overcoming her mother's opposition – she thought that her daughter should make a socially better match – got engaged at nineteen and married Hans at the age of twenty in 1905. Hans and Lotte's birth certificates record them as being Jewish. Though they came from backgrounds of secularization and assimilation, marriage to a Jewish spouse was still expected in their generation. They married in a civil ceremony.

My grandparents with friends in Bring auf Rugen, Germany,
1919. My grandfather in striped swimsuit, my grandmother below
him holding Ilse, my aunt, my father bottom far right

My father Werner was born in 1906, his sister Ilse in 1909. Werner inherited his grandfather Elias Sachs's stubborn spirit and Hans's scientific curiosity and analytic skills. Ilse was, like her father, gently tolerant towards others; Werner from all accounts had a short temper and an obsessional side to his nature as a child. He famously flew into a rage aged eleven when Ilse failed to put his ruler back in exactly the right place. He once tried to throttle a hated governess.

The household they grew up in was steeped in German culture. On the bookcases that lined the sitting room in their tall house in Frankfurt's Bockenheimer Landstraße were the German classics of the eighteenth and nineteenth century, Thomas Mann and Rilke from the twentieth, as well as biographies, political memoirs and letters. English literature was represented by Shakespeare (in translation), some Dickens, Scott and Galsworthy and Lotte's taste in racier novels – Elinor Glyn and Grant Allen's *The Woman Who Did*. They bought Hitler's *Mein Kampf* from the first printing in 1933. There was no outward evidence of an interest in Jewish religion – their menorah was used as a candlestick – and there were no Jewish religious or devotional books, just a book of Jewish history on their shelves, together with a text of Luther's, a copy of Freud's *Moses and Monotheism* and six sermons given by Pastor Niemöller.

A Bechstein grand sat in the corner. Hans was a good pianist and accompanied friends regularly at musical evenings. Werner had flute lessons and became an accomplished player. Ilse learned the piano. There were scores for Wagner operas, the libretto for the *Ring of the Nibelungen*, piano scores arranged for four hands of all the main German classical composers which I got to know well when my father and I later played them together, he taking the bass part, thumping away and counting loudly – '*eins, zwei, drei, vier*' – in his repeated attempts to make me better at sight reading.

Grandmother Lotte Sachs with Werner and Ilse, 1919

Assimilation in my mother's family also involved making fortunes – this time in America during the gold rush. My mother talked to me often of her American heritage; she was proud of it and to a young adolescent the stories of her family's rise to riches on another continent were extraordinarily romantic.

Her grandfather, Feist Livingstone, grew up near Frankfurt and joined his brother, Marks, in California in 1849, where they set up a trading company supplying the gold miners with the goods they needed. It was a highly profitable business, the payments sometimes made in gold dust.

California at that time was flooded with adventurers and fortune seekers. Hundreds of Jews joined the westward movement in search of economic and political opportunity, coming from centuries of oppression and discrimination in Europe.

The original reasons for the brothers going to America are unclear, though Marks was thought to be fleeing debts in Germany, which he later repaid. In America they made their fortune. Around 1870 the brothers went back to Frankfurt to live. They felt they were German and belonged in Germany. Frankfurt had become a lively and liberal metropolis, developing a rich and sophisticated Jewish cultural life – the ghetto abolished, in 1853 Jewish people had been confirmed as having full and equal rights with other citizens. And Jews were playing an increasingly important part in the industrial and commercial life of the city. It was a good time for Feist, now called Frank, to return with his wife Emma and their children. There were three boys and eight girls. The boys all died young, the daughters all survived. The story we were told was that all their marriages were arranged, but only my grandmother Marta's to Henry Boehm was happy. Her sister Flora apparently advised her four daughters never to marry: they never did.

4

MY PARENTS

THREE YEARS APART in age, my parents grew up in those tall bourgeois houses characteristic of Frankfurt's Westend, where about a third of Frankfurt's Jews, roughly 4,000 of them, lived. These were the wealthier Jews, the reformist Liberals and those like my grandparents who didn't practise Jewish rituals at all. Years later when, exhausted after a week at the Frankfurt Bookfair, I met my father there, he took me on a tour of the streets. The exhaustion dropped away as, riveted, I listened to him naming everyone who had lived in the neighbourhood at the time – and what had become of them after the Nazis arrived – exiled to England or America, or taken to the camps.

My mother, a tomboy as a child, was nicknamed Fips after the monkey in the children's book *Max und Moritz*. The name stuck with her for the rest of her life. She grew up in an elegant apartment where tea was served at the same time every day from

*Marta Boehm, my maternal grandmother, with my
mother Fips (left) and her sister Elizabeth, 1912*

a silver teapot. Her sister Elizabeth, to whom she was never close,
was two years older. Fips was devoted to her mother Marta and
very dependent on her support. On my kitchen wall is a photograph of Marta, grave expression, hair swept back, elegant in her
lacey white blouse, arms round the two dark-haired girls sitting
in their long white dresses.

Fips and Werner lived in shouting distance of each other in the
same street, Bockenheimer Landstraße. Some friends described
her as bold, *'ein mutiges madchen'* and outspoken. But according
to others, including her classmate and close friend Ilse, my father's
sister, she was often anxious and insecure, needing a good deal of
reassurance about what she'd said or done. Exceptionally beautiful,

when she was young she wore her dark hair short, later in a fashionable bun; high forehead, freckled nose, full lips and when she was happy, a warm smile. She was a bright pupil, particularly good at maths, persistently late for school, exasperating Ilse, who called to pick her up every day.

Fips was eighteen when her mother died of cervical cancer aged forty-seven. Fips's father Henry was a doctor whose practice in Frankfurt, unusually, included working class as well as middle class patients – though, as my mother would tell me with embarrassment, they came into the practice through separate entrances. His patients called him the 'Jesus of Bockenheim.' Marta operated the radium lamps on Henry's patients – a common practice at the time when the effects of radium were not yet understood. It seems likely that her cancer resulted from this.

Her mother's death left Fips utterly bereft: it was probably the greatest trauma of her life. Even as an old woman she expressed her grief over the death of Marta as if it had happened yesterday.

She remembered nothing about her mother's death, nor of her funeral: she wasn't even sure she had gone to the funeral. Her father withdrew into his grief, while her older sister, already engaged, spent most of her time with her fiancé. 'I survived by going as often as I could to stay with Ilse in the Sachs household,' she told me. She felt welcome there and never forgot the relief of going somewhere where people were laughing and talking; in her own home there had for a long time been only silence and gloom.

The death of her mother left Fips not just grief-stricken – a grief that never became bearable, never seemed to be resolved – but also stranded. Her mother, she recalled, had intended her to go to finishing school, but her father was too stunned by his bereavement to be able to attend to her needs and my mother was too devastated to organize things for herself. What she did was to take up Mensendieck, a fashionable form of gymnastics at the time, popular among some Hollywood stars, in which the participants learn to use their will to relax muscles and release tension, all performed naked in front of mirrors. Fips acquired a diploma as a Mensendieck teacher, but she hated it and pursued this career reluctantly and not for long. What saved her at this difficult time were her friends, young men and women, most of them Jewish, who formed a strong group around her; and particularly the Sachs's, who offered her a haven of cheerful family life.

So it was that, in the late Twenties, my parents began to see more of each other. Their backgrounds were similar culturally – both of them from professional, secularised families who felt themselves to be Jewish and German and saw assimilation as a positive good.

༖

Despite the death of Marta, my parents' accounts of their teenage years and early twenties had idyllic qualities. They were part of a close-knit group of lively and talented young men and women – one of them a future Nobel Prize winner, Hans Bethe, a theoretical physicist who worked on the formula for the H-bomb and for the rest of his life sat on committees to try and prevent the bomb being dropped. He fell in love with my mother though she turned him down because he had dirty finger nails: 'I was stupid,'

Fips and Werner, second and third from left, Ilse second from right,
with companions on a winter ski trip in Switzerland, 1931

she told me. Siblings (though noticeably not my mother's sister), cousins, intimate friends went to dancing classes and on ski trips together – the photo albums tell the story. Ten or twelve laughing young people lined up with their skis, in shirt sleeves, waistcoats and ties – the girls as well as the boys – in beautiful mountain scenery; or sitting, with goggles on their heads, in deckchairs and on sledges in front of mountain huts and small hotels. They produced a cyclostyled magazine, *Die Lawine* (the Avalanche), with witty accounts of their ski trips, their friendships, who was flirting with whom, in prose and poetry.

My mother featured prominently. There are photos of her in her early twenties, sploshing in the sea, black hair dishevelled, arms waving in the air, or standing on her skis, relaxed, slim with broad hips, in deep snow. She is often laughing, sometimes shyly but often with a directness of gaze and a defiant boldness which eclipses the others.

By then my father and mother had been seeing a lot of each other. My father, a talented scientist, after leaving school attended the Max Planck Institute in Munich, becoming one of its star pupils, studying chemical engineering. In 1932 they married. I see in the wedding photos this handsome couple, my father solemn and serious, his black hair parted, my mother in a short white dress with a veil keeping her smooth hair drawn back, smiling tentatively, looking like Ingrid Bergman. Both are looking straight ahead. To me now there are omens in these photographs of their difficult later times – of anxieties and incomprehension.

My parents, Fips and Werner, on their wedding day, Frankfurt, October 11th 1932

Over all this was the shadow of Nazism. In 1933, the year Hitler won power, Werner and Fips moved to Berlin. My father had joined the family firm owned by his uncle Paul Grunfeld. The non-ferrous metal industry was rapidly developing in Germany, not least under the spur of the secret rearmament programme. Gesellschaft für Electrometallurgie was involved in the manufacture of armour-piercing bullets, a programme that increased demand for tungsten ores and the business of the family's Nurnberg works. (Ironically, a decade later my father was working for the same purpose for the British Ministry of Supply).

My mother disliked the set-up in Berlin: the Grunfelds were a rich and powerful family and seemed to dominate their lives too much. She felt marginalized, less at home in Berlin than Frankfurt at first; she remembers being reproached for telephoning my father at the office. My father went to work every day. My mother, by now pregnant with Peter, stayed at home.

A few months after my father had moved to the head office, the offices of one of the constituent firms in the Ruhr were ransacked by SA storm troopers. Several of the senior Jewish scientists and managers had to withdraw from the works in Nurnberg, where anti-Semitism was particularly rife.

By April 1933, Jewish students were forbidden to attend schools and universities. By September 1935, the anti-Semitic Nuremberg Laws were passed, those endless dirges of horrifying bureaucracy, which were the basis for the exclusion of Jews from all public business life. By November that year Jewish children were banned from using the same playgrounds and locker rooms as other children.

❧

I try to imagine my parents' life in Berlin. I read memoirs of the time, look again and again at family photographs, at letters, try to remember conversations. I want to know what they felt and thought, what they knew, what they talked about to each other. Standing in the garden of what was their villa in Dahlem in 1981, when I was forty-four, I wondered whether I'd imbibed through being their child a generational feeling of that time. Fips and Werner told anecdotes, often vivid, about their lives. But they were part of a generation, and a class, that didn't encourage questions, that avoided probing, difficult conversations, taboo subjects. And yet I know too that some of this was about protecting us – above all from fear. I wish I'd asked more questions. Did they encounter anti-Semitism in their private lives? Did their assimilation protect them? How much did fear interfere in their daily lives? Perhaps they understood exactly what the parameters of their world were and stuck to them. How were they affected by being forbidden certain areas, socially and professionally? Unlike my grandparents, I never heard them say that they thought the Nazi influence would pass, that people would come to their senses. I think they understood the lure that the Nazis offered – a sort of liberation from the self into mindless belonging – and recognised its power.

How was their cultural life affected as the Nazi edicts against Jews grew? Berlin was an extraordinary cultural hub. For Fips and Werner classical concerts and theatre were the main features of their cultural life and Jews were not forbidden to attend such events until September 1938. They'd been well-educated in German and to some extent in English literature, with their leather-bound Shakespeare, Schiller and Goethe on the bookshelves. They didn't go to the cabaret performances in the bars of Berlin that I read about later in Christopher Isherwood's books; that was not their world. My father in particular always had strong views on what was 'good' in culture and shied away from anything too provocative. Years later, I asked him what he thought about a performance he'd seen of Strindberg's *The Dance of Death*, a savage account of a disastrous marriage. 'For me', he said loftily, 'this play need not have been written'.

When in 2011, I visit the Topography of Terror museum in Berlin, which lays out in devastating detail the speed with which the Nazi Party acted to change things, I wonder what my parents' responses were: to the establishment of Dachau, after thousands had been taken into 'preventive detention', sometimes using bars and people's front rooms for this, after the Reichstag fire; the street battles; the public book burning, the political murders, the removal of opposition parties, the banning of Jewish physicians and lawyers. They certainly knew of the boycott of Jewish shops in 1933; my mother told me how she deliberately went into them – and how that wasn't always welcome for the frightened shopkeepers.

My mother insisted later that she saw dangers everywhere but that my father didn't want to talk about them or even necessarily recognize them. Perhaps by not talking about his fears he could manage them. He was able to work till 1937 and when Fips talked about how late she felt they had left Germany, he insisted that it had taken a lot of time and organizing to do the necessary things – get exit visas, hand over the company, prepare for exile. They never agreed about this.

5

A NEW-FOUND LAND

Ah, what an age it is
When to speak of trees is almost a crime
For it is a kind of silence about injustice
BERTOLT BRECHT

THE RELIEF MY parents Fips and Werner felt at being in England was palpable – they told me later of the pleasure they felt at taking refuge in a country where, in 1938, arriving from Nazi Germany, the burning issue in the Letters columns of *The Times* concerned the condition of laburnum trees. My mother warmed to the English and particularly liked what she saw as an English tendency to play down tension and chaos, to be quiet and calm and above all humorous in the face of troubles. It was not the German way – both my parents were inclined to respond expressively, even explosively to what was happening around them.

Considering how disorientated they must have felt, how cut off from their old world, how traumatic the recognition that there was no place for them in their own country, they seemed to have adjusted to their new circumstances – with the support of the four Hesse sisters, my mother's cousins, all musicians, whose parents had emigrated in an earlier generation. And on the surface at least they adjusted fast.

For them the most important matter was that their children should become integrated into English life. North London, where many Jewish refugees had settled was not, in their eyes, the route to assimilation.

They found a house in a suburban street in South West London, which they first rented and later bought. 19 Tideswell Road in Putney was a plain Edwardian house, a solid yellow and red brick affair two storeys high, detached, double fronted. Two small squares of grass with bordering beds full of primulas and grape hyacinths made up the front garden; a pyracantha, bright orange berries in winter, surrounded the porch. At the back of the house the French windows led on to a lawn surrounded by beds where spring brought daffodils and tulips and my father grew roses and tomato plants for summer ripening. He loved gardening, mowed the lawn regularly, in straight lines, tipping the cut grass on to a compost heap under the apple tree. We were assigned weeding jobs, which for a long time discouraged me from garden-ing altogether. At the end of the garden a large pear tree stood next to the high brick wall, separating us from the grander houses in parallel Gwendolen Avenue where, in adolescence, I spent hours after school batting a tennis ball till it was too dark to see.

Downstairs in the house the dark hallway was made darker by the coloured glass in the windows. The rooms were filled with our large furniture from Germany – the matching dining table, chairs, sideboard and glass cupboard, all in cherry wood – wedding presents to my parents which now live with me – and the desk and grand piano in my father's study.

Apart from the kitchen, I never felt much comfort in that house. An observant friend once said that she felt it had no history – that it seemed frozen, with no past or future. The rooms were tidy and somehow empty of life. If they expressed anything it was a kind of careful feeling of the way – not much intimacy, no bold statements, no comfortable places to settle into, no objects scattered about to catch the attention or make you feel at home, hardly any photographs – a few rather drab framed photographs of Riemenschneider carvings on the wall up the staircase, a photo of my grandfather on my father's desk – that was all. There were some signs of my parents' past life – they had after all brought many of their belongings from Germany. Yet somehow these things didn't seem to connect us with each other or our history.

Perhaps the house reflected the isolation Fips and Werner felt at leaving their life behind. Later, when my parents divorced, my mother chose to fill her new flat with family photos and objects from her past. Later still, I filled my own house to overflowing with photographs, obsessively, on every shelf, fading and bending, my grandparents, parents, my daughter, friends, lovers – constant, perhaps rather anxious reminders of who I was, where I came from, where I placed myself.

It was a strange social mix, this street my parents had chosen to live in, with its pollarded plane trees and small, neat front gardens, its little plots of tidy suburbanism more tightly congregated than the spacious villas they were used to in Königin-Luise-Straße. They found comfort in the kind, reserved and austere neighbourliness.

At the top of the road sat the Catholic Church. On the dot of twelve on Sunday mornings the church doors opened and streams of people came out of Mass, down our street and scattering in all directions. As a wistful and moody teenager I leaned out of my bedroom window watching them till they had all disappeared, thinking how fired up they seemed, how full of energy.

The people who now live in Tideswell Road are lawyers, television executives, marketing directors. In the 1940 and 50s they were bank clerks, accountants, teachers, people running small businesses, many of them outsiders and eccentrics. The houses exuded a rather melancholy mystery, secrets I felt I would never understand; the shell-shocked man in the house opposite, ill and unshaven, in his darkened house; the friendly Plymouth Brethren family next door, with their six children who weren't allowed to play with me because of their religious beliefs, but who kept a careful eye on my mother during air raids when my father was away. Two doors down, the Dickensian spinster sisters: grim, upright, dressed in tweed suits and spotless white blouses. Their long-suffering live-in servant Nellie, tiny, her face full of sadness and anxiety, was a friend of Dolly's, our daily help.

Dolly, barely five feet tall, with her elfin weathered face and equable temperament, never vehement or angry, became intertwined in the dailiness of our life so quickly that it was hard for me to remember when she first came and what it had been like before her. She was something of a rock for us.

I was close to Dolly. As I became a teenager she would bring me her women's magazines – 'books' she called them – which I devoured, each one, knitting patterns, features about birth, children, illness, make up, recipes and, above all, stories, love stories, usually about difficult but fascinating men and adoring women learning to understand them. I stopped reading books. My father began to despair about my reading habits and tried to thrust classic novels at me. None of it worked.

And I confided in Dolly. She listened patiently, never making judgements, while I told her things I was feeling about my family, my jealousy of my sister, my anxiety about my mother, my fear of exclusion with friends at school. And she told stories about her life as a single mother, of her mother's life in service, regularly beaten once a week by her employer just to remind her of her place. Dolly confided in me that Nellie too was beaten, by the sisters. I was haunted by that.

Ours is a bilingual household – they speak German to us, we speak English back. We learn each other's languages and in my head they merge into one. Much later, I realize that I don't feel entirely at home in English, that I have a small vocabulary, that I often speak in translation. 'I had three eggs already and Grandpa often does accompany me at the piano,' I write to my parents when I am eight years old. Jokes, rather German-style, about the English language feature regularly when my parents are with their refugee friends, producing gales of laughter. 'A refugee from Germany is asked by an acquaintance what his name is. "Mackintosh," he replies.

'Yes, but what was your name before that?'

⁂

Fips and Werner had always been interested in the Christian opposition to Hitler – they read theologians Dietrich Bonhoeffer and Pastor Niemöller and heard them preach. Now, in England, they joined the Anglican Church. So it was that on a sunny day in the spring of 1939 Fips and Werner were confirmed and Peter and I were christened, in St Mary's Church in the High Street in Oxford. My mother started teaching at Sunday School. They had personal support from Canon Cockin of Winchester Cathedral, who gave so much help to Jewish immigrants. Werner Simonson, my parent's friend who had been a judge in Germany, was re-training to become an enthusiastic Anglican vicar, his first parish in working class Dalston in East London. He supported their conversion.

It's easy to dismiss my parents' conversion as a somewhat craven desire to belong, but nothing as simple as that makes sense to me. Christianity continued to mean something to them both for the rest of their lives. We regularly walked to the church bordering on Wimbledon Common for Sunday morning services when we were children. I liked the hymns and can still recite most of them by heart, but apart from a brief flirtation with Billy Graham's ideas (learned from a school friend) in my teens, I felt unengaged with Anglicanism, finding the sermons dull and my confirmation lessons uninspiring, engaging with rather banal versions of girlhood and adolescence while I had by then read *Peter Abelard* by Helen Waddell and wanted to engage in passionate issues of faith, sex and love. My sister was drawn to a Christian community in her teens where she escaped from home and spent holidays; my brother became a seriously committed Christian at his boarding school and has remained one ever since.

Once we had grown up, my father stopped being much of a churchgoer, but he kept up with changing ideas in Christianity, reading Teilhard de Chardin and Bishop Robinson's *Honest to God* when they came out. For my mother, in her later years, the church near her house in Oxford and its vicar, became a central part of her life.

But for both of them being Jewish remained an integral part of their identity and it continued to be the way they described themselves to themselves and to other people.

I suppose in Germany in the Thirties my parents would have seen themselves as Isaac Deutscher's 'non-Jewish Jew' – solidarity with the persecuted, feeling the pulse of Jewish history, supporting the security and self-respect of the Jews. And culturally they lived lives as German Jews which for them had a distinctive though unreligious quality.

What happened, when they converted to Christianity, to their embracing of Jewish race and culture? We as children growing up in England learned a great deal about the place of Christianity in our cultural life, much of it at school and from our peers. Jewish culture, imbibed from our parents and other relatives, was always separated from Jewish religion. And was it Jewish culture? Or for us simply the cultural life of a certain kind of bourgeois German?

Though they'd decided to settle where few Jews were living, Fips and Werner's closest friends during the war were fellow Jewish refugees, who regularly came over for supper. I remember particularly a lawyer and his wife, also converts to Christianity, she an outspoken woman with sharp features and a startlingly blue nose, witty but often depressed and anxious, talking more openly about the horrors of Nazi Germany than my parents. When I was old enough to be at table, I made myself as inconspicuous as possible and sat silently listening to their stories of narrow escapes, of German collusion with the Nazis and, memorably, of encounters with Germans who 'behaved well' - work colleagues, people in the streets, casual encounters with officialdom.

And like all good stories, they were told often and each time I waited for the endings as if I'd never heard them before. They were relieved to be safe and there were roars of laughter about their attempts to make sense of their new life. They were learning the funny side of being exiles - my parent's handbook being George Mikes' *How to Be an Alien*, from which they read extracts at the supper table. These evenings were rare periods when I saw my parents being playful.

There were dark stories and dark thoughts, certainly and fears for people who were not yet safe. Werner Simonson in particular was permanently worried about his wife and son while they were still in Germany. Most of our family had managed to get out. But there were two relatives for whom there were serious concerns. My mother's aunt from Zoppot – I still picture my mother saying angrily, in sadness and exasperation, 'she couldn't keep her mouth shut about what she thought about the Nazis' – had been taken from her house and no one knew where she was. Eventually we learned she'd been killed in Auschwitz. The other relative was my grandmother's brother, Kurt, whose reluctance to grasp what Hitler had in mind for Jews meant that he left the attempt to emigrate too late. He and his wife Greta sent their children to safety, to a private boarding school in Switzerland, in 1939. Kurt was arrested while on a visit to Belgium in May 1940, deported to France and interned in various camps. His wife, who was not Jewish, went to join him there in 1941 and together they tried to get visas to Switzerland. The family made every attempt to help them. But all efforts failed. They were sent to Auschwitz in 1942 and were killed there the same year.

※

For these suppers, my mother made the most of wartime rations, putting on her white cotton apron, tucking her hair behind her ears when it escaped from her neat bun. She'd brought her handwritten recipe books with her from Germany. She was a good cook and resourceful at managing on what there was – sieving sour milk through muslin cloths to make into a sort of yoghurt, making soups with meat bones, Verschleiretes Bauernmadchen pudding with a few precious eggs, apfelmus, using the apples and pears we'd wrapped in newspaper in the summer to preserve them. She seemed to organise domestic life in her new surroundings without too much difficulty; she was touched by the slightly remote friend-liness she found around her, the gentleness and understatement of English people, their non-authoritarian way of speaking.

❦

My father quickly settled into work. Within six weeks of arriving in England and even though they had come out of Germany with no money, he and his cousins had been able, with financial support from the Swedish branch of the company and some income from the tungsten mines in Bolivia and Turkey, to set up new offices for the family firm in London. They began with portable type-writers in the drawing room of 3 Hyde Park Gate but soon moved what was now called the London and Scandinavian Metallurgical Company to Wimbledon.

And so their new life began. My father's behaviour remained much more German – peremptory, talking loudly, charming, bossy. They both spoke and read English competently, my mother the more fluent, though they kept their guttural accents to the end of their lives. Fips got to know neighbours and local shopkeepers, though not without anxiety – she was often unsure whether she had got things right, whether she'd offended. While my brother was at school, she took me shopping with her, sometimes walking, sometimes riding on the back of her bike. I was often cold and chilblains were a constant part of my life in winter. At breakfast Werner read *The Times*. The news on the radio was switched on most evenings, news from Germany eagerly awaited. Later, I became aware of other regular radio favourites too – Tommy Handley in *ITMA*, Kenneth Horne in *Much Binding in the Marsh* and the Trollope play on Sunday night – all routes to learning about England, especially about the English sense of humour, which had acquired something of a mythical status in our family.

By late 1938 there was still family in Germany, unsafe, a cause of worry. In November 1938, the night of Kristallnacht, my mother's sister, her two children and husband left Germany and came to stay. We heard the drama of their story again and again over the years. Having been warned by telephone that they would be rounded up by the police, Otto and Elizabeth and the children took a train for Holland. At the German border, they were made to get off, detained all day, without food or drink till my aunt insisted on milk for the children. One of the storm troopers asked whether anyone had anything of value. Dot, aged eight, spoke up brightly. 'I do.' Everyone froze until her thing of value turned out to be a gold-coloured paper ring. They arrived in England penniless.

The sisters had always been rather at odds with each other; there was tension in the house, sharp words, raised voices. We all felt it. My parents found Alex, my five-year-old cousin, wild and naughty. He wore T-shirts, of which they disapproved, was naturally defiant, cut the tassels on the living room Persian carpet, threw a pair of scissors at my brother. I watched, a fascinated two-year-old, as the two boys fought. To Fips and Werner's relief the Wormsers moved to Wimbledon after a few weeks. There their possessions from Germany arrived – the Opel car, the baby grand Steinway, art that Otto had collected over the years. America was where they wanted to go but US immigration policy didn't allow whole families to immigrate. In 1940 the children and Otto found places on a boat. Elizabeth had to stay, and found a job in the Lake District as a hotel maid. Finally, in 1942, she was allowed to go to the USA. It took three months for the boat to get across the Atlantic and by the time she arrived in Montreal her visa had expired and she was put in jail for a week before she was finally reunited with her family. Her hair had turned completely white over the two years she was separated from her family and she would later say that she feared that her children wouldn't like her when they were reunited. She needn't have worried.

And then in late December 1938 my grandparents arrived in London. It had been a long, protracted leaving. By 1934, a publication ban for Jews had been brought in; the number of students in Hans's classes was dwindling; and two of his most important co-workers, both Jewish, had emigrated. He was still able to travel, but in 1935 Jews lost equal citizenship under the Nuremberg racial laws and he was categorically dismissed. The letter he received translates 'The Home Secretary for the Reich and for Prussia has decreed that, in accordance with the Law of September 15 1935, employees with either three or four grandparents of Jewish race or religion, will be placed on immediate retirement. In accordance with instructions from the Education Minister in Karlsruhe you meet the requirements of this law. You are therefore given leave of absence from service'.

He now saw the writing on the wall and started looking for academic jobs abroad, Britain being his first choice; but all attempts failed, perhaps partly because he was by then considered an old man (he was fifty-eight).

Peter and I had left Lotte and Hans for England in early September. Friends begged them to leave. They were still reluctant.

Then, on November 9, Kristallnacht. One thousand synagogues were destroyed or damaged, 7,000 Jewish-owned shops were vandalized; 30,000 Jewish men were arrested and taken to camps at Buchenwald, Dachau and Sachsenhausen. At 5.00 a.m. there was a knock on my grandparents' door. A Gestapo officer stood on the doorstep. Hans and Lotte both thought this was the end for them, that they would be taken away. But Otto Westphal was a former pupil of my grandfather's, who had joined the Nazi Party in 1933 in a spirit of hope, believing that Hitler would save Germany. His disillusionment came quickly, but he couldn't leave the Party. He had made it his business to knock on people's doors in the early hours to warn them to flee. Finally, my grandparents knew they had to leave.

There followed an anxious time, not least because of the cat and mouse games the authorities played over granting the permits needed to emigrate, which involved giving up all their financial assets. Hans and Lotte were still having trouble getting British visas. Finally, the British Consul in Frankfurt, Mr Smallbones, wrote: 'The organization in the Home Office has broken down and there is no hope of getting a decision from them about your case in a reasonable time'. Upon which Mr Smallbones issued the visa himself. He was one of the officials commemorated by Rabbi

Julia Neuberger in her book *On Being Jewish,* for their 'kindness and actions beyond the call of duty, against government policy.' He issued, with other colleagues, over 50,000 visas to Jewish immigrants to Britain.

My grandfather, filled with apprehension and pessimism, went from room to room, trying to decide which books and belongings to take, calling out '*Ecrasez, ecrasez!*' Lotte, less introspective and less involved in the emigration formalities, remained calmer and more optimistic.

I was so excited the day they arrived in London, going to look in the street again and again to see whether there were here yet. Relieved to be safe, they were overwhelmed with pleasure at seeing us again. But they were still not certain where they would eventually settle. They were short of money, most of it having been seized by the Nazis and deposited into the Nazi Golddiskontbank.

In February 1939, Hans was offered a post at the Institute for Advanced Studies in Dublin. It meant he and Lotte would be separated from the family and from German-speaking company. But the job was interesting and he hadn't received any offers in England.

He went to Dublin in March on an exploratory visit. A few weeks later, he and Lotte rented a flat at 3 Palmerston Villas. In May he wrote to his banker friend, Frau Brenning, 'We are finding things rather difficult, as we are really lonely here and have no contact with any Germans, which we certainly had in London. But at least we are glad to be living again amongst our own furniture although much of these were damaged during their long travels.'

The grant Hans received, £500 a year, allowed them to rent a spacious flat in a nice part of Dublin. They could afford domestic help. They seem to have recreated much of the setting of their life in Heidelberg. In my grandfather's obituary, Kees Van Joek, a colleague, wrote 'no other Dublin house had, quite like his, the atmosphere of Continental culture from all the wall-covering bookcases to the graceful porcelain in which coffee was served – it remained Heidelberg, transported to Dublin.'

There were also, Hans wrote to my mother Fips, 'the pleasures of curiosity which prevailed at first.' They quickly established a musical evening at their house every Monday, with Hans accompanying his singer friends. Above all they made friends. They were warm, gregarious, particularly Lotte, and hospitable, their friendships eventually developed in both the German-speaking Jewish refugee community in Dublin and with a large circle of Irish people.

They had found some sort of a home.

6

OUR WAR

MY PARENTS DISCOVER the route to assimilation early. We, their children, will be their English representatives in their new-found land. They won't try to be English themselves – they're shrewd enough to know they'd never succeed.

I turn out to be a brilliant assimilator. A conformist child, I learn the rules assiduously and take to them easily. I work hard at being a little English girl – antennae alert, imitative behaviour where it seems appropriate and a good deal of silence. And I live a double life without being conscious of it. It isn't until my late teens that I begin to understand I am in an important way a foreigner. Later still, in my work and political interests, I begin to see that being an outsider is a sort of gift, bringing a particular sort of energy. With hindsight I see that politics entered my life long before I had the faintest notion of what politics was.

Is it justified to feel an exile in a country in which I was born and returned to at the age of eighteen months? Looking back, the odd thing is that I felt so English for so long. My parents spoke with strong German accents and small English vocabularies, we ate German food, our cultural and family life was almost entirely German/Jewish in its patterns and habits – the rather rigid, black and white opinions about people, books, politics: the reluctance to break routines; our traditional Christmas celebrations on Christmas Eve; my father the orderly, patriarchal figure. Great emphasis was placed on punctuality and I have been anxious about being late all my life. My parents both had short tempers and had no hesitation in shouting when they were annoyed or angry. For them it was not a social taboo, as it was in their adopted country. I inherited this shouting characteristic and have always felt disapproval for it.

In *English Journey*, published in 1933, J. B. Priestley writes that in England there was depression, unemployment and 'liberty not as much as I'd like but a good deal more than in other countries'; he describes England as 'a country of a free and generous temper.' The English are a decent people and they will give some people refuge from some situations, some of the time. But, like most host nations, they have problems when immigrants stand out, don't become enough like their hosts, don't fit in. In 1989, I heard the historian Bill Williams give a talk on Jewish immigration to Britain at the end of the nineteenth century. He described a list that was produced by the indigenous Jewish community for the new immigrants, telling them what to avoid – speaking their own language in public places, talking loudly in the street, wearing the wrong clothes – anything that made them appear un-English. I recognized all these as features my own family had failed to avoid.

The average Briton knew very little, if anything, about the horrors of Nazi Germany, which were officially played down in Britain. Though I was too young to be aware of it, Germans in England at the outbreak of war were, as enemy nationals, particularly vulnerable; and for German Jews there was also anti-Semitism to deal with. Harold Nicholson, the writer and diplomat, said at the time 'Although I loathe anti-Semitism, I do dislike Jews.' He was not alone. There are many personal accounts of asides about money, casual references to the size of Jewish noses, the odd disparaging remark about flashiness, how clever Jews are, how good at making money. These were irritating rather than seriously hostile or threatening remarks, or so I was led to believe. My parents never talked about experiencing anti-Semitism in England.

By the time war broke out in 1939, my father's company was helping the British war effort by supplying non-ferrous metals and alloys to the British steel industry. There was never any question of Werner being interned, because of his useful expertise, though his cousin Ernst was sent to the Isle of Man for a while because he wasn't, as my father was, qualified as a metallurgical expert. In a world of paranoid suspicion aroused by the wartime Defence of the Realm Act ('See Everything, Hear Everything, Say Nothing') the story goes that Ernst stopped a policeman in the street and pointed to a star, saying he thought it was a German plane and was immediately taken in for internment. My mother's elderly aunt Adele was sent to Holloway Prison for no explicable reason but was rescued by her niece after a week.

I was too young to be frightened by the early air raids. In 1940, when my father was away on business, our Plymouth Brethren neighbours fetched us over to their house in the middle of a night attack of incendiary bombs. Peter was terrified. I was three and as my mother carried me next door I saw the bombs raining down as pretty lights twinkling in the sky. But I still remember the frozen fear in my parents' eyes four years later, when they sat with me, in bed with flu, as a V1, an unmanned flying bomb, came noisily over our house; the sound cut off, as it always did, then the terrifying bang as it dropped about half a mile away, destroying houses and shops and creating a huge crater near the railway line.

In 1941, the Blitz at its height, Peter and I were evacuated to

With brother Peter, Oxford 1940

Oxford with my mother. Ilse was still living there, now with her new physicist husband Arthur. She helped us find a home with the Grensteds, a charming but daunting elderly English couple, he a pillar of the Oxford Movement, the High Church movement of the Church of England.

I was four years old and was sent to Oxford High School round the corner, where I remained overwhelmingly shy and was regularly teased by a pugnacious boy in my class. An early report read: 'Ursula seems to be an intelligent girl but she does not speak.' My aunt Gitta, a professional photographer, took photos of us at the time – my brother and I huddled affectionately together, he in a checked shirt, his arm slung round my shoulder looking confidently at the camera, me in a long sleeved Viyella dress with a necklace, black hair parted at the side with a slide, giggling.

But I was bemused by everything, alert to every change in our lives, the move and living in this strange household with these kindly but strict people, very Christian and with rules and routines very different from our normal family life. One day I was sent home from school early because it was snowing and I walked home but didn't dare ring the bell, too worried about breaking the routine, being a nuisance. My mother eventually found me shivering on the doorstep.

After eighteen months we moved back to London, where, now five years old, I went to Putney High School Junior School in Lytton Grove, still overwhelmingly shy, with a strong desire to please – always punctual for classes, always neat, standing up straight, always doing my work, waiting to hear what others said before I spoke.

1942 was a bad year for the family. It was then that they finally heard that Lotte's brother Kurt, who had been arrested and interned as an enemy alien in Brussels where he was working in 1940, then sent to Vichy France where he had written to them from various prison camps – had, with his wife, who had joined him, not wanting to be separated from him, been transported east and was therefore beyond help. The chilling narrative of their journey to Auschwitz is inscribed on the monument erected by the French government in Roglit, in Israel.

That same year Ilse had a stillborn child. Hans's letters from Ireland to my father and mother also dwelled on anxieties – he had prostrate and kidney trouble – and he asked Ilse to send medicines from England. And he was increasingly aware that he wasn't working as he wished. 'It was always clear to me that I am not a pure researcher. I do not have the broad talents for that.' He missed working in partnership with others, feeling at times his work life as full of 'restrictions and impossibilities'.

And he was missing the family. He wrote to my mother that same year: 'I feel more and more the loneliness to which we are sentenced. Yesterday we were on the pier at Kingstown and attended the arrival of the mailboat. It was very crowded with holiday-makers and we watched if somebody of our children or grandchildren would alight. But no surprise! This is perhaps the most characteristic feature of the life in advanced age that no surprises happen. Although I am well aware of the situation it is sometimes very difficult to be accustomed. This may, however, not be altered and we must be satisfied with the relatively good conditions in which we live. So we are.'

What I remember most vividly about the war is the arrival of my sister Ruth, born in 1943, in a small nursing home in Wimbledon, in the middle of an air raid. My mother regaled us with stories about the nursing home – that she had to find a phone and ring the doctor herself when her contractions started in the middle of the night, that there wasn't a nurse around. After the birth, my brother and I were sent away so that my mother would have time to recover at home with the new baby. I went to stay with a grim elderly Jewish émigré couple who lived close to my father's office in Wimbledon – he small and with a hunchback, she tall and heavily made-up – a new experience for me. They didn't know what to do with me or how to talk to me, and had a habit of resting every afternoon after lunch while I wandered unhappily around their rather grand house. My father visited regularly but to me it seemed an endless and unhappy exile, though it was probably no more than a week.

What I had to face when I got back home was the most intense jealousy. I was overwhelmed with it. I have memories of going into a front garden in our street where there was another baby in her pram – I didn't dare do it to my sister – and pinching her to make her cry.

My sister was a charming baby, curly haired and sunny; I was a sombre, silent six-year-old. I was expected to play with her and to push her around in the pram for walks. Before this interloper arrived, I had been trying to be a support for my mother. I already had some sense that I needed to check her mood, that she was prone to anxiety and somehow that it was my job to take care of this. My ebullient little sister had no such needs. She was just her own charming self. There may already have been some signs of the mental illness that would develop so fiercely in my mother six or seven years later. Certainly, she was preoccupied and seems, in retrospect, to have found it hard to be absorbed in the life of her new baby. A nurse, Fraulein Wolf, was hired to help. My sister once told me that she never really felt she had a mother, adding brightly: 'But that's all right!'

In spite of my jealousy, which remained intermittently fierce for some years – for a while I had a habit of covering my sister's mouth with my hand to stop her talking – I also felt protective of her. Years later I described these feelings to an aunt and she replied that I was perfectly right to be jealous, that Ruth was the most adorable child, one 'you wanted to pick up and take home'. It was a relief to have my feelings confirmed.

Soon after she was born Ruth got scarlet fever and once again I was sent away from home. This time I went to my Great Aunt Grete, a formidable matriarch, the wealthy widow of Uncle Paul, the founder of the family firm. She had been a supporter of Bismarck's son and had agreed in 1917 to have tanks parked in her back garden in Berlin in case they were needed to help what became a bloody suppression of the brief revolution. When she left Germany, by train, in August 1938, with her eldest son Herbert, her carriage was filled with violets from well-wishers. She was a handsome woman, dressed in elegant and expensive clothes, a great supporter of Churchill's (she had several photographs of him in her house in Wimbledon) and a patron of the arts, especially of musicians. When I was thirteen she took me to the last night of the Proms, where one of her protégés, Iso Elinson, was playing a Beethoven piano concerto. When they played Elgar's 'Land of Hope and Glory', the scale of the orchestra, the mood of the audience and the emotional patriotism the music inspired embarrassingly made me weep. Then we went backstage to meet the pianist and Sir Malcolm Sargent, who I noticed looked at himself in the mirror all the time.

Aunt Grete lived with her maid and cook. Valuable antique furniture and gloomy but important pictures filled the rooms; the house was quiet and orderly. She had a rest after lunch – by now I realized this was a common German habit – and once again I did a lot of mooching in the house and garden, obsessively playing competitive games with myself which involved balancing on rockeries and walking on paving stones. She was kind and interested in me and tried to make me feel at home in her grand and formal way. But I was unhappy being away from home and unhappy too that my sister's illness was the cause.

And then early in 1944 we were evacuated for a second time. This time my mother, Ruth and I went to the Peak District, close to my father's factory near Sheffield, where we stayed with a working class Derbyshire family in their stone house with its huge vegetable garden in Castleton. I went to the local school, where I was amazed to discover that children were hit with a cane on

With my parents and baby sister Ruth, in Castleton,
Derbyshire, where we were evacuated in 1944

the knuckles. I became good friends with Keith, the son of the house, a small, naughty boy the same age as me with a mop of brown hair, and tried hard to join in, hanging around with the local children after school, learning to whizz fearlessly in a go-cart down the steep main road into the village. I was acutely conscious of the differences in the way of life between us and our hosts, of my mother's attempts to make a life there. Keith's parents were warm and welcoming; every morning his father, a big man who wore brown braces, sang 'I'll Walk Beside You' in a rich baritone around the house and as he tended his vegetable garden. Only the older daughter of the house resented our presence. My brother meanwhile was sent to a Catholic boarding school nearby. He wept bitterly when he went, but later said that he enjoyed himself there.

Strange dislocations for a family already dislocated, but they were the familiar currency of wartime lives.

After nine months we returned to London where air raids became a regular part of our life. Incendiary bombs, though small, were often responsible for burning houses down because the owners had left the city. We had a large cellar, with a room for coal and a larder where our milk was kept cool in a jug with a lace cover weighted with beads. But cellars with one exit weren't safe. When the sirens started we went down to the kitchen, bleary with sleep, in our dressing gowns, where we huddled under the kitchen table till the all clear sounded. My father, in his striped black and red silk dressing gown and blue pyjamas, sat at the table seemingly calm – there wasn't room for him underneath. One night, with the bombs raining down, we heard a crackling sound. My father went upstairs to investigate and found an incendiary bomb had come through the bathroom ceiling, hit the basin and landed between the bathroom floor and kitchen ceiling, just above where he had been sitting. He doused it with water and the danger was over. My father was visibly shaken.

After this my parents installed a Morrison shelter in the dining room, a huge rectangular metal box with an open side which almost filled the room and which could accommodate all of us when necessary. We children often slept there, with or without air raids – a strange dark claustrophobic world which intimidated me, the dark grey metal exuding coldness and a slightly bitter smell.

I remember being wrapped up warm in coat and scarves, gloves on and being sent shopping, sometimes pushing my sister in her pram. I made regular journeys to the cheerful red-faced butcher in

Lacey Road, passing the bomb crater on the way, to pick up large bags of bones for my mother. These were boiled for hours, filling the house with a pungent sour smell. I hated the soup. I was still overwhelmed with shyness, but the butcher greeted me with warm raucous affection, which I secretly loved.

I came back through the side gate, along the narrow side passage and from the back door into the comforting kitchen, with its capacious store cupboard and, above the large kitchen table, covered in cream and green patterned oilcloth, the laundry pulley with its wrought iron brackets hung with washing. The old upright stove served the whole house, fed by my father first thing in the morning and last thing at night with the coal and coke he shovelled into the scuttle, the stove making its contribution to the thick greenish fogs which were a regular part of our winters. I often walked along pavements without being able to see the next lamp post.

⁂

Late in 1944, when I was nearly eight, I went to stay with Hans and Lotte in Dublin. By this time they'd been settled there for five years. The conductor Havelock Nelson, a musical and scientific friend of Hans and Lotte, had been in England and took me back with him to Ireland by boat. It was a stormy crossing; he, a tall, gentle man, tried to keep his balance, the boat tipping in the waves, as he lifted me to pee in the cabin basin.

I loved being with Hans and Lotte in that Dublin flat, the long row of steps leading up to the heavy front door, the large living room full of books.

They had by then established a comfortable life, retaining their bourgeois lifestyle, remaining within a social cocoon of educated people, keeping their distance from politics and religion. A maid came every day (my grandmother never learnt to cook). Lotte got up early, bustled around the house, alert to everything that was going on, emphatic and bossy about the plans for the day, her hair tied back in a bun with wisps escaping at the nape of her neck. Hans, quiet and tolerant as ever, with his genial square face, his bald head and trim moustache, put on his rimless spectacles at breakfast and ate two boiled eggs every morning – astonishing for a child living in wartime Britain. We played a regular game pretending that the empty eggs were not yet eaten. I wrote to my parents: 'I am very happy here.'

At times they talked as if they regarded their stay as temporary. And yet, even at my age, I was aware of how gregarious and hospitable they were.

Lotte was clearly the organizing spirit of their social life. Hans went along with it and probably enjoyed it more than he admitted. He also liked doing things alone. He wrote to my mother that 'I spent this night without my wife. I appreciated it very much to be free and without any influences. At first, I attended a meeting in Trinity College. After that I was invited by the President to a party. I returned at 1.00 a.m, what is not quite easy because buses stop already at 11.00 p.m. and lifts are not available'.

My visit gave my grandparents huge pleasure, Hans particularly feeling the absence of his children and grandchildren. He seemed always to carry with him the sense of loss that uprooting brings. He seemed not to find any advantages to being an outsider. Lotte

My grandfather Hans Sachs at his desk, 1942

insisted on a certain level of optimism and always conveyed to us that she was having the happiest time in Ireland; while he was inclined to speak more about the cost of their exile. My mother must have written to him about my quietness, because he speculated that I might have inherited this quality from him. He wrote to my mother that he 'never was, unfortunately, a chatterbox. I believe that it is better to be one than not to be. For I always felt a little unhappy during my school time because not having enough connections with the others.'

Hans died in March 1945, two months before the end of the war, after a prostatectomy, at that time a dangerous operation, and acute heart failure. He was sixty-seven. He was buried in Dublin, a secular ceremony. His funeral was packed with their friends and Lotte retained many of them for the rest of her life. She returned to England after he died, staying first with us in Putney and then with Ilse and her family in Oxford. She corresponded with German friends constantly in the late 1940s and early 1950s. Letters arrived from the different occupation zones in Germany and Lotte sent them food parcels and presents even though she was far from well off herself at that point. I meanwhile rushed to the door when the postman rang because in that same period my parents were getting regular food parcels from Germany – sent by my father's work colleagues, who clearly were not suffering the severe privations that many Germans went through. I still remember cutting through the package and discovering those delicious smoked hams, neatly tied up with string, wrapped impeccably in brown paper.

For me the proper end of the war was VE Day. I was eight and off we went to Buckingham Palace – me clinging to my parents' hands as we weaved our way through the crowds, eyes glued to the balcony as we waited for Churchill to come out and join the king and queen. People danced wildly in the streets, singing and shouting and climbing lamp posts, women with their flowered wartime turbans, men in their uniforms. I was breathless with excitement.

For my father there was more to come.

When I was fourteen years old, I came across a photograph of him in British army uniform. My father had never been in the British army. But as a German speaking industrialist he was sent by the British government in December 1945 with the Control Commission to look into the state of German industry and they dressed him in colonel's uniform to make him look the part.

But the photo had another significance for me. When I first saw it I was a teenager battling with an autocratic father who very much expected his will to be done. And here was this same man, in uniform, looking uncharacteristically anxious, even sheepish. The expression on his face was one I didn't recognize; my father looked vulnerable. The photographer had caught him off guard. I suddenly saw a man not always in control; what's more, I felt I knew things that he didn't. I'd by then been initiated into a world of women where feelings were more freely expressed. By the time I left home a few years later I recognized that some of his vulnerability lay in the fact that, like many men, he seemed ill at ease with his own emotions.

And then, when I was writing this memoir, I unexpectedly came across in my brother's attic some letters of his. They were the nine letters he sent to my mother on his trip round Germany in December 1945. Apart from the remarkable journey they describe, as he looked at the devastated country he had been forced to leave, the letters told me other things about my father, which touched me deeply. Some of them I knew: his competence in doing an extremely difficult job; his capacity to focus on the telling details, which revealed so much about the traumatised lives in post-war Germany. Others less so: his love of the landscapes he had left behind; his surprisingly expressive affection for my mother and his children.

It was, he wrote to my mother, 'certainly the most interesting experience I ever had but it is difficult to digest all the manifold impressions on the human and technical side.' His letters were long, informative and written in English – the language presumably required by the Control Commission. They are remarkable, revealing the condition of Germany at the end of the war, the relations between the British and Americans, the physical devastation of cities and the psychological reaction of Germans to their lost war and the Nazi regime. The letters were also poignant for the expression of his feelings, rarely very demonstrative but there nevertheless, for the country he had had to leave.

His trip lasted several weeks, including Christmas, mostly in conditions of snow, ice, fog and cold wind. Accommodation varied from comparative luxury in hotels to sleeping in dormitories. In Austria he used DDT powder to counter the fleas – 'because I have no confidence in the Austrian bed.' He writes with relish about the landscapes they pass through, especially the views of the snow-covered mountains of his youth, the Alps and the Dolomites. Food varied too, always better when the Americans were providing it, and there seemed to be regular entertainment – they went to musicals, cabaret, the occasional opera and concerts. In Frankfurt, he went in search of the family's houses – 'completely down, empty shells. Westend looks dreadful'. Heidelberg, on the other hand, was 'like an oasis in the desert, not a single bomb, no houses damaged, practically no change from seven years ago.' He continued on to Munich and then to Nurnberg, where the Grand Hotel was 'reserved for the big bosses in the trial' and 'the inner town is completely destroyed.' He walked through the Berghof, Hitler's house in Obersalzburg – 'Unfortunately we did not meet the Fuhrer' – that had been mostly destroyed by bombs. 'It was a curious feeling to walk through this ruin. But the view from there is one of the nicest I have ever seen. He certainly chose a good spot.' His mode of writing was to underplay everything, the physical desecration, the effects of the brutal Nazi time, his own emotions about his homeland. But the force of his feelings are very present.

He and his colleagues visited factories, laboratories, offices, talked to hundreds of people about the conditions of their lives and work, including my father's own company works in Nurnberg. For some, life was very difficult, houses and possessions bombed and serious food shortages; for others, especially in Bavaria, food was reasonably plentiful. Work conditions varied – many factories and power stations were bombed and not functioning. Others were back to some sort of normality and paying wages.

He commented carefully but repeatedly on the way the Germans addressed their situation and the political experiences of the past few years. 'Life is of course not easy and the worst is, that the Germans start already now again all their petty intrigues against each other as they did after 1918.' His attempts not to judge are remarkable. 'The whole development (the rise of the Nazis) is un-understandable to the people I speak to, as it is to us and especially to my English colleagues. In spite of all criticisms, one hears however, too often, the self-pity, that all this happened to them, though they were against the Nazis. The question is never raised, what was wrong with them that this could happen. I know of course that this is only human, but it is nevertheless regrettable. I could easily write a book on this problem, if I had the time.'

How remarkably rational he seemed to me in these letters, how seemingly lacking in bitterness and anger and even incomprehension my father was about what the Nazis had done to the Jews, the death camps, the gassing, the collusion of some of the German population – and of course what they'd done to his own life. Memories of my childhood confirmed this– the ways my parents talked about leaving Germany, being Jewish, what had happened to them. In these letters he expresses a kind of calm, more-in-sorrow-than-in-anger attitude, which I find both moving and hard to grasp. Not that he was without contempt for the German's embracing of the Nazis and their self-pity at the end of the war. But he had a kind of acceptance, a disinclination to dwell on what had happened, a powerful drive to get on with the new reality of his life.

7

THE YEARS BETWEEN

W HY DO I remember so little about my life from the ages of eight to 12? Memory loops backwards and forwards, comes in sly selective flashes; my ninth birthday party where I wore a gold-coloured wool dress when I had longed for a pink frothy one with a wide skirt which my mother didn't approve of; Miss Hartnell, the stern head of my junior school, telling me off for joining in a silly giggle in assembly about my Burmese friend Jane; Miss Sawyer and Miss Wyatt, athletic committed teachers who lived together – I knew nothing about lesbians and accepted this without question, liked them for their boisterous energy.

A strange memory about me and my father: in our bathroom, lying on a shelf in the cupboard was a small red rubber syringe, which my mother must have used as a douche, presumably for birth control purposes. I had no idea what it was and one day, when I was eight, I took it to the basin and filled it with ink and

squeezed it in and out. When my father discovered it, he took me
to the living room, sat down in an armchair and cross-examined
me – had I filled it with ink? I denied it. He asked me again and
again whether I had done it and I repeatedly – just as relentlessly
– denied it. I never understood why he was so upset about it – I
couldn't have known it was used as a douche, did he think I'd done
something deliberately, perhaps he simply feared losing control,
something that was so much part of his nature.

Eventually I admitted it. I didn't really understand what I'd
done. I didn't think to ask him. I wasn't exactly afraid of him
though he unquestionably had power over me and he was a formidable person to encounter – set in his opinions and authoritarian
in his manner. I didn't feel seriously able to challenge him until
much later in my life.

Eight to twelve is Freud's latent period, which he describes as
a time of relative stability, where 'cultural skills and values' are
acquired and the child becomes 'a more reasonable human being',
developing complex feelings such as shame, guilt, disgust.

What I remember are the struggles with self-worth. I repeatedly compared myself with others, mostly finding myself wanting.
It seemed that everyone else was confident, happy, at ease with
themselves; real life seemed to be elsewhere and was going on
without me. I enjoyed playing with my brother and his friends
well enough, when they allowed it, but by the time I was ten he
had left his day school in Wimbledon to go to boarding school
in Shrewsbury and I saw much less of him. He flourished at his
public school, went mountain climbing, stayed with friends in the
holidays and spent very little time at home. This school, he said

later, was where he became English. After five years there he had
no sense that he had to assimilate or that he was in any way an
outsider; he became a Christian, though he remained clear that
he was in some way Jewish. He finds my interest in assimilation
intriguing but incomprehensible.

My sister and I didn't do things together much, though for
several years we shared a room, with its sap green patterned wall-
paper and curtains to match. We didn't talk much either. She
seemed confident, certain of what she wanted, self-sufficient.

I collected glass animals which I kept on my mantelpiece.
I brought friends home for tea occasionally and went to their
houses in return. I practiced the piano. I went to friends' parties,
a memorable one where Sid Field the comedian, the father of my
great friend, presided; another grand one for my Jewish friend
Jean, elaborate food and posh presents. At my birthday parties we
played musical bumps and Kim's game; my father put objects on
to a tray – a pencil, a pack of cards, a bowl of jelly, a handkerchief,
brought in uncovered for half a minute and then covered with a
cloth; we all had to write down what we remembered

Children accept the normality of their lives. My father went
to work, my mother managed the household, they seemed on the
surface to be all right together. We went on family holidays to
North Wales. I did well at school. But I had no sense of who I
was or what I wanted.

At home my parents were assertive about things they wanted
from us – to do well at school, to be punctual, to read, to listen
to classical music. And to be orderly. To get my weekly pocket
money, I had to produce my cash book, the money I'd received

on the left page, what I'd spent it on on the right. I always forgot to keep records, so invented it. Mostly it didn't occur to me to disobey my parents. When I got home from school I told my mother about my day, not confidentially but in rather formal ways. If I was naughty my mother would sometimes say wait till your father gets home.

As I grew older, influence became more significant. Fips and Werner wanted things for their children, but perhaps more ardently and anxiously because we were the outward and visible signs of their success in coping with exile. They listened out very intently for the signals, which were not always easy to read – especially those of class.

Although some working-class girls got in on scholarships, my school was overwhelmingly middle-class in population and attitudes. At the age of 11, I made friends with Margaret, the daughter of Christian Scientists living in our street, her father unsmiling and disapproving. She was not, as my parents made clear, of our class. One awful day Margaret and I dared each other to hide under my mother's bed while she was in the bathroom and then watched her dress, hooking up her long corset. We were bound to be caught and we were. My parents were shocked and angry, but the brunt of their anger was for my friend, who they said was vulgar and a bad influence. They more or less forbade me to see her and I capitulated, stopped seeing Margaret – I never explained why to her and assumed she must have known. I didn't like being disapproved of.

And I came to realize, even at the time, that my parents were truly afraid. They couldn't read the signs. As immigrants and outsiders they felt they had even less understanding and control than other parents over what was happening in their children's lives. I worked extra hard at being good at school, good at the piano, good at being a daughter, good at everything.

⳯

I think of my early life as hugely dominated by my mother and her illness and unhappiness. I send an early draft of this memoir to my friend Adam, who says my mother isn't really present, doesn't come alive on the page. I am surprised. I have written so much about her, she feels to me so much centre stage and she has had a powerful effect on my thinking and behaviour. Why is she not present?

My mother's life was in the home; she didn't work outside the house, didn't pursue interests of her own, apart from playing music with the family. She looked after our daily needs, making sure we had our clothes ready for school, taking care of the household, the cooking, the laundry, overseeing Dolly's work, cycling to the shops on her tall bicycle with my sister strapped into the back seat – all these things keeping her busy, all perfectly ordinary conditions for a middle class wife in the 1940s.

Later, when I understood more, I would have a sense of how difficult such a life can be and how much it must have inclined her to brooding and to living through her children. These things weren't talked about, indeed weren't understood. It took another fifteen years for Betty Friedan's book *The Feminine Mystique* to come out in 1963 and famously address 'the problem that has no name.' What Friedan observed was that many American women, while seeming to have everything they ever wanted, husband, children, a home, were suffering from a 'nameless, aching dissatisfaction, each one thinking that she was alone.' When Friedan wrote of her own 'terror' at being alone in the house, she commented that she had never once seen a woman who worked and also had a family.

Friedan talks of women's yearning and sense of dissatisfaction and their fear of asking themselves the question 'Is this all?' She made many hundreds of thousands of women realise they were not alone, were not wicked, were not useless, were not mad.

I began to be aware of my mother's periods of unhappiness and withdrawal quite early. There is a photo of the two us, me at the age of three, where she is staring ahead at the camera, beautiful, inward looking and remote, unconnected physically or in any other way to me; I look vigilant, as if I'm anxiously wondering – what next?

One of the difficulties I've had with writing about her as a person is that I didn't experience this much as I was growing up. There were few obvious intimacies between us, though I knew she loved me. We didn't much do things together, play together, talk to each other. And increasingly less so as time went on. I read other women's memoirs about their difficult or warm relationships with their mothers and they are about arguments, intimacies, disagreements, misunderstandings, expressed in words. My experience of childhood with my mother is mostly dealing with silences – trying to interpret them, feeling frozen and anxious about them, hanging on to them to try and make sense of what my mother was feeling, what she wanted, was disappointed or unhappy about, where she felt excluded, looking for clues about how to make it right.

All this became more so when I was in my early teens. There were times when she couldn't focus on what was going on around her, or on anything but her own feelings. On many days she would get up late, wander down the stairs in her green flowing dressing gown, her expression preoccupied, her brown eyes sad, her hands pale and fragile, always strangely expressive, and sit silently at the kitchen table eating her porridge. Mealtimes were more and more often silent and tense, though she would from time to time come out with an unhappy, angry statement, about a person she'd met that day, about something happening in the family, about my father. We were all silenced by her at these times, sitting rigidly in our chairs, none of us able to cheer her up or daring to make jokes about things.

I grew acutely attuned to these moods and began to feel a responsibility for them. I absorbed her fears and behaviours long before I could understand them. In this way my mother had power over me. I felt I had been chosen by her to be the child who cared for her and at some level I must have agreed to it. I learned to watch lives.

I realised that the way I was writing about her was as the sad, depressed, ill mother who I had to look after. The rest of her was invisible on the page. So I spent a day pacing up and down, trying to put together a few paragraphs about her as a person in her own right, struggling to find things to say, looking at photographs of her as a young woman, with that direct gaze of hers at the camera, that sense of her as a bold if anxious young woman, and then thinking about what she'd encountered as an exile and as a woman of her time. And then I tried to think about her as my mother without the depression and withdrawals. I finally managed to send Adam three paragraphs about her. I spent the next thirty-six hours weeping.

After my mother died, we found boxes of letters in her flat, some going back to 1914. She had brought them to England in 1938 and continued to keep much of her correspondence to the end of her life. The letters brought home to me how many people she had contact with, one way or another, while she lived in Germany. She was part of an extended family and a group of friends who had known each other since adolescence or earlier. From what I learned from relatives, her insecurities and anxieties were part of her life even then. But in retrospect I'm shocked at how casually I diminished the effect that exile must have had on her, the disappearance of the sense of family and friends in a country and a culture she knew. With exile, several categories of identity must have disappeared for her and even though she liked England and the English, there wasn't much magic to replace them. But the pressures to adapt, try to understand, sometimes to pretend must have been enormous. And apart from being a wife and mother, which Friedan made clear can in its own way be desolate and lonely territory, she had no obvious place in the new world she inhabited. There were some friends in England and some family. But many were dispersed, to America in particular. And though she had a few women friends, I don't think she called on them to confide in when things were difficult, or just propose they have a good time together.

She became more anxious and needy and ill. I would arrive home from school and look into her eyes over the kitchen table, hoping that I wouldn't see that pleading look she so often had. I found it hard to hug her – overwhelmed by the feeling of her desire to be reassured, that what she said was all right, what people said to her wasn't hostile – her body awkward and somehow unmotherly for me. At weekends I'd talk to her when she had her bath after breakfast, watching her drip water gently from her delicate fingers on to her full breasts, preoccupied. She didn't laugh often though she was sometimes able to laugh at herself, self-deprecatingly, which touched me. She was more at ease playing the violin when the family made music together, though even here she was tentative.

The starker reality of my mother's condition begins to affect me when I become aware that there are family secrets.

Towards the end of 1949, when I am twelve, my parents start going on mysterious trips. They called it 'going to town'. Once a week they get into their Austin 16, looking solemn, and drive into central London. These are gloomy times, my mother often withdrawn and angry, my father brusque and tense. My room is next to my parents and as I lie in bed at night I half hear their quarrels, usually about something my father has or hasn't said, something he hasn't understood about her, hasn't been sensitive to, my father shouting, my mother shouting and crying. Both are in anguish.

I try to work out where each of them stands, who is right, who is having the harder time and feel a sense of hopelessness at how little they seem to understand each other. My father doesn't want trouble, especially emotional trouble. My mother finds this difficult. Her attempts to elicit an emotional response are never calm, they are demanding and agitated. He deals with this by trying to minimise them and the more he does that the more she continues with her anguished criticism – about people they know, about social occasions when she feels awkward or slighted; about domestic matters where she wants changes in the house.

⁂

The easiest times I have with my mother is when we speak of the past. She doesn't talk to me about my life, about what I'm thinking, feeling about things. But she has some good stories to tell. I sometimes try to delve more deeply each time a particular story comes up, to get a new angle on it, but it rarely works. She's become stuck in a version of reality (don't we all?) and I don't want to risk pushing her because anxiety is always close to the surface for her and I hate dealing with it, hate the business of reassuring her though I know that's what she needs.

The fact is I often understood my mother's desperation, which of course exacerbated my fears of being like her. But then I found myself sympathizing with my father's resistance to her and his longing to find a peaceful way of living with her. When my mother showed more explicit signs of what would later be described to us as mental illness, delusions, ideas of reference, irrationality – she would, for instance, refer to the way an uncle was sitting in his chair as being significant about what he felt about her – I tried to understand those too in terms of her unhappiness.

My mother was much more critical of my father than he of her. Behind the rows I felt that my mother wanted my father to be someone he wasn't. She wasn't very interested in his work, didn't much like or respect the business world or his colleagues. My father was very good at business and loved it. She still resented my father's cousins, who owned the family business he worked in and who were rich. We visited them from time to time and swum in their pool, but my mother felt we were the poor relations and she didn't like it. And though Fips and Werner had much in common culturally, temperamentally they were very different. He was robust and authoritarian, outgoing, direct in his dealings with the world, charming but not subtle. She liked quietness and wit, was sensitive, often hypersensitive, to mood, very aware of how people were reacting to her, though she had her own authoritarian ways. And unlike my father, she liked people who lived the life of the mind – like many of their friends from adolescence who she had lost when they moved to America from Germany.

I was convinced that their trips into town were to a divorce lawyer – a strange certainty, as I knew nothing about divorce or that lawyers were involved. After a particularly bad time between them, I went with my father one morning to visit his cousin Ernst and his wife Gitta in their smart modern flat nearby in Putney. As we sat in their living room and drank tea, there was music on the radio and I watched them as they spontaneously started dancing together. I remember thinking – that's what happiness is.

The regular trips to town lasted for about four years. I eventually found out that my mother was seeing a psychoanalyst, Dr Loewenstein. She kept his letters – they wrote to each other, she telling him details of her week and candidly telling him when he had upset her (I can only guess at what she wrote from his replies, we have no letters from her), he sometimes apologetic that she'd been upset by him and giving his explanation about what was going on between them. His letters were reassuring and affectionate. It all seems rather unorthodox, but my impression was that she found him helpful and it was clear from his letters that he was robust as well as supportive in his dealings with her. He asked to talk to me some years later, when I was seventeen, as my mother's closest confidante. He was direct; he felt my parents' marriage was a contributory factor in her illness. I didn't disagree with him, but it was hard to know what to do with the information. I never told my parents or my siblings about the conversation.

8

THE SHADOW OF ILLNESS

SOMETIME IN MY mid-teens, I began to have more regular thoughts that I would, like my mother, go mad. There were reasons for my identification: I looked like her, she felt I understood her and relied on me emotionally. I was often anxious. I understood her need for emotional responsiveness, though I didn't always like it. I was the eldest daughter and I was at home. I was her ally and something of a lifeline for her. She was proud of me and wanted me to succeed and to represent her. I benefited from her attention, but I also resented it. But I didn't resist – I don't think I knew how to.

By this time, I had passed from the junior to the senior school at Putney High. We were given solemn talks on how life was going to be more grown up, how we had to take responsibility in a new way – learning to use the library, being in charge of our own work – which I found frightening. In my first year I asked

With Peter and Ruth on holiday in Southwold, 1949

the maths teacher, with her cold blue eyes, a question; she paused for a while and then said, 'It's funny that you should ask that question, Ursula, I always thought you were an intelligent child.' Her gaunt face turned away. The phrase chilled me and I never forgot it; it was a kind of marker for my insecurities and I stopped asking questions.

The all-girls school was in a prosperous part of Putney, conventional in its ethos, conservative in outlook. Each day we poured into the Victorian building on Putney Hill, wearing our purple tunics, white blouses, purple striped ties; on the street we had to wear hats and were forbidden to eat. Occasionally I would be the pianist who played the hymn at the daily assembly. I can still recite the verses of the hymns we sang. I sat very upright, my posture was good, my teeth were straight, I was good at games, this was the late Forties and early Fifties. There was a sense of peacetime recovery in the air, of families living together again after the trauma of war – and the notion of women being educated to be good wives. Many of the older teachers had probably encountered feminism in some form earlier in their lives and may well have been part of peace movement or anti-fascist groups, but they never talked about it and there were no discussions about equal opportunity or choices for women. And yet we were encouraged to have a good education for its own sake, ambitiously so; much more attention was paid to girls trying to get into university than those who chose nursing, as my sister did, or secretarial careers. It was a strange mix of messages.

To our cruel schoolgirl eyes most of the teachers seemed dry, rather distant spinsters. My biology teacher, though, made no secret of the fact that she lived with a woman, called Ursula and she always took rather a special interest in me. I was fascinated by our English teacher's deep-set passionate eyes and long, heavy, masculine face, though I failed to respond to her awkward and shy attempts to convey her love of literature. The younger married teachers were more glamorous, tougher in class, they wore lipstick, high heels and smart clothes and we had a sort of awed respect for the fact that they had husbands and children and lived a domestic life outside school hours.

What was absent was any sense of the extraordinary political transformations of those post-war years – the welfare state legislation set up between 1945 and 1948 specifically to create more equality and to help combat the five 'Giant Evils' – squalor, ignorance, want, idleness and disease – that the economist William

Beveridge talked about in his 1942 report and which radically changed people's lives – their health, education, security in old age. None of the regular talks at assembly addressed these changes or what they might mean for us. There was more of a harking back to the war – Peter Churchill telling us about the heroism of his wife Odette Churchill in the Resistance, for instance – though no mention of the Holocaust, the death camps, the Nazis. No one referred to Jews as the victims of the Nazi regime and I must have been so determined to be part of things, to be not different, that I have no memory of being surprised by that. If anything, the occasional girl would make a reference to my being German, but never Jewish.

But I was also living a split life. I had my English friends, but I grew close to two girls in my class whose parents had also escaped from the Nazis. They were from Vienna. I went to tea with them, in rather grander houses than ours and discovered very different exiled worlds. Jean was glamorous, seemed more at ease with her aspirations towards Englishness than I and eventually moved on to Sherborne School. Elizabeth was short, wore spectacles and unlike most of us was totally uninterested in clothes or how she looked. She spoke slowly and, though I only realized it later, was a serious intellectual. Her parents both worked (as dentists) and seemed completely at ease with their foreignness.

But spending time with these refugee families sometimes made me feel uneasy. The accents, the food, the aspirations – they were deeply familiar and yet they jarred. These families were candid and outspoken about their aspirations – educational, social – in a way that English families never were. I was busy with my apprenticeship in assimilation, my attempts at belonging, which required reticence about these matters.

I also gravitated towards the most English of friends, two of them brilliant at tennis, playing at Junior Wimbledon. They lived their lives out of school at their local tennis club, where there were dances on Saturday nights. They seemed supremely confident, in the way they dressed and talked, seemed to know what they wanted, seemed to acquire boyfriends without difficulty. I went to their homes and felt drawn to their mothers, with their comforting big bosoms and brisk affection, seemingly so relaxed, easy with their daughters and with me. Of course I discovered there were tensions. But to me, then, these homes were the epitome of calm – their living rooms with their comfortable sofas, their easy relationships.

With rare exceptions, the teaching at my school seemed unexciting. Or perhaps that was what I experienced – I felt dull and flat myself. I had friends who were more responsive and so it often felt like my failure. My clever friend Jane, half Burmese, half English, wrote poetry and exuded energy in lessons – she was obviously a joy to teach. I worked hard and wanted to do well. I knew how to be a good girl but felt little passion for what I was learning. I stayed near the top of the class for a while.

I escaped from home as often as I could. I loved people who felt confident about the world, who could laugh at things. My friend Janet, small, pretty, curly hair and snub nose, travelled for an hour from Shepperton every day to come to school. She recounted endless exciting stories about the boys she met on the train.

Her parents were both head teachers of schools for handicapped children. When I went to stay with them in their bungalow on Shepperton towpath, they told stories about the children at their schools full of black humour laced with affection. Nothing fazed them. They managed to make comedy out of tragic situations. This was a revelation. At home I was used to conversations that avoided difficulties, were full of anxious evasions and smoothings over. My mother was sensitive to anything that she interpreted as 'tough', used by her as a derogatory word. Janet's parents were tough – they had to be – and I loved them for it. I wanted to learn how to be tough.

As time went on I brought friends back to the house less and less as my mother spent more time in her dressing gown and I found it harder to deal with her fragility. At the end of the summer term in 1952 – I was fifteen – I brought a friend home. It was late morning. We came into the house in our purple blazers and hats; and there was my mother waiting in her pale green dressing gown– every day I hoped that she'd be up and dressed. I handed her my school report. It was disappointing; I wasn't doing as well as I should, the kind of disappointment she found particularly hard to bear. She became very agitated, couldn't stop talking about it, her voice more and more querulous. 'You and I must go and see the teachers, but not with Daddy.'

My friend was silent and baffled and I, filled with embarrassment at my mother's increasing distress and loss of control, escaped with my friend to my room as soon as I could.

The fact was that mental illness was a taboo subject for conversation or even acknowledgement in the milieu in which we lived. Even inside the family the conversations about my mother were awkward and hedged around with silences and the unspoken. It was if she inhabited a different country. My grandmother Lotte, who before settling in Oxford with Ilse, had lived with us briefly after she was widowed and was in constant touch with my father, showed a good deal of concern about my mother. She was a passionate family person and made it her business to know what was going on with every member. In some ways she was the most straightforward about addressing my mother's illness, but there was a patronizing tone to her sympathy that made me uncomfortable.

At school I was silent on the matter. When my mother was first in hospital the school had been informed by my father. My biology teacher tried to engage me on the subject: I was embarrassed and bemused as to how to respond. A friend invited me to tea; her mother was divorced from her Indian army husband. It was the most English of houses and we had tea in the gloomy drawing room, out of china cups, with polite chat and sandwiches with the crusts cut off. Her mother was tall and angular, her blonde hair in a roll; she was very friendly, very proper. I thought – this must be one version of normality, how it is to be English. We went to my friend's room, talked about school and the teams we were in (we were both sporty) and who we liked and who we didn't, the usual chatter of teenage girls. Years later, this friend told me she desperately wanted to talk to me about how isolated she felt, having divorced parents. She felt I had a secret too though she didn't know what it was and hoped we could talk more easily. But we never did talk till all those years later. It was enough to cope with being an outsider, too dangerous to acknowledge a problem or to share it.

And as for home, Peter was away at boarding school and often during the holidays too. When he came home he sometimes brought friends from school, exciting for me, these boys who seemed so worldly, so handsome. I was thrilled when they allowed me into their conversations. But family matters weren't talked about. I felt Peter had separated himself from the mother who'd become so sadly self-preoccupied and I accepted that. I was after all the older girl, at home, and he was a boy finding a life out in a new world. I had some sense that this was how the world worked – the beginnings of becoming a woman. Ruth, being much younger and not so connected with my mother, felt freer to be rebellious and not to engage with what was going on between our parents.

So the three of us observed what was going on and reacted in our different ways, but never talked to each other about any of it.

9

DAILINESS

MY FATHER'S ROUTINE was regular – he left for the office in Wimbledon after breakfast, wearing his double-breasted suit, smoking a cigarette and was back in time for supper except when he was travelling. On occasions in school holidays he would take me to the office, where I met his colleagues, most of them fellow refugees from Germany – Dispeker, Schwabach, Grunfeld. I thought they were enormously glamorous – laid back, good-looking men in smart suits sitting at their desks, on the phone, smoking cigars and cigarettes, worldly, in control.

At intervals my father went by train to Sheffield to oversee the office there as well as the factory they had set up in Rotherham, which made alloys for hardening steel with non-ferrous metals, particularly for shells, which they now supplied to the British. Each time he brought back Lilliput, a small monthly magazine with cartoons, short stories and photographs of female nudes. He left it lying around and I was riveted by the nudes and wondered about my father and whether he liked them.

Still managing to take care of the house and domestic life, with Dolly's help, my mother's routine was that of a middle-class housewife and mother of the time. Her life beyond the confines of the home was, apart from the occasional lunch with a friend, associated with my father – she had no life of her own as far as I knew, though she always had her own opinions. My parents' refugee friends and my father's colleagues sometimes came for supper, though more rarely than before. The monthly musical evenings that my father had set up continued. And from time to time Fips and Werner went out in the evenings, to concerts, to the theatre, my mother wearing her long fur coat in winter, her fox fur with its hard-pointed head round her neck, both sent into storage in Harrods for the summer. I loved touching the fur when she came to say goodnight. On these occasions I was left to baby sit and never dared tell them how terrified I was of the dark. I dealt with my obsessional fear by going round the house with my sister, over and over again, ritualistically checking the locks on the windows, my sister mildly amused by my anxiety.

As a young man my father smoked sixty cigarettes a day. Though a strong, fleshy man, he was physically quite vulnerable. On several occasions I saw him dislocate his shoulder, in great pain, sometimes managing to put it back himself. And he had hollows behind his ears where, before the discovery of penicillin, he'd had operations to remove the bone for repeated inner ear infections.

Each morning he woke us up, drawing the curtains back,

shouting good morning; then he went to the bathroom, to shave, stripping to the waist, coughing loudly. We children shared the bathroom with him in turn, cleaning our teeth and washing our faces over the bathtub. On one occasion, when I was sixteen, my father and I began an argument, he with shaving soap on his face, and started shouting at each other. I stormed out of the bathroom, he followed me. I remember saying 'don't touch me, don't touch me!'

At mealtimes he was a dominating presence, a noisy eater, a soup slurper. He had his personal rituals – mashing up his break-fast boiled egg with butter and bread in his special glass cup – *eier im glas*. He was likely to be angry if we were even a little late for meals. If he wanted a fork at table, he announced it and someone leapt up to get it for him.

Talk at meals tended to be formal, sometimes educational. One day it was revealed that I knew nothing about the Peloponnesian Wars and didn't know where the Peloponnese was. My father ordered me to bring down the atlas and proceeded to show me. In his later, mellower years, I could tease him about not being able to catch out my daughter, when she was doing Ancient History at A-level. But teasing was not part of our family life. There was too much at stake. Both my parents had strong feelings, strongly expressed, about how one should behave. *Das tut man nicht* was a phrase I heard repeatedly.

And control was so important to my parents, especially to my father. It was manifest through tones of voice, sometimes shouting and an assumption that adults made the decisions in the family, that children didn't on the whole have choices – decisions about where we were going on holiday, which play we were going to see, which concert to hear and there was no argument possible. At Christmas, which we celebrated German-style, on December 24, my father was in sole charge. He put holders on the tree with real candles, prepared the tables of presents and lit the candles. We waited outside the closed door. When everything was ready, the door opened and in we went. At the far end of the room the tree stood, glittering. I sat down at the piano and we sang a carol. Then we opened our presents. It was all very orderly. I longed to have an English Christmas, like my friends, with stockings at the end of the bed and tearing open parcels chaotically early on Christmas morning.

I was nervous of my father's controlling impulses. Later I wondered how much his tendency to control was exacerbated by being a refugee, an outsider, by my mother's increasing lack of control?

And Fips was becoming more distressed and withdrawn. I still saw myself as the child responsible for her. There were rarely explicit demands or requests from her, more unspoken matters – that I was required to watch her moods, which I picked up through her body language, her lack of engagement when she was withdrawn, her sadness. It made me feel anxious and sometimes irritable, but it had become part of my life.

We began to have au pair girls to help out. Gisela, from Germany, with her alert pale face and who always managed to see the funny side of whatever was going on, was a rock of warmth and sympathy. She became good friends with us all but went back after a year to marry an East German doctor. Edda, also from

Germany, curly haired and very young, was like an older sister to us. I missed Gisela.

In 1950, my parents' childhood friend Annemarie, who'd lived through the war in Germany, married unhappily to a Nazi sympathiser, came to stay. This was an old friendship – she had been to school with my mother – and her visit brought a kind of lightness and humour to the house. They talked about memories of childhood and shared their very different experiences of the war. My mother emerged from her shell a bit.

And it was the year I began to have rages. They usually came suddenly, out of the blue. I was swamped by a panicky despair, shouting and weeping, losing control, feeling no one could reach me. It was not always clear to me who I was raging at. Afterwards I felt limp and empty, often for hours. My parents had no idea how to address this anger, which I suppose frightened them too; they simply waited till it was over and things went on as before.

These rages continued intermittently into my adult life. It was years before I could talk about them, to friends and later to therapists, before I began to understand them better – a sense of loss and abandonment, a fear of not being understood, of being invisible, of insecure attachments, which left me drained and always touched on my fear of mental illness.

Culturally, there were elements of my parents' taste and their past lives that they really wanted us to embrace – classical music above all. We were taken to concerts and operas from an early age. My parents were clever about introducing us to opera – taking us to the tuneful, easier ones first and gradually to more difficult ones. I have loved opera ever since.

Concerts were different – I often didn't want to go, but to protest would have been inconceivable. Aged fourteen, I was dragged off to the late Beethoven Quartets at the Victoria and Albert Museum. I was bored and wanted to be somewhere else. The fact that we were given no choice simplified matters. Gradually, without my noticing, classical music embedded itself into my life. And later I felt huge gratitude to my parents for their insistence on taking me.

We all played instruments. My mother was a competent vio-linist, my father an excellent flautist; the gentle side of his nature, hidden at other times, emerged when he was playing. My sister, like me, played the piano, but I, being older and better at it, played more. My brother was a good cellist. We played chamber music, Telemann, Bach, Mozart, Beethoven, Schubert, Haydn, trios, quartets, duets. It was part of our life and I accepted it as that, initially not always enthusiastically. But then, as we played, I became absorbed in the pleasure of the music and music making. At times of great tension between my mother and father it some-times even seemed a solution to the unhappiness, however tem-porary. Sometimes we played in small local concerts, in charming drawing rooms in suburban Putney. There was no doubting how much we all got out of those afternoons and evenings, even though the sense of the united family, in tune with each other, was by no means the whole picture. But music was a family bond – and remained so for the rest of our lives.

I started piano lessons when I was ten. My piano teacher, Dorrie Hesse, a large, warm, endlessly patient woman, was utterly committed to her pupils. She was my mother's cousin – the one who met Peter and I when we first arrived in England – one of eight children who came to England a generation before my parents. Dorrie, who made something of a mark as a concert pianist and then turned to teaching, chose the Tobias Matthai method, which involved developing a particular clinging touch to the keys. 'Now drop the fingers and *cliiinnng*' was her constant call.

Once a week I took the bus for my lesson to Earl's Court, usually with my mother. Dorrie had some talented pupils, many of whom took up music as a profession. I was quite a good pianist – '*Sehr musikalisch*' my relatives nodded to each other – though I was lazy about practicing scales and never acquired enough technical skills. I practiced the classical pieces diligently, but I sneaked off to spend my pocket money on sheet music – Frank Sinatra's 'Love and Marriage', Frankie Vaughan 'Give Me You', Doris Day 'Che Sera Sera' – which I played defiantly at the end of the practice time.

Each year Dorrie held a concert at the Wigmore Hall for her best pupils. I first played there when I was thirteen. The hall looked very much as it looks now – the plush red seats and above the stage the nearly-naked figure, arms raised, rays of the sun behind him; the door to the right of the stage, through which we had to come on to the platform. What I mostly remember is the terror of performing, a terror that I knew I didn't want to have as a regular part of my life.

The last time I played in the Wigmore Hall, aged fifteen, fell on the same day as the final of an important rounders match at school. My mother said I had to miss the match as it would affect my playing in the evening. I insisted that I couldn't miss it. How could I possibly explain to my mother the impossibility of not playing in that match – how absurd it would seem to my fellow team mates that I should choose not to because of a concert. A serious clash of cultures – not for the first time. Even the idea of proposing such a thing was humiliating.

So, I defied my parents. We won the match and then, in the evening, I walked through the door on to the platform in my flowered frock and shiny black shoes, full of the usual terror and I made a mistake in the Mozart *Rondo*. I recovered myself, but when I saw my mother in the interval I could see that she was in agony. I had let her down and she couldn't conceal her feelings. The hall was buzzing with proud, aspirational parents of talented children and I was the only one to have made a mistake, or at least one that showed.

I was angry at myself and miserable at my less than perfect playing. I knew my mother blamed the rounders match for my mistake. But I felt, as I often did, that this person who my parents wanted to be so proud of was mysterious to me. Who was it they were praising anyway? What did this person really want? We went home in silence. It was a disastrous evening and it made it clear to me that I was not going to make it as a musician and I was more certain than ever that I didn't want to. I had anyway begun to feel my fellow pupils' lives were too centred on music and found their lack of interest in other things frustrating. I was ready to find out what was going on in the wider world.

⚜

Our living room, never very cosy or lived in, was nevertheless the place I spent a lot of time. I did my homework diligently at the cherry wood desk in the corner, the Van Gogh print over the mantlepiece, the etching of a horse race and the drawing of my mother as a young girl on the wall. A strip of linoleum separated the wall from the grey pile carpet. My mother longed for the carpet to be fitted; it was one of the recurring arguments between her and my father. Every weekday evening I rushed upstairs at 6.45 to catch the stirring signature tune of *Dick Barton, Special Agent*. On Sundays we sat and listened to the evening play. It was where we played endless games of canasta. In the Forties, my father bought a radiogram on which you could stack six 78 rpm records; they dropped down in perfect sequence and transformed our listening habits – no need any longer to get up after each side had played and turn the record over. My parent's collection was entirely classical, played by their tried and trusted performers, Schnabel, the Busch Quartet, Otto Klemperer, with the occasional Viennese operetta and the Comedian Harmonists. I have these records still.

I listened to this music because that's what was expected of me, liked it well enough at the time, knew it was part of my world. Now it's something I can't manage without. I bought my own first

The family on holiday in Switzerland, 1951

record with pocket money when I was thirteen, a 45 single called *The Cuckoo Waltz*. I became obsessed with this banal little tune and listened to it endlessly.

❦

In the late Forties we began to go on family holidays to Switzerland, my father driving the Austin 12. This was postwar Europe and as we passed through towns and villages in North West France, still showing devastating signs of war and poverty, the French children, seeing our British number plates, held up their fingers in the V for Victory sign and we excitedly held up ours in return. At a time when food was still rationed in England, the meals we ate were astonishing. I remember an unforgettable meringue Chantilly, enormous, crumbling, smothered in whipped cream, in a small restaurant near the cathedral in Rheims.

My parents wanted us to have a taste of the landscapes they knew as children and adolescents in Germany. They found hotels high up in the mountains, unpretentious, comfortable places with wonderful views. Walking was an important feature of these holidays. My father wore his usual plus fours, my mother a scarf round her head; they both carried walking sticks. Sometimes we walked high into cold, dense mist, stumbling on to huts serving pea soup and rye bread. It was hard going, but, as ever, complaining wasn't possible and I grew to love the climbs and the views and the triumph of reaching the top of ridges and mountains.

I felt Fips and Werner's attachment to these landscapes and their ease and familiarity with them. They were in charge of things here, while in England they were often still strangers where we children knew our way around.

On the last holiday, in 1951, my mother's mental health was fragile and there were particularly painful tensions between my parents that couldn't be disguised, my father hitting my mother on her bottom with his walking stick in a moment of total frustration and anger. I was shocked but felt his despair and hers.

*

In the summer of 1952, my mother took my sister and I on holiday to Dawlish Warren in Devon. By now there was so much unhappiness between my parents that they'd decided on separate holidays; my father took the son, my mother the daughters. Arriving on a hot July day at Dawlish station, we took a taxi to the smart hotel we were staying in, the gardens with lawns and tennis courts, full of jolly young people. I walked up the drive, my feet kicking the gravel disconsolately, watching them play tennis and talk loudly with such confidence, so at ease with themselves and each other. I felt a hopeless alienation rising, a recognition that I could do nothing to turn myself into these people. I envied my sister her happy seven-year-old's oblivion.

That evening there was a fancy dress competition after supper. My mother, admirably, for I could see that she too felt out of things and had no husband to support her, encouraged me to enter. All I could think of was to dress up in my pyjamas. The music played and we walked round in a circle being judged, the other children in pretty dresses or fancy trousers, in funny hats and with make-up on their faces. I slumped round and round, dragging my feet, looking as awkward as I felt. Somehow, I was given second prize. Were they sorry for me? Or did I do a rather brilliant unintentional imitation of a street urchin? I shall never know. It was a consolation to be given a prize, but it did nothing to bring me closer to those golden girls and boys.

Perhaps because it was the first time I realized the gulf between my parents was unbridgeable, that holiday imprinted otherness with particular intensity. The next day we walked down towards the sea and my mother went swimming across the river estuary, which turned out to have dangerous tides. A man in a rowing boat went to rescue her, though she herself felt in no danger. As she was brought back to us on the beach, I noticed she had forgotten to take off her pearl necklace. She was embarrassed about this, indeed about the whole episode. She clutched the necklace and giggled a little. Her big breasts were half-exposed and she looked beautiful and vulnerable in her black bathing suit. Her accent seemed stronger than ever. I was mortified, on her behalf as well as mine.

This absurd scene seemed to confirm our otherness. It was so obvious that I stopped aspiring to the condition of a Joan Hunter Dunn tennis girl and began, at least on that holiday, to accept things as they were. It was a sullen and depressed acceptance, but some sort of acknowledgement of the reality of my life. I was far from seeing the strange gifts of alienation – Adorno once warned his fellow refugees that if they lost their alienation they'd lose their souls – but it was a beginning.

10

ABSENCE

MY MOTHER FIRST went into a residential hospital when I was sixteen. I remember her extreme and frightening unhappiness that October morning in 1953, her distraught talk and then, looking down at the floor, her complete withdrawals. My sister had gone to a children's concert that morning, returning home before lunch to find me sitting at the bottom of the stairs. My father had driven my mother off to the clinic. He came home shortly after lunch and explained that my mother was unwell and he'd left her in the clinic. I have no memory of what he said to me before he left. He spoke very little about our mother's illness. I think he thought he would protect us by saying as little as possible about it. Given his generation and with his experiences, he seemed to have a tendency not to talk about the most important things. He may have been advised not to disclose too much to the children. He may have given the impression that my mother would soon be better. He definitely gave the impression that life would go on as normal. I didn't emerge from this period having any great understanding of what was going on or what my mother was suffering from. I did discover that I hated silence and secrecy and longed for us to talk about it all. But I never talked to my sister about this – though talking to her now I realise she felt the same.

At weekends I sometimes went with my father to visit my mother in her quiet room, white walls with the occasional bland print. For some reason my sister didn't come – maybe my father was protecting her again. Fips was withdrawn and we made desperate attempts to cheer her up and tell her what we'd been doing. I learned later that she was being given insulin shock treatment there, repeated injections of large doses of insulin to produce spasms, convulsions, comas which supposedly might jar her out of her condition – a form of treatment used, before ECT replaced it, in the 1940s and 50s, mainly for depression and schizophrenia.

At home, without her, I felt bleak and confused. I didn't dare to ask questions of my father, for fear they would be diverted. I felt complicated about him, as ever, resentful that he didn't understand her better or be more direct about his own emotions, but sympathetic to his attempts to help her, love her, make life workable, manageable.

For me, it was a guilty relief not to be wondering how her mood might be at the next meal, or how to try and make her join in when her head was bowed down with gloom or anger. My father's determination for life to go on as normal worked up to a point, though domestic life was strange and disrupted; Dolly came more often and was there when we got home from school. Soon after, my father took on Nell as a live-in housekeeper and the reality of my mother's absence began to sink in.

A few weeks later, I saw a headline in the *Evening Standard* as I was coming home from school – 'Mental Patients in Fire'. I rushed home full of indignation and told my father how outrageous it was for the paper to call them mental patients. Looking bemused, he tried to explain that this was a reasonably accurate way to describe people with mental illness. And so I began to take in that my mother was something called mentally ill, that she was, I supposed, mad. Somehow the words had not been articulated up to then and it made a difference that I knew them. And the fear that I would be like her, become mentally ill myself, became more deeply embedded.

She was diagnosed, repeatedly over the next many years, as schizophrenic or paranoid schizophrenic. Diagnosis in the 1950s for mental illness was, as we discovered in retrospect, unreliable. I witnessed symptoms my mother displayed – paranoid feelings about what people were saying, ascribing significance to how people were sitting or standing, a high level of anxiety, some depression, some anger. Being curious and with a certain compulsion, I started reading about schizophrenia. I thought I might have all the symptoms the books described. I had already experienced anger and anxiety and was at times ritualistic in my anxious thoughts. It was not difficult for me to exaggerate the fears I had about whether other people liked me and turn them into some version of paranoia. I was still very shy and often silent. So it was that I managed to find endless examples of symptoms that were proof of my incipient madness.

Though I tended to cut the information short, I read enough to convince me that I would end up schizophrenic. One day I asked my father whether schizophrenia was inherited, as many of the books said it was, and would I get it? He hesitated fractionally and in that moment I felt sure that he thought I was like my mother and might be at risk.

❧

With all this going on at home and perhaps the more so because of it, at school and in my social life I continued, in a sort of daze, to work hard at belonging. Being a good girl and an achiever, that was part of the enterprise and to the extent that I was successful some of my sense of otherness was kept at bay. But it was all precarious and I never really felt safe. Aspirations to be good are not uncommon in girls. But I was representing more than myself. I had my parents' desires to consider.

I was diligent and reasonably clever; but I was in an exceptionally clever class and had to work hard to keep up. My confidence in coping with work was at an all-time low. My quiet bespectacled maths teacher at the time took me to one side one day and said, as gently as she could, that I must stop copying my friends' homework, that it wouldn't get me through. I was mortified.

We were all grappling with puberty too. I was very thin and my parents had been feeding me hot chocolate every night to fatten me up. I was the last person in my class to menstruate. It was a competition between me and Diana, an even thinner girl and waiting to see who would get there first became a subject for public discussion. I was last. We were studying Julius Caesar for O-levels and some of my classmates suggested that I must be Calpurnia because she was barren. I didn't feel it as particularly cruel, but I was relieved when the blood finally flowed.

I threw myself into sporting activities, ending up as hockey captain, a member of nearly every school team and head of house. Putney High School, an all-girls school, had four houses, named after successful male politicians, Pitt, Cromwell, Argyll, Fairfax. We were all assigned to one of them. Competition between them was a major part of school life, mostly around games. On the day of house matches, girls in the teams were allowed to wear girdles in their house colour – a matter of enormous pride. The house that won the most matches over the year was, astonishingly, called Cock House. This was all very important to me. I was devastated when later I was made only Deputy Head, not Head Girl.

Meanwhile, I'd moved on to Lonnie Donegan and Chris Barber, and it was now Johnny Ray's 'Just Walkin' in the Rain', Perry Como's 'Don't Let the Stars Get in Your Eyes' and Doris Day's 'It's a Lovely Day' that I played on the piano at the end of my classical practice period. I began to write an opera with my friend Gill, a good pianist herself. We pored over the manuscript and the piano for hours. An only child of parents who were desperate for her to achieve academic success, she started going out with a boy, got pregnant and married him and that was the end of our opera enterprise.

Belonging meant doing my best to be a success at the local tennis club, to acquire boyfriends, to be a star at the youth club dance, to make jokes in the best colloquial English. I didn't feel easy expressing myself even though I spoke English without an accent. My attempted verbal subtleties were earnestly imitated from friends. I was awkward and unglamorous. I apologised too often. I didn't have the patter, the inflections, the speedy responses. I didn't dress right, still much under the influence of my parents who remained resolutely continental and old-fashioned in their tastes.

There were miserable Saturday evenings at the youth club in East Sheen, dancing with a foxy boy who, unbelievably, seemed to like me a bit. I went through these evenings as if sleepwalking.

My first school dance was due a few weeks after my mother went into the clinic. Frau Rosenblatt, the wife of my father's colleague and a friend of my mother's, was designated to help me buy what was to be my first ball gown. Our destination was Harrods. I was familiar with its huge arched halls, their thick pile carpets lit with a rosy glow, the shop assistants dressed in black, standing watching attentively.

I was not used to dressing up. I tried on endless dresses in the cubicle. I stared at myself in the mirror. I was skinny and awkward but after a while I began to enjoy it, to feel that perhaps I could look pretty. Finally, with the help of the kindly Frau Rosenblatt, I chose a long pale blue slipper satin dress with a halter neck. I felt good in it.

I'd been having dancing classes at the local boys' school, Emmanuel, for a year and had got friendly with a boy there, Richard Marquand. He had a pock-marked face and he was very attractive. The boys all came to our dance and Richard quickly took me on to the floor in the main school hall and I was happy.

After a few dances we sat down together and another boy came and asked me to dance. I said yes immediately and got up. It never occurred to me to say anything to Richard, to make some acknowledgement that we were together. I was innocent, naïve, clumsy about such things. So that was the end of our evening together – he assumed I had lost interest in him and wandered off. It didn't occur to me to go after him. I never saw him again.

Surely I exaggerate my feelings of not belonging? All children have to assimilate to something. I sometimes enjoyed my school life, I had friends. But I was precarious in particular ways. I was not making sense of the two worlds that I was growing up in. I was never sure why people liked me or whether they would go on liking me, whether I would go on coping with work or stay in the school teams. My friends knew my parents were refugees from Germany, but they weren't very interested, nor did they think it made me different. But I did. One skin too few, someone once said. I needed too much to be part of things that didn't seem to be available to me. Later, I wanted to discard some of the very things I had wanted so much to belong to.

And there were times when I rebelled against this need to be part of a world that eluded me. In my mid-teens, I regularly went to stay with a Jewish friend in Golders Green, a year younger than me, the daughter of Frau Rosenblatt who had helped me buy the ball dress. I loved the Friday night Shabbat ceremonies. She was an only child, with parents who were happy with each other; her mother mothered me and giggled with us. It all felt very safe. On Sunday mornings her father retired to the bath for two hours, reading the papers, head leaning against a rubber cushion, given cups of tea by his wife at regular intervals. We giggled at that too. My friend wrote in my autograph book: 'Stay as sweet as you are today' – we all had autograph books in those days and wrote in them with this absurd formality.

Being with them was another kind of certainty and I tried it out on myself. It never lasted much beyond the visits, but it was some recognition that there were alternative worlds to join, although I knew that this was not really a possible alternative for me. Much as I enjoyed these visits, I felt a stranger to their world. I was Jewish but not practicing. They never commented on my parents' conversion to Christianity, but I could talk about my mother's illness, which, ironically, sometimes made me feel more estranged.

But there were drawbacks to these efforts to belong, to knowing so little about what I wanted. I didn't have a sense of how to judge things for myself. I was often sure I wasn't normal and I wanted to be. I seemed to live with such extremes of feelings, though I found it hard to understand what they meant. I wanted life to seem less black and white. I wanted to accept myself more. It was years before I acknowledged that there was no such thing as normality and where I thought there was, it was rarely useful to me.

11

HOUSEKEEPERS AND
MENTAL HOSPITALS

O VER THE EIGHT years of my mother's absence in mental
hospitals, domestic life in Putney was overseen by live-in
housekeepers. They didn't offer me much emotional comfort, but
they were not unpleasant and they kept things going. First, in
1954, there was well-meaning and humourless Nell, who stayed for
two years, followed by a period of a few months when my mother
was well enough to be at home. My father's own attempts to keep
family life going were, in their own way, impressive. He threw
himself into work, but always came back for the evening meal:
sometimes he travelled, to Germany, to Sheffield, to Sweden, but
he was in contact with us, made sure we were being looked after
properly in material ways, that routines were established.

Emotional matters were another thing: he tended to avoid
them. He was interested in what we were doing, if not always

approving. I felt protective towards my sister in all this, though in retrospect I wonder whether she dealt with the disruptions of our lives rather better than me.

When I was sixteen my father felt he ought, in my mother's absence, to talk to me about sex. He took me for a walk across Wimbledon Common and tried to explain how it 'worked', ending with the assertion that 'one should never feel tired after sex' – something I assumed was in the spirit of German athleticism. It never worked for me: I always fell fast asleep after sex.

Nell, with her pale face and sombre brown sweaters, was competent and calm but kept her distance from the family, going off at weekends with her twin sister. Miss Berenz came three years later, after my mother had returned to hospital, unable to sustain life at home. By that time I was already at college, at home for the holidays. Miss Berenz stayed for six years. A handsome, stiff German woman from a distinguished family, she felt acutely that she'd come down in the world. Though she was not in the least anti-Semitic, I detected in the bitter way she talked a resentment that we, a Jewish family, were living a comfortable life while she was in reduced circumstances, not in keeping with her class position.

She told us many stories – of her escape from the Russians at the end of the war on a cart with a few belongings, how she'd offered herself to Russian soldiers when they tried to rape younger women, of how she adored her divorced diplomat brother and tried to help bring up his daughter, how she felt that her life was hard and unfair and not what she'd expected.

Her attitudes to life were dogmatic and bourgeois and she was obsessively tidy around the house. If I put a newspaper on the table it would be tidied away when I came back twenty minutes later. She left notes for my sister reminding her that she'd failed to tie back her curtains before she went to school. It was impossible for me to ask a friend home for a meal at short notice if she hadn't catered for them being there. She was also capable of kindness and concern. I was exasperated by her and felt sorry for her. And her position was impossible. She wanted above all to be part of our family and after the evening meal the awkward moment would come when she went to her room and we went to our living room with my father. It felt deeply uncomfortable and yet I didn't want her with us either. Occasionally my father would ask her to join us. And, inevitably, she fell in love with my father.

When she was well enough, my mother came home at weekends. The difficulties for her were enormous. She was faced with a housekeeper ensconced in the household, running daily life, being in charge of meals and organizing things. My mother was left without a role in her own house, having to adjust to a woman she didn't know well, recognising that her husband and children were being looked after by someone she saw as a stranger. For the housekeepers it was also not easy. I put myself on special alert on these occasions, watchful, protective and irritated by the fact that I was participating in the situation.

On one occasion a close friend of the family came for tea. Miss Berenz had laid the dining room table which was only used for formal occasions, had made the sandwiches and put the cakes out. For one awful moment she and my mother tussled physically over who would pass the plate of sandwiches to our guest.

It was an insoluble and intolerable situation. My father was trying to make the household work on a day-to-day basis in my mother's absence. My mother felt excluded from her life and who could blame her? My father wanted, above all, to avoid emotional conflict and though I was unsympathetic to that at the time and tried to persuade him to be more open about how things were to my mother and Miss Berenz, he was in his own way trying to survive. My parents couldn't talk to each other without desperation or anger. Added to which Miss Berenz's feelings of exclusion and her growing attraction to my father, which he chose to ignore, created more tension.

On weekends when my mother didn't come home, my father, Ruth and I went on weekly Sunday visits to whichever hospital she was in. By then my brother was hardly ever at home. I came back in the university holidays and took part in the weekend rituals again.

For those eight years my mother was in several hospitals, all of them old Victorian asylums on the edge of London. Our visits followed the same pattern. We drove to the hospital, through the gate towards the monumental red brick buildings, with their strange turrets and modern extensions. Solitary people passed each other without recognition, solitary figures too walking in the gardens among the rhododendron bushes and holly trees, or on the lawns bordered by formal flower beds. It looked peaceful enough, until you got closer and heard the mutterings, saw the sad drawn faces, the wrinkled stockings, the nicotine-stained fingers.

Inside, we walked down the long corridors with their faint

smell of disinfectant mixed with urine, their cream-coloured walls and strip lighting throwing grey shadows, making everything look bleached, to pick my mother up in her ward. The staff kept up a bustle of cheerfulness and friendliness, but there were also the layers of silences – women sitting at the table in the day room, bewilderment and confusion on their faces, the odd burst of anger or slightly manic laughter from one or another. There was a good deal of curious staring at us.

My mother wanted us to meet the nurses; she enjoyed the regular sessions making baskets and knitting and introduced us to the occupational therapists she'd befriended and the patients she particularly liked. Here I discovered that my mother was at home with people she would never have spent time with outside the hospital; here, sharing her moods with others whose feelings she understood was what was important to her, regardless of who they were. Her closest friend was Mrs B, a large working class woman wrapped in warm cardigans, cigarette permanently hanging from her mouth, whose warmth and understanding towards my mother was palpable. Slowly it dawned on me that being in a place where she didn't have to relate to her husband and children or deal with her life at home, or feel she was the ill one, was a huge relief for her. Her ability to sustain the giving of love had been diminished. The hospital was a safe haven. Such places, now almost disappeared, were in their way true sanctuaries for people with mental illness.

I became used to what seemed at first extremely frightening places and unpredictable people. I dealt with the drives to and from the hospitals by sitting in the back of the car and having fantasies – about the boy at the tennis club, about imagined heroic acts where I saved friends' lives, about possible and impossible futures, hugging my emotions to myself. We took my mother to smart, comfortable hotels for roast Sunday lunches and, after a country drive, for cream teas in pretty cottages with flower-filled gardens, all over the home counties in South East England. Conversation was an effort and often felt forced. I thought there were many taboo subjects which would make my mother sad or anxious. Yet not talking carried the heavy weight of guilt. There were often long silences. In the early evening we took my mother back to the hospital. I felt relief and guilt and sadness.

My father drove home. Going into our house, I went immediately to turn on the lights that made the rooms seem warm and friendly – no central overheads. I opened a can of Fray Bentos steak and kidney pie and put some frozen peas in a saucepan of hot water. That was supper, a ritual that was repeated Sunday after Sunday. We never talked about my mother, but there was some sense of relief – from tension, from distress at my mother's unhappiness, from not having to be careful about what we said.

I kept my fears, the same old fears, to myself – that I understood my mother too well, that I was too close to her, that I would inevitably be as unhappy and as mad as she sometimes was. I believed this to be possible and even likely, until I was forty, the age I calculated my mother had first gone into mental hospital. (I'd miscalculated – she was forty-four.)

Perhaps, looking back, I was more resourceful than I thought in the situation I found myself. I was sensitive to my mother's moods and learned to adapt to them in ways that earned me affection. I tried to become someone who was able to identify with others. I built myself a world outside the family that helped me to cope with my fears. I discovered to my surprise I had a strong will to survive.

It was when R. D. Laing's writings came out in the early sixties that I began to believe it was possible that I might not go mad. I read them voraciously. *Sanity, Madness and the Family*, the book Laing wrote with Esterson, was an early exposition of the idea that mental illnesses can be the result of social interaction, can be largely social creations, that families may sometimes choose someone from their number to be ill for them, that some illness is to do with the denial of experiences. At least it offered alternative views and didn't doom me categorically to heredity. It was probably the first book to politicize me, giving me an understanding of social constructions and how society plays its part in an individual's life.

In a sense, the whole family colluded with the secrets around my mother's illness. Peter, Ruth and I shared hardly any confidences over those years: we survived as best we could, in our separate ways. After the death of our parents, we began, tentatively, to exchange information. We realised that we had seen things in utterly different ways. My brother didn't accept my view that my mother, as well as being distressed, was often angry. My sister told me her fantasies about the mysterious trips into town. They were more benign than mine – she believed they were going off to see Frau Rosenblatt.

I always assumed my sister was more protected, less engaged

in my parents' troubles. Because I was in effect mothering my mother (the therapists call it the parentified child) – I felt that I was a buffer between my sister and my parents' problems and in some ways I was. But one evening, when I was in my seventies, she in her sixties, Ruth told me of the time when she was still living at home and I had left for university. My parents had had one of their enormous night rows and in the course of it my mother had pulled down the curtain rail. In the morning, they left together in the car. My father was taking my mother to the mental hospital, which required her first to be certified (now called sectioned).

My sister went into their bedroom and put back the curtain rail. Some hours later, my father returned, went to bed and stayed there for three days, weeping. My sister was thirteen. She made him porridge for breakfast and took him regular small meals.

This story of the collapse of my tough, authoritarian, autocratic father and my sister's attempts to look after him shocked me deeply. The fact that she'd never told me the story was a measure of how my mother's illness and all that surrounded it separated us rather than brought us together. Concealments and secrets were part of the way we lived. We listened in on telephone conversations, or outside doors, to find out what was going on, but we didn't tell each other what we found out.

My sister and I both felt sorry for my father because we assumed (I think rightly) that he didn't have any sex in his life for years. But we didn't talk to each other about it at all. Nor did I tell her of the occasion where my father read out a letter to me from a German woman, the wife of a colleague of his, who was very much obsessed and in love with him. He read it with a hint that she was a troubled woman. He asked me what he should do about it. I was twenty. All I remember is saying with great feeling that he had to answer it and not leave her hanging (I'm not sure I'd advise him that way now!). In this and other strange ways he demonstrated the vulnerability which went along with his quite abrasive authoritarianism.

In my mother's letter collection there were many from my father. Some are from their early years together – he often addressed her as '*Mein geliebtes kind*' (my beloved child). During her times in mental hospitals he wrote to her regularly, this time '*Mein liebster Fips*' sometimes once a week, addressing her health and state of mind in careful, concerned ways, responding affectionately to her letters to him, telling her news about us, the children, making arrangements to come and visit, talking about what the doctors were suggesting, always signing off with 'love and kisses.' They are rather formal and careful but I am struck by the consistent loving tone in them, the attempt to reassure her. I believe he loved her more than she loved him. She seemed so often to be disappointed in him. He was dutiful and, as far as I know, faithful to her till I was twenty-one, when, after another huge row, he gave up. It was only then, when my father finally felt that he could do nothing to help her, that he passed me some typewritten notes on some of the milestones of her illness. I was horrified – partly because the typing gave them such an impersonal tone (I wondered, uncharitably, whether he'd got his secretary to type them up), mainly because I didn't want to know.

I remember nothing of what the notes said.

She remained largely my responsibility, though less so in later years when I called on my brother and sister to take a larger part in caring for her. She was fragile, needy, responding to life with high levels of anxiety. I loved her in my way, took care of her as I felt I should. But it was hard for me to spend more than a few days with her at a time. I rarely confided in her because her anxiety would immediately take the conversation over. I found that hard to bear.

When, after her death, I read some of my letters to her that she had kept - from Egypt, America, London, Lebanon - I was surprised and relieved, that I had been affectionate and chatty, happy to tell her what we were doing and seeing, inviting her to stay. But I hardly ever told her what I was thinking or feeling - that would have been dangerous territory. I still wonder whether I should have risked telling her more, stepped back a bit, not be so stuck in my fears. Everyone deserves to be seen with fresh eyes.

After she died, the irritation, to my amazement, dropped away. I was left with the sense of her heroism - of her ability to survive awful things and terrible times; living under the Nazis, being exiled, starting again with a young family in a strange land, surviving insulin treatment and ECT, being certified more than once and spending many years in mental hospitals. And then taking on living alone with courage.

In February 2012, I heard a radio programme on schizophrenia. The psychiatrist talked of the unbridgeable rift in the Seventies and Eighties between those who believed that schizophrenia was a genetic or constitutional affair and those who thought it was socially induced. He discussed his recent work on schizophrenia and immigration, mainly done with Caribbean immigrants. It demonstrated clearly that vulnerability to schizophrenia is considerably increased if you are an immigrant.

12

LEAVING HOME

I DON'T REMEMBER thinking much about my decision to study medicine at university. Science was a tradition in the family – two grandparents and an aunt had been doctors, my father a chemical engineer, my uncle a physicist, my brother a mathematician. I was reasonably competent at science, I didn't feel drawn to any subject in particular, so doing medicine seemed as good a choice as any.

I got a place at Edinburgh and St Andrews universities and applied to two London hospitals, which I failed to get into. I was told later that there was not only a women's quota but also a Jewish quota (my surname was Sachs, a Jewish enough name), both unofficial. My parents, aspirational as they were for us, wanted me to go to Oxford, which meant taking an entrance exam. They set out to find contacts who might help and advise – very characteristic of my particular refugee community. There was also an expectation that I stood a good chance of getting in, not shared by me. In the autumn of 1955, I went to tea in one of the handsome houses in Park Town in Oxford with my godmother Mary Black and her friend, Miss Bannister, a physiology don at Somerville. We sat in the pretty living room overlooking the crescent gardens, me bolt upright in the chintz-covered armchair, knees together as I'd been taught, on anxious tenterhooks. Miss Bannister was intimidating. 'We had such an interesting student last year who wrote her entrance exam on Hebrew palaeontology,' she announced grandly, addressing my godmother. I didn't know what palaeontology was and felt crushed by her tone and obvious lack of interest in me.

But some small rod of steel I didn't know I had was angry and rebelled at her indifference. I'd show her. I was a child of exiles and at some level I'd absorbed with my mother's milk how to try and make things happen in a world I didn't by any means understand.

The next week I set off alone for the Royal Academy. I had no idea what was showing there. It was an exhibition of Portuguese art. I looked at the pictures, bought the catalogue and by the time of the general paper for Oxford entrance a few weeks later, I had learnt its contents by heart. I can remember some of it to this day. The information was easy to fit into the essays we had to do for the general paper. And it was almost certainly this essay that got me an interview. I turned up in an ochre-coloured hat and a neat beige suit, eyeing my fellow candidates on the bench in the gloomy St Hugh's corridor. In the end I slid in by the skin of my teeth; Oxford took twelve women in medicine, I was thirteenth and someone dropped out. I was pleased enough to get it, but felt a kind of numbness about what I was doing and little sense of excitement about the future.

So, nearly nineteen, I left school with a place at Oxford and with some months to fill in. In January 1956 I went to live with my aunt Ilse and her family and my grandmother Lotte, in Oxford. It was arranged that I would work as a lab assistant in the pharmacology laboratory where Mary Black's husband Hugh Blaschko was a distinguished research scientist whose field was chemical transmission in the nervous system. I have no memory of choosing this for myself, but I fell in with the plan.

I worked in the lab for six months. I cleaned out the cages with the rats on whom research was being done, made sure the instruments were kept clean; I paid a weekly visit to the abattoir in South Oxford, a visit I dreaded because of the killing and the smell, where I picked up adrenal glands from newly slaughtered cows and took them back to the labs. In some ways I felt in limbo, though I enjoyed the company of the young researchers, who talked to me about the research they were doing, and briefly fell in love with one of them – a tentative and innocent affair with someone I think was probably gay.

But I was also feeling safe. I was sharing a warm, welcoming family life, which was deeply reassuring, with my kind, tolerant aunt Ilse, her sweet, concerned nature and utter lack of pretension, her brown cardigans and sensible shoes, as attentive to me as she was to her two boys, her husband and Lotte. She was the person everyone relied on. I could confide in her about my mother – a huge relief – and she understood the conflicting emotions I felt, the mixture of irritation, concern and love and the sense of carrying a burden.

My cousins, younger than me, shared with me their comics and affectionate jokes about Lotte. And Lotte was the dominant figure in the household, small, vociferous, by now bent almost double, her frizzy grey hair tied up in bun, a genial but bossy matriarch, demanding to know what we were all doing, insisting that she must know exactly what time Ilse would be back whenever she went out, insisting too that we were all present for high tea every day at 5.00 p.m. When she disapproved of me she would say 'you are the worst of the trio.' She was interested in my life and she talked, often candidly, about her own past with Hans, who she loved, and about falling in love with her neighbour as a young married woman, about her life in Heidelberg as a professor's wife.

There were the usual disagreements and irritations in this family. But no huge tensions or arguments, no withdrawals. Routine family life – and I felt much gratitude to my aunt for supplying me with something I hadn't experienced for a long time, if ever – a life with other people where I wasn't watching out for difficult undercurrents or changing moods.

In October 1956, I left home for university. My father and mother drove me to Oxford and we filled the car with my belongings – a few novels, a textbook of physiology and biochemistry, trousers and sweaters, a white shirt and a pleated skirt, sheets and pillow-cases, a couple of indifferent watercolours of Cornwall, a vase and some music. We stopped for lunch in a hotel by the river, when we talked nervously about what my new life might be. They deposited me at The Lawn, in Banbury Road, the St Hugh's annexe I'd been designated, where we unloaded my stuff and took it up to the first floor, to my long, thin, gloomy room with its narrow truckle bed and faded armchair, the grey curtains matching the grey bed cover, a small desk at the window.

My mother had had a period of some months at home in the summer and was managing the household with the help of Dolly. But she was showing signs of getting withdrawn and agitated again. I was apprehensive about this, but much too excited about escaping from my parent's life and starting one of my own to let it affect me too much, though I did worry about my sister, by then a confident thirteen-year-old.

Autumn 1956 was the time of the Middle Eastern Suez crisis. I arrived in Oxford and everywhere – in colleges, on the streets, in lecture rooms – there were people protesting about the British government's attitude to Nasser, the President of Egypt and about Soviet tanks in Hungary and the arrest and subsequent execution of the Hungarian prime minister, Imre Nagy.

It was a revelation. Politics had been no part of my life so far: at home there was little talk of what was going on in the world and my school had not encouraged it. None of my friends were interested and nor, I thought, was I. As I left home for Oxford my father's words rang in my ears – his outrage at Nasser's claiming of the Suez Canal and later, in October, when Britain, France and Israel attacked Egypt, his defence of Anthony Eden the Prime Minister – 'the only thing he did wrong was not going far enough.' At the time I thought that sounded fine.

❦

A kind of liberal conservatism was a given position in my family. I knew nothing about socialism and had never met a socialist. The history of my family in Germany was mostly conservative, sometimes arch conservative, apart from my great-grandfather, Richard Grelling, the radical lawyer. My family were proud of him, but at a safe historical distance. I knew of only one girl at school whose parents voted Labour. We regarded her with a mixture of pity and amazement.

I was overwhelmed with excitement about the protests in Oxford, but even more about the fact that people were engaging in political argument at all – about these events, about the welfare state, about banning the bomb – and that they were interested in what I had to say. I had a family understanding from early on of what Nazism had done to my family. But I had read very little history at school or at home. Now I began to fit things together with other events in the world where people were oppressed and persecuted.

I was easily influenced, unclear as to what I believed, and above all happy to be among people who seemed to be passionate. I was longing to be passionate about the world. My teens had been too much spent thinking about personal emotions, my own and others, erratic and often disturbing. Now I heard people getting stirred up about ideas and the world was transformed. I'd never heard anything like it. My chameleon nature absorbed it all. Within a few weeks I was radicalized.

The sense that I might have a place in the scheme of things

began in those first weeks at Oxford. I was separated from the life of my parents, I began to have a sense of exhilarated freedom, much of it inside my head - where I had secret thoughts which separated me from my parents even more.

13

COLLEGE LIFE

THERE WERE TWELVE of us living in The Lawn. Our communal breakfast was overseen by the distinguished classics don who lived in the house with us, unsmiling and shy and severely disabled – one leg supported by an iron frame. Conversation with her was austere and difficult. She wasn't the only one in college who conveyed a sense of austerity in those first weeks. The new students were gathered together to be addressed by the principal, Miss Proctor, a tall, gaunt woman, born in the nineteenth century, part of the generation who slowly and painfully fought for the education of women. Oxford only finally allowed women to take degrees in 1921 (in Cambridge it took till 1947) and this was the world she came from.

None of us were in any doubt that work was part of why we were there, but for most of us it was only part. Miss Proctor seemed bemused by us, young women wearing trousers, keen to have a rich social as well as an intellectual life at Oxford. There was no real connection between her and us.

I fell in with college life easily. I loved everything about it – being with my fellow students, the structure of the day – lectures and laboratory work, then lunch in college and more labs and libraries, evenings in or out with friends. I even loved the disagreeable smell of the cooked mushroom stalks offered for breakfast, the long dark corridors with their old linoleum, the gloomy bedrooms and scruffy kitchens.

We drank a lot of coffee and cocoa in each other's rooms, late into the night. How uncool that sounds now. Alcohol was no part of college life amongst my friends. Some of us smoked, none of us took drugs. We took it in turns to make open fires in our tiny grates, two buckets of coal a week supplied. And we talked and talked. I felt as if I'd been observing the world in bottled up silence from an early age and for me at least this talk was a great release. We were hungry for ideas; I began to try and make sense of the world; I began to think.

I first encountered the three women who were to become my closest friends in the queue for lunch, laughing together after a tutorial, Jane, Veronica and Marianne, in one of those long St Hugh's corridors.

We soon began to share confidences and early on all three of them tried to shake my annoying tendency to apologise. We'd arrived in Oxford via different routes. Veronica, red haired and beautiful, with a deep roaring laugh, had rejected being a debutante and persuaded her father to let her come to Oxford. I was struck by her immense tolerance (except for anything that smacked of snobbery). Marianne had a German father and an English mother and a background more similar to mine; she had been to Cheltenham Ladies College; her intellectual confidence was often buried in giggles and shyness. Jane had been living in a hostel from the age of sixteen because she didn't want to side with one or other of her separated parents and made her own decisions about coming to Oxford. For a long time I was intimidated by the firmness of her opinions, then realized that sometimes she was, like us all, just testing them out. She was a convinced Christian, loved her father, a small wild man with gypsy origins who was a commercial traveller in postcards. Her mother, she told us, had warned her that about sex all men were like animals.

I was envious of their life studying English and longed to be doing it, I think as much as anything because I loved their company. There was often helpless laughter – what about it wasn't always clear – some expressive reading aloud and what seemed to me worldly and sophisticated discussions about love and religion.

What else did we talk about? Literature, our childhoods, music, our tutors, asthma, our parents and siblings, men, though cautiously, sex. Veronica told a story of her aunt on honeymoon, sending a telegram to her mother saying 'Help, help, John is going mad!' We roared with laughter, but we were fifties girls, pretty ignorant and inexperienced about sex ourselves.

There were some things we didn't talk about. When the four of us met in later years, my friends were surprised at the account I gave of my mother's illness and shocked that they didn't know more about it at the time. Even with them it had been a taboo subject for me – all the more striking because one evening in my first term I was called to the college phone (mobiles were years away) – my father told me that my mother had gone back into hospital. I can still feel that cold, small, dark phone booth in the hall and the dread I felt as I heard the news. He told me that he was looking for a new housekeeper, and in January the next year Miss Berenz arrived.

The anatomy labs to which I cycled each day, along the Banbury Road and the cherry tree lined road by the parks, were Victorian, the rooms huge and filled with the pungent, irritating smell of formaldehyde. Tables were lined up on each side of the room and on each lay a body, stiff and greenish in colour. They seemed so far removed from being human beings, these cadavers. I couldn't imagine them as men and women with their own stories. Only when the dissections were completed and the cars arrived with the coffins to place the remains in, to be buried or cremated, did it hit me that these bodies which we'd been poking and scrutinizing, cutting and laying open, had once been people who had had lives.

In my year, we were a class of sixty male medical students and twelve women. We were paired off, each pair given one part of the body every term to dissect – leg, arm, abdomen, head and neck, thorax. With our scalpels we carefully followed for hours the routes of blood vessels, nerves, unearthing the muscles and ligaments, making clear in death how the body works in life. Drawings are one way of doing this, but it's almost impossible to get the level of detail (or messiness) that one sees in the flesh. Without the cadaver you don't get the texture, the variation, the reality of what bodies are like.

The smell of formaldehyde hovered in the air. Each week we were tested on our progress – an exercise in learning by rote from a small brown book – or at least it was for me, as I could never find much logic in how the body was laid out. From time to time an anatomy professor would come and ask us questions. Most memorable was Professor Alice Stewart, small, glamorous, outspoken and brilliant, who famously asked us all "what is the position of the uterus?' As we mumbled our attempts at answers, she'd say brightly – 'Men say it's up and in and women say it's down and out'.

I was not much drawn to my fellow medical students. Many seemed pompous and arrogant. The attitudes around medicine at the time were authoritarian and old fashioned– even into the 1960s some of the men interviewing young doctors for jobs wore wing collars and junior doctors were often required to serve lunch to their seniors. This was fifties Britain and the profession was very much at home in a society where deference ran deep – towards traditional institutions, in hierarchical structures, in the young to their elders, the poor to the rich, women to men. In the Oxford medical school I was very much a woman in a man's world.

Not that I understood this well at the time. I was not much aware of the obvious lack of freedoms and choices for women compared with those of men, I didn't talk about it with my friends and certainly didn't rail against it. At some level I accepted that my future would be guided more by the man I married – I took it for granted that I would marry – than by any choices I might make about my own life. Gloria Steinem, the American feminist and founder of *Ms* magazine, said in the Sixties that 'women then were supposed to live the lives of their husbands, to marry an identity rather than become one themselves, to live secondary lives.' The writer Jessica Mann, a contemporary of mine, wrote about the Fifties: 'The fact is that we didn't long for things to change. We had no idea that posterity would be shocked by the way females were always, automatically, secondary and we didn't even notice. We just took it for granted. After all, there was nothing new about it. In fact I have a horrible suspicion that we actually felt perhaps deferential, or perhaps inferior.' It was in Oxford that I felt the first stirrings of what it was to become a woman, but it was years before it I felt it had much relevance to me, personally or politically.

It's hard to convey quite how marginal women felt in the fifties. It was rarely remarked on that there were few women in Parliament or in high positions in medicine or the law or on company boards. Women's territory was still fundamentally confined to the domestic – birth, death, marriage, motherhood, children – and the emotional – love, friendship, nurturing, caring. Most of the feminine stereotypes were firmly in place – passivity, irrationality, compliance, formlessness. In 1949, Simone de Beauvoir had demolished the notion that a women's biology determines her way of thinking in *The Second Sex* ('One is not born a woman, but becomes one'). But her insights were not enough at that time to change things and women were still in their biological cage. Juliet Mitchell reports that when she tried to buy a copy of *The Second*

Sex in the 1950s she was asked to leave the bookshop because it was thought to be pornography (not helped by an early cover that had naked women on it). Jane Miller, in her book Seductions, brought to life the excitement of the intellectual ideas of the Fifties, but pointed out that the ideas were almost exclusively male. She wrote of her time at Cambridge: 'Cambridge was a city of men. She was welcome here so long as she laughed and danced for them in the way its literature assured them women could and did. Let her beware though of asking for quarter in the examination hall or of asserting her difference from them in ways that might seem to question their absolute right to be where they were.'

And though there were individual women – Katherine Whitehorn was one – who described feeling confident of their place in that world, who experienced above all an opening up of things after the war – the optimism of the Festival of Britain, the possibility of careers for married women – they were rare. It was not a female world.

And yet at Oxford we were being educated by people who expected us to achieve intellectually. We were intensely aware of our privilege – we knew that only five per cent of the population went to university and an even smaller percentage of girls – were excited by ideas, engaged in argument and debate. Even so, when we thought about it, most of us were conscious that it would be our husband's work lives that would dominate our marriages, when we made them. Not that we talked about it at the time, perhaps because we thought such conversations frivolous. We took work seriously and for me that was complicated because it was not the work I wanted to do. I felt uneasy in my medical student world.

Not so with my friends who were reading English and languages. I was fascinated by their conversations, their witty deconstructions of their tutors, their accounts of the authors they loved and the ones they hated.

The talk among medical students seemed in comparison complacent, boisterous, dull. Being scientists, we spent a good deal more time in structured work, having to fit in laboratory work with lectures. So I missed out on the life of the Bodleian, where writing essays on Chaucer was interspersed with the passing of notes for assignations with men.

Though I made friends with other medical students, it was never a world I was comfortable in. I struggled with some of the syllabus, especially the parts which required a good grasp of physics. I wrote an essay a week and read them to my tutors. I did it competently but rarely felt inspired by the work and much of the writing I did was extracted from textbooks. I wasn't really engaged with medicine and I knew it. At one point I considered changing subjects, but I was discouraged from doing this.

Excitement came later, in my third year when I studied neurophysiology with an inspiring teacher Marian Fillenz; she made the connections between mind and body come alive, she talked to me about memory and brain chemistry and in her tutorials I began to understand people's passion for scientific research – which had been such a tradition in my family. She triggered in me an understanding of how much good science requires the imagination.

At the back of my mind I feared that if I became a doctor the business of diagnosis might cripple me with anxiety. In the end I did the pre-clinical work, took my degree in Physiology and was glad to have done that. I remained intrigued by medical matters and to this day am still drawn to hospitals. I got a bad degree, but I didn't really care. By the time I reached my third year, I had become much more interested in politics, psychology and the social sciences.

⁂

Though the terms at Oxford were short, we lived them intensely. The friendships I made in those three years were transforming and much of my sense of reinvention came from a feeling that with these women I could be myself, that I didn't need to perform or try too hard, that I would be accepted for what I was. They made me feel safe.

We shared our clothes, selecting them from a collective pile each morning. I more or less took over a turquoise polo necked sweater of Veronica's. We had our moments of wanting to dress smartly – the pleasure of a full-pleated skirt over several layers of starched petticoats and wraparound white shirt, with black winkle picker shoes; and my first sack dress, bright red linen. But they were rare – none of the four of us was particularly fashionable. We usually wore trousers and the fashionable trouser suit had yet to be invented. I wore a roll-on corset every day.

In between tutorials, medical lectures and anatomy classes, I tried to get myself educated in other subjects. Translation from Ronald Knox, the theologian and detective story writer, whose brilliant lectures he continued to give when he was dying of cancer, his face with a strange yellow tinge: the Renaissance from

Professor Wind, a man equally at home in art, literature, history and philosophy: painting from Kenneth Clark: the imagination in science from the charismatic Peter Medawar, the immunologist.

I had tea and crumpets in people's rooms, in front of sputtering gas fires. In summer I went out in punts on the river and on walks in the countryside at weekends. There were occasional sherry parties. I gave up sport, out of a sort of snobbery that associated sport with not being cool, though all the men I knew were happily engaged in it.

Music was a large part of my life. For a while I had a Jewish friend, Ursula, and we talked a lot about being the children of refugees, a mix of protectiveness for what our parents had gone through, embarrassment at their 'otherness' and the desire to escape into our own worlds of assimilation. I accompanied her on the piano, Schubert and Schumann songs, straight out of the culture of my family and hers; with Veronica, I learned seventeenth and eighteenth century English and Italian songs, quite new to me but which she particularly loved.; I joined choirs, especially Laszlo Heltay's, a glamorous and hugely talented Hungarian who'd just fled from his country. I often tagged along with Veronica, who had a really good voice and was instantly accepted into the choirs, sometimes, she irritatedly suspected, because of her beauty as well as her voice.

I began my lifelong addiction to movies in Oxford – early memories in black and white gradually turning to colour – from Ingmar Bergman, Antonioni and Elia Kazan to Elvis in *Jailhouse Rock* and Henry Fonda in *Twelve Angry Men*. I saw more plays in those three years than at any time in my life, Restoration comedies, Shakespeare, Chekhov, Strindberg, Pirandello, Tennessee Williams. Several of my friends were talented actors and I went with them to rehearsals, too shy and inhibited to act myself, thrilled at my contemporaries' theatrical skills.

And I felt distinct comfort in having Ilse and my grandmother nearby. I saw them every week for tea, cycling from college down to their large rambling house in the centre of town, sitting round the large oval kitchen table with its cream oil cloth and having teasing exchanges with my cousins, hearing my grandmother's regularly forthright opinions on everyone, both she and Ilse asking many questions about my life at Oxford. And, as ever, I could talk to them about my mother, whose health wasn't good, as I found out in regular phone calls I had, sometimes reluctantly, with my father. Ilse was always sympathetic, so was Lotte, but more to the situation than to me. I thought: Why don't they say how hard it must be for me? Nobody did. Maybe they felt it. We were not a family good at expressing our feelings.

⁂

Mine was an unexceptional Oxford time, not particularly glamorous or dramatic or smart. I didn't shine at work. I was simply happy there, my days filled with work and friendship and talk.

And I discovered a life of my own, not being responsible to others, sheltered from powerful and sometimes overpowering cultural messages from my parents. I learned new things from people who came from different backgrounds. I began to worry less about getting things wrong. I no longer felt so much need to please. Spontaneity had not been my strong suit so far but I began to feel I could try things out, take some risks. Now, slowly, I began to talk less tentatively, to try out new ideas. I became intoxicated with words, discovered what I thought by saying it out loud. I needed to make myself understood and used words experimentally, testing them out on what I thought of as my critical audience (I was well into my thirties when an irritated friend told me that I used swear words as if I was a child, with a desire to shock but without any real conviction).

Up to now, silences and interpreting silences had been a huge part of my life. Now I discovered that words were an important source of comfort, and formulating what I was feeling, sometimes to the point of obsession, began to matter to me. There were times when I found it hard to contain my thoughts. When I was unhappy I thought that unless I spilled the words out they would eat me up, devour me from inside. Or I would endlessly write my thoughts down, in tiny writing, cramming them on to small pieces of paper, on both sides, down the margins, in an attempt to understand what I was thinking, to alleviate the anxiety.

⁂

One autumn afternoon in 1957, Veronica and I went to the matinee of *Look Back in Anger* by John Osborne at the Oxford Playhouse. Kenneth Tynan, the theatre critic, had been one of the few who had admired it as 'a minor miracle with all the qualities one had despaired of ever seeing on the stage – the drift towards anarchy, the instinctive leftishness, the automatic rejection of "official" at-

titudes, the surrealist sense of humour, the casual promiscuity
. . . the determination that no one who dies shall go unmourned.'
Perhaps things were beginning to change. Veronica and I sat in
front of two middle aged women. When the play was over, one
said to the other 'Well, that's what happens when you marry a
man like that!' We giggled helplessly.

14

FIRST LOVE

M Y MOTHER SAID 'I don't understand why you haven't got a boyfriend when all your friends have.' I was seventeen and I was letting her down and I hated the conversation, which confirmed what I already knew – that I was awkward and plain and had no chance of having a boyfriend.

Two years later, I found myself at a university where women were in a striking minority. To my amazement, many men asked me out. The sense of confidence this gave me was an altogether new experience. I was flattered and it didn't occur to me not to accept.

Two of the men I stepped out with were medical students, good looking, gentle and, in stark contrast to many of those future doctors, neither cocksure nor patronizing. One of them became a regular companion that year. For a while I also went for tea and crumpets to the room of a shy historian in New College where he told me of his doubts about inheriting the family business. I had a brief disastrous encounter with a man in cavalry twills from Oriel who took me out in a punt, steered it up a small tributary of the river Cherwell and pounced on me. I fought him off, as it turned out without much difficulty, he was rather half hearted about it and not in the least bit seductive, and we punted back in a state of acute embarrassment.

Apart from the biochemist in my gap year, which hardly counted – the rare kiss and holding hands – I hadn't had any boyfriends, though I'd been aware of having sexual feelings for men who were hopelessly out of reach since I was about sixteen. And travelling alone on a train from Oxford in my mid-teens, I had discovered, to my astonishment, how to masturbate, which at least introduced me to orgasms.

Now I occasionally had strong feelings for people I was actually connected with. What that meant for me was more kissing and holding hands, a lot of hugging in front of gas fires in college rooms, but no more. Sexual intercourse was not even on the agenda for me – too risky on too many fronts.

I quite quickly lost interest in most of the men I met, though I sometimes went on seeing them, often feeling restless, dissatisfied, aware that there was something unsatisfactory in the relationship, wishing for more, more intensity, more certainty, knowing this wasn't the person for me, but not wanting to be without a man either.

I saw myself as Jewish and in some ways defined myself by that. But at that time I had no particular interest in finding out more about the Jewish religion. A few friends at Oxford were similarly children of Jewish refugees and we exchanged family stories. None of the men I went out with were Jewish – something I became aware of later, when I noticed how none of my siblings or cousins married Jews, how assimilation seemed to be instinctive, part of the collective unconscious in the family.

One damp autumn day (low-lying Oxford was often damp and I regularly got bronchitis) at the beginning of my second year, I was walking through Worcester College quadrangle with a boyfriend who was studying forestry and passionate about the countryside. He was very serious and turned his earnest bespectacled face to me as we argued about what a good life might be.

Just as we were leaving through the main gate we bumped into a friend of his from school. I was drawn to him immediately; striking looking, with a triangular Welsh head, deep-set green eyes and a Roman nose, he was wearing an elegant black coat over his broad, rugger-playing shoulders. His talk was quiet and intense, full of flashes of ironic humour. Aware that he seemed interested in me – the way he looked at me and asked me questions – and knowing that he was at Magdalen College, I decided to take matters into my own hands and two nights later I cycled down there. After enquiries at the porter's lodge, I threw stones at his window in the Old Grammar Hall building. He was there, opened the window and invited me in – his living quarters a good deal grander than my single room at St Hugh's, comfortable armchairs, separate bedroom and kitchen. And I was allowed to be there even though it was 9.00 in the evening. We drank coffee and we talked.

Later that night I cycled back to college in a state of excitement, heart thudding, but this time with other, new feelings jostling in my head and a strong desire to see this man again. He was interesting and ironic, withdrawn and hard to reach. He seemed to want to know who I was and I wanted to go on trying to draw him out. Speeding back through the wet streets, I was aware of how beautiful the buildings in Broad Street were looking. I was very happy. I reported some of this excitement to my friends back in college, though in moderation. We were rather reticent about matters of the heart with each other, though I would have liked to be more outspoken and confessional about love.

The next week I explained to the forester from Worcester College what had happened and ruthlessly dumped him.

Roger and I began to see each other regularly. I was drawn to his cleverness and what I saw as a certain worldliness. He was studying Politics, Philosophy and Economics, he read poetry, he'd been in love before and he was a socialist. And when he told me his stories, he seemed to have experienced life in a way that was unthinkable for me.

As part of National Service, he'd been sent to Cyprus as an army officer in a radio engineering unit. In his first few weeks on the island he was ambushed driving a jeep; miraculously, he and his colleague were unhurt. He was left standing by the jeep, gun in hand. The feeling of holding a gun and having the power to kill, left him, he said, with 'a sense of elation that lasted a couple of days, with my body more alive than I could ever remember and the colours more intense.' He described a sense of triumph: his enemies – he felt it very personally – had tried to kill him but had not succeeded.

I was fascinated and shocked – at his account of violence

and near-death and his feelings of elation. I wasn't used to such candour and, as a woman in love, I invested the whole story with immense romanticism.

Cyprus was Roger's first taste of the Middle East. It was where he began to love the terrain – rocky, dry, hot landscapes and beyond them the intoxicating blue of the Mediterranean – and became interested in the politics and history of the region. Lawrence Durrell was working as the government Information Officer on the island at the time and had just finished writing his novel Justine. They met on social occasions, in particular at horse races.

Anarchic, hedonistic, scornful of traditional English middle-class values, Durrell represented something deeply attractive to Roger. He told him to give up the idea of going to Oxford – which he regarded as a waste of time – 'and live.' His words made their mark and though he didn't take Durrell's advice Roger arrived at university feeling he'd already experienced things more significant than anything Oxford could offer, feeling older and wiser and rather distant from the whole business of being an undergraduate.

At the time I met Roger, one of his friends was orchestrating a campaign in Oxford against nuclear disarmament. We were a generation living with the fear of nuclear war. The campaign included a Lysistrata strand where girls were required to refuse to sleep with their boyfriends if they didn't support nuclear disarmament (more likely to have been a refusal to kiss their boyfriends as few of us were sleeping with men at that time). Roger was the quiet man behind the campaign, very organized but not very visible. I admired his arms-length involvement, the fact that he didn't seem to need the limelight. He saw himself as an observer, objective, full of healthy scepticism, a bit distanced from things. In retrospect, I think I was attracted by the reticence, the tendency to withdraw, the distancing. I saw it as grown up, something about depth of feeling, about a sense of privacy, about some sort of self-sufficiency, about someone in charge of himself. The distancing, of a different kind, was something I'd experienced with my father, but it was far from the familiar and overt neediness I felt from my mother. It felt like a relief, and attractive. It was, ironically, these qualities which I later found difficult in our relationship.

Roger was good at asking questions. His reticence went together with a deep curiosity and interest in who I was. He wanted to know about my Jewishness, what I felt about it, about my family's history and exile. His own parents, both socialists, brought him up to be politically aware and it was easy to talk to him about the more difficult aspects of being part of a refugee family. He asked questions about my sister and brother, my parents, my friends, about what I thought about studying medicine. I told him about my mother's illness and my parents' difficult marriage. I told him pretty much anything, though I occasionally sensed some disapproval as well as interest in what I was saying – for instance, about my rather conservative politics, or my desire to be good. His responses were not always easy to read, never vehement, sometimes ironic. He made me feel interesting and desirable. He made me happy. He was unlike anyone I'd ever met. I was pleased that such an interesting man was interested in me.

I began to introduce him to my friends, acutely conscious of their reactions to him. Some of them liked him, others found his reticence difficult. Our first kiss was outside Oxford High School, on a long walk home from the movies on a moonlit night. I wanted this man to be part of my life.

He talked to me about socialism and I became interested in ideas I knew nothing about. Gradually he told me more intimate things about himself – about his parents' divorce and how painful it had been, how they had come to his boarding school to tell him they were separating when he was thirteen and how awful it felt to be left at school afterwards. He was told by his parent's friends that he must now look after his mother and it weighed heavily on him.

I shared my twenty-first birthday party with my friend Ursula and we threw a large party and dance at the local army hall. The other Ursula had many theatrical friends, who dressed flamboyantly and seemed to me enormously witty and sociable. Dudley Moore came and played the piano. I wore a green satin strapless dress and was overwhelmed with excitement. Roger looked handsome and rather grave and we talked and danced and when everyone had gone, he walked me back to college where I had dispensation to get back late.

So we became a couple. We did all the usual undergraduate things – going to the cinema and the theatre, meeting each other's friends, listening to music. On Saturdays he'd play rugger, once returning to his rooms with his ear hanging by a thread. That winter was exceptionally cold and we skated together, sometimes late into the evening, on the frozen floods of Port Meadow looking like a Breughel painting. In spring we walked round Addison's Walk when the purple-headed fritillaries were out and as summer came I learnt how to punt along the willow-lined river Cherwell.

We met often in his college rooms – no curfew for men, though I had to be back at St Hugh's by 10.30 at night. I didn't dare stay the night: had I been caught I would have been sent down. He wouldn't – the disparity between women and men was striking. At St Hugh's that year a medical student became pregnant and she was sent down even though she married her partner.

We kissed and touched and made love more and more often, arousing each other in many different ways, but avoiding penetration, which Roger wanted but I resisted. Fear of pregnancy (birth control for women undergraduates was very hard to find); fear of being sent down; and, perhaps most potent as well as most hard to define, fear of not being a good girl. I'd been brought up Christian, had been confirmed in the Anglican Church and though I had no great interest or passion for religion and hardly ever went to church, I was still imbued with things I'd been taught – one of which was you don't sleep with people till you're married. I wanted to be on the safe side, even now I was in love, perhaps more than ever. I couldn't shake it off.

And so our early sex life was rather like Mary Quant's, who graphically described something very similar in her first autobiography *Quant by Quant*. Plenty of erotic feeling, plenty of orgasms and no penetration. What now seems strange and neurotic and rather ungenerous seemed to me right at the time.

Roger and I introduced each other to our families. His was Welsh, both grandfathers non-conformist clergymen. His father, remarried now to an American woman twenty years younger, was a successful executive in the UN, living in New York. My first glimpse of him was through the darkened windows of a limousine, in which he came to sweep Roger and me out of Oxford to lunch by the river at the country house of his friend David Astor. A small, twinkly man, he was charming and easy to talk to and we immediately liked each other. Roger's sister, two years younger than him, was also in the car. I knew how close she was to her brother and was acutely aware of her examining me carefully, wondering about my suitability for her adored brother.

Roger's mother, a warm, handsome, rather formidable-looking woman, was outspoken and direct, with a tendency to giggle. A Quaker and a socialist, she lived in Manchester with her second husband, a paediatrician. She and Roger wrote to each other every week. He teased her mercilessly, often about her instinct to do good works, her capacity to fill her house with lonely Africans and Indians at all times of year, especially Christmas.

From my first visit, in the spring of 1958, I loved talking to her. She was a strange mixture: on the one hand ready with stern judgments about how life should be lived, but also full of doubt, especially self doubt. Difficult emotional matters were no problem for her and I couldn't believe my luck. Here was someone I could talk to about my mother and how difficult I found the business of mothering her. She often said about my mother – 'poor woman'

– but even she never said 'poor you.' I tried to dismiss the self pitying thought.

Though we talked as equals, I also turned Roger's mother into the mother I longed to have, someone in whom I could confide. She in turn seemed to feel she could talk to me about intimate matters – her divorce, her relationship with her sisters, her children.

The general mood of closeness and fun in Roger's family was, for me, nothing short of wonderful. Of course there were tensions, some not so hidden. But family gatherings were large, immensely jolly events. The aunts and uncles were warm and friendly. At Christmas we played games and dressed up in silly clothes and put on film slides of old family photographs, with endless noisy commentary. They were so clearly fond of each other, yet they could be rude to each other in a jocular way – something out of the question in my family. I was falling in love, not just with Roger, but with his family as well.

And with this family came, for me, a sense of belonging, that old need, still there, being satisfied.

The first time I brought Roger home to meet my father (my mother was in hospital), the occasion was a catastrophe.

By then we had been together for some months. I sensed very quickly that Roger was too quiet, too inward, not outgoing or formal enough for my father. When my father left the house briefly, Roger didn't rush to help him on with his coat. I could tell that he was, with his ironies and his quiet intensity, rather frightening to my father, who clearly couldn't make any sense of who this person was. They were poles apart and neither was prepared to modify their behaviour. My sister told me later, with some glee, that she had overheard a telephone conversation between my father and his sister Ilse after Roger's visit. My father told her that he had met Roger, that he didn't like him and that he hoped I wouldn't marry him.

My father, the powerful patriarch, could often express his disapproval with words; in this case, in my presence he expressed it wordlessly. I was young and in love and in a way there was no serious competition. But there was conflict. I was living in borderlands, where two cultures encountered each other and made no sense to each other. I was the go-between, though I was never in any doubt that I was on Roger's side.

The relationship between them was never good. Later, Roger wrote this about my father:

'I knew something about Werner from Ursula before I met him, for example about how he taught her to drive very slowly by walking in front of the family car. But none of this had prepared me for the man himself, a self-confident, well-groomed bulky presence, secure, or so it seemed, in his opinions, his successful business life and his patriarchal domination of an almost exact replica of his previous German homes down to the books, the furniture, the practices – parents decorating Christmas trees not the children – and the cooking, all of which seemed very foreign to me. I felt welcomed into this unusual ménage but very much as an outsider, there on sufferance as a friend of his daughter.

Then, as I got to know the house better, I began to think of him as both more bullying and controlling than I had first experienced and also as someone I secretly wished to stand up to and resist – but feared to do so because of my position as guest and suitor. Yet it was also difficult not to feel sorry for him as he struggled to keep things going in the absence of a wife whose erratic and painful behaviour after her illness was a constant threat to his well-ordered world.

Only later, after Ursula and I got married, did I begin to recognize the extent of his hold over her as the epitome of a certain kind of fearsome brute masculinity, the very opposite of my own, much more tentative version. I could try to belittle him with ridicule, but I could not compete directly in terms of his power in both its physical and its tragic manifestations.'

I was profoundly shaken by these thoughts.

⚛

On our regular visits to Putney, Roger met my mother at weekends when she came home from the hospital. He was good at coping with the complicated emotional situations these weekends created – with my mother and Miss Berenz, the housekeeper, uneasily dancing round each other – and I was grateful for that, though I noticed that I also expected him to deal with it. Growing up in the nineteen fifties had its drawbacks, but one assumption for me was that the man in my life would be my companion, a friend who would understand.

My mother liked Roger from the start – his quietness, sense of humour, cleverness. He and I began to talk of love and then of marriage and in the spring of 1959, he proposed to me, upstairs in the living room in Putney, on the sofa overlooking the garden.

I had once told him (it became a joke between us) that the two most important men in my life were my father and Albert Schweitzer, the theologian and medical missionary. I was still, it seemed, inexorably committed to being a Good Girl. There was a moment in my last year at college when I was walking down the Banbury Road with Veronica, Marianne and Jane. We were discussing whether we wanted to be good or happy, a conversation that would be inconceivable even a few years later. Properly interpreted, it was really about whether we wanted to do good in the world or marry. At some rather absurd level it still seemed to us to be a choice. My friends decided they would choose to be good. I said, emphatically, I wanted to be happy.

My position was hardly one of an outsider. Marriage in the Fifties was still most women's idea of the next step, the way forward and my three friends were all in serious relationships with men. At the time it didn't seem a debate for me. Nothing in my upbringing, even my parents' evidently unhappy marriage, made me ambivalent about the happy-ever-after scenario. I want to get married, I said. My friends were surprised at my vehemence. For a moment the old fear returned. I had made a mistake. I would be cast out of the magic circle, belong nowhere. But we simply went on arguing about the good/happy divide.

By the end of our final year in Oxford in 1959, my three friends and I were engaged to be married. So were many other students at St Hugh's – coming down to breakfast with their new sparkling rings. It was a familiar pattern for girls like us – going to university, falling in love, getting engaged, getting married. For those who didn't follow this route, it could be lonely at least for a while. It was harder in those days to go out into the world as single women.

The four of us were curiously reticent with each other about our emotional lives and future marriages. Perhaps we knew in our hearts that we were young and ignorant about what marriage might be. By then we knew each other's men, but we didn't socialize together. We were shy, anxious not to be intrusive, perhaps afraid of being sentimental and I'm not sure we knew how to talk about it all – odd, since we confided in each other about many other things.

The conversations I had with my school friend Jane, who went to Somerville College, were altogether different. I hadn't seen her much over the three years in Oxford but I knew she'd become a Catholic, had been taught by a Catholic philosophy don and by the end of her Oxford time had made the decision to join the Carmelites – a contemplative, enclosed order devoted to prayer, community and service. Though I was amazed at this decision, I was also impressed that someone of our age so clearly knew what she wanted.

Her family felt no such thing. They were devastated. I had an uncomfortable conversation with her mother, who hated what had happened, was contemptuous about my sitting on the fence about it and felt her daughter must be in some huge distress about the world, perhaps about sex and that the nuns were making sure she would come to them before she was ready to make a proper decision for herself.

And so our Oxford years ended in the summer of 1959 – the summer that Bob Dylan graduated from high school, Allen Ginsberg wrote his poem 'Lysergic Acid' and *Advertisements for*

Myself by Norman Mailer came out, with his famous story about a Jewish woman's multiple orgasms, 'The Time of Her Time'. I learnt a lot about sex from that story. The era of drugs, sex and rock and roll was about to begin.

❧

We had all taken finals. Marianne got a congratulatory first. She had no idea what was happening when at the viva her examiners stood up and clapped. Jane and Veronica got good degrees. I got a third. I hadn't expected more. I knew my abilities in my subject were patchy. I wasn't particularly unhappy about it. My parents would have liked me to have done better. Three years back my brother had also got a third in Mathematics at Cambridge and my mother was distressed about that at the time. Forewarned by this, I didn't give them much opportunity to discuss my degree. By then I already knew that I wanted to study social sciences, psychology and politics, to work with people with social problems and I had got myself a place on the Social Science and Social Administration Diploma course at Bedford College in London.

Veronica, who had got on to a similar course at LSE (I had tried to get there too, but failed), asked me to share a huge flat she had found above a furniture store in Brixton. I hesitated. I was still very involved in my parents' lives. I wavered between feelings of guilt about my mother's health and the need to break away. My mother was going through another bad period and I felt I should be at home, even though she was in hospital most of the time. I said this to Veronica, who expressed bafflement. I hadn't revealed much about my mother's illness and she couldn't understand why I would make such a choice. And somehow that pushed me into saying yes to sharing the flat, to making what was a more final break from home.

My parents accepted the decision and to their credit didn't put pressure on me to stay. All of us had left home, my sister at nursing school and my brother married to his first wife, a Dutch woman and living in Leicestershire.

For a year I lived a life which was the closest I got to being a bit bohemian, with Veronica and with Dinah, a beautifully-dressed student from St Clare's. The three of us each had a room and we had an assortment of visitors – each of us had a man in our lives – and others who were temporary and for whom there was always plenty of room. We shared this wonderful, ugly, rambling three-storey flat opposite Brixton Town Hall where the clock struck not once but twice as it bounced off the walls of our building, lovers coming and going, visitors at all times of day and night, much cooking of food I'd never tasted, garlic, olive oil, haricot beans, stews marinated with wine left for hours on the stove. And people doing things I'd never encountered, Dinah's Greek boyfriend a film maker, Dinah writing novels, visitors returning from travels to Iran, to Turkey, to America. The casual and generous hospitality, the relaxed attitude to who was there – it took me a while before I felt confident with it but it felt very good.

Each morning I made my way down the spiral staircase, past the furniture store and on to busy, scruffy Brixton Road to catch the bus to Regent's Park and college. It was a time of transformation in the teaching of social work. Richard Titmuss at the LSE was one of the biggest influence in these changes. His writings of the 1950s had helped to define Britain's post-war welfare state. He focused particularly on the idea of social justice, on altruism and the value of public as opposed to private service in social and health care.

The teaching at Bedford was imbued with these principles. Our teachers were full of energy and enthusiasm. I loved the course and flourished there. At last I was making sense of a world I wanted to work in. And it was only now that I think I properly began to attend to my mind, dimly aware that it would be my companion through life and that it was mine.

Between classes in economics, politics, social psychology and much else, we were sent for social work practice all over London, working with children, the old, the disabled. For someone who'd had a more or less sheltered life, the people and situations I encountered opened my eyes – families coping with a severely disabled child, rehabilitation centres where people were recovering from devastating strokes – and where poverty coloured everything.

I did well in the course, the only one to get a distinction in my final exams, very different from my Oxford achievements. And I was now qualified to be a social worker.

✿

Roger had got a good degree, though not the First he'd hoped for. He'd failed to get into the Foreign Office, which turned out to be a blessing for him. For a time he was unemployed, uncertain what he was going to do. He spent some time at his mother's house in Sale, some in Brixton with me and after a few months, in early 1960, rented a flat near Swiss Cottage, where I would regularly stay. We were engaged, though he was a bit vague about getting an engagement ring and I eventually persuaded him to buy me a pretty antique one in an Oxfam shop. We made plans to marry in the summer.

I was happy but also anxious. We were friends, we talked a lot and I was very conscious that we were growing up together. Some of the more obvious differences between us – me outgoing, he withdrawn – were clearer now and though I was intrigued by them I worried about them. I felt plenty of self doubt but in public I was outgoing, gregarious, friendly. Roger, more confident than I in some ways, was reserved and careful and I felt his reticences were barriers to closeness. I felt a lack of intimacy and even though I tried to understand it in him, it was painful.

I was probably replaying some of the things between my father and mother and combined with my Fifties' upbringing, where a woman's place was seen to be primarily domestic, this led me to be frightened at any dissatisfaction I felt and to anxiety when Roger and I disagreed about things. I wanted him to be some sort of total, perfect companion. After seeing a movie I would sometimes sit up till three in the morning arguing, trying to find agreement. Partly we enjoyed argument. But there was a darker side for me – I found it painful when deeper differences seemed to be reflected in the arguments. I could be obsessive and ritualistic, asking Roger to repeat things six times, my head from time to time filled with dark ruminative thoughts and imaginings. I was confused about love and fantasies of normality. I couldn't leave things alone, didn't have the confidence to let things go.

This desire to be in total harmony also came out of some of the ideas about love at the time, out of the way that women were expected to live with men, and memories of my mother trying desperately to turn my father into someone he wasn't, someone she thought she could relate to better. Although I was in no doubt about Roger's love for me, he had a tendency to shut doors, to remove himself from anything too directly emotional or difficult.

I found help in a surprising place. Jane, my friend from college, was a great admirer of Simone Weil, the French philosopher and theologian. She introduced me to *Gravity and Grace*, a collection of long aphorisms on themes taken from her notebooks. There is a chapter on love and one particular extract struck me with great force. 'The beautiful is that which we cannot wish to change. To assume power is to soil. To possess is to soil. To love purely is to consent to distance, is to adore the distance between ourselves and that which we love.' It was an austere revelation, written by someone who loved God but as far as I knew had not known sexual love. It helped me to see something that I had not under-stood – the possibility of loving someone *because* of their differ-ence, their distance.

The possibility that I would end up like my mother was never far from my mind. The same old thoughts – the same freckles on my face and arms, the same dark hair, brown eyes. I was exasper-ated by her but I understood her. She relied on me emotionally. Therefore I must be like her. She was often on my mind, not always benignly. She could talk to me about her anxieties and I often hated it – the weight of it, the feeling that I needed to reassure her, that not to do so would only make the burden greater.

Perhaps most frightening was that I so rarely remembered seeing my mother happy, or even relaxed. And I was aware that during my time in Oxford my parents' relationship had been getting worse.

I could talk to Roger about all this. He listened, asked questions, as ever, and engaged with what I was saying. His involvement was real. The withdrawn side of him manifested itself in other ways, resisting what he saw as excessive emotion or enthusiasm, not going out to me to encourage me in things in my life, feeling strongly that people must make their own decisions, uninfluenced. It was in its way admirable, in theory giving me space. But there was an element of 'I will be me and you will be you' and it wasn't always space he gave but an arm's-length watching.

It was hard to talk to him about things that were difficult between us. But then my own behaviour was not the easiest, the anger, anxiety, the need for togetherness – although I sometimes told myself this was intensity, rather than the tension it often was – but I found his dug-in removal of himself from things perplexing and difficult.

But I *could* confide in him that if I was able to survive without going mad till I was forty, perhaps I'd be all right. And that, for me, was serious support.

15

SCENES FROM MARRIED LIFE

O NE WINTER WEEKEND in Putney in 1959, Roger and I witnessed the final fallout between my parents. It was our last year at Oxford: my mother was home from hospital. My parents had one of their terrible rows – Fips weeping, Werner shouting and desperate, leaving the house, slamming the door. He rang me from his office, to say that he couldn't go on. He asked me to take Fips back to the hospital. So on a dark Sunday night Roger and I drove her back to West Park Hospital in Epsom and left her in the looming red brick Victorian building which was for the time being her home. She was quiet and calm but it was a sombre drive and Roger and I didn't talk much on the journey back

And that was the end of their marriage. I had thought for quite a while that their marriage was not helping Fips, but faced with the reality of Werner no longer being in her life, I felt flashes of sadness and fear. From then on, my mother would be mine, Peter's and Ruth's responsibility – and, for some years, particularly mine. Roger was solidly reliable about all this. I knew I could ask him for support and help. He knew how dependent my mother was on me. He had become fond of her and though he recognised that for me she was a burden, he didn't find it difficult to relate to her or help her. And so we took her out from the hospital at weekends, alternating from time to time with Peter and Ruth. And life with her took on a new pattern.

The following spring my mother came from Epsom into London for the day and we went on an expedition to Harrods, always her department store of choice, to choose my wedding dress – long cream-coloured satin, plain and round necked, and a veil; and to pick the linen for our future flat, she insisting on ordering our initials to be sewn into the sheets and pillow cases, though rather more simply than the beautifully embroidered initials on my grandparents' linen which I had inherited. I had a sense that she was calmer, less agitated since she'd separated from my father.

And on August 9 1960 Roger and I married, in a beautiful small twelfth century church in Oxford. I was still influenced enough by my Christian upbringing to want a church wedding. Roger, an agnostic, reluctantly agreed. He wore a suit. Our sisters, neither of them yet married, were our bridesmaids in deep red dresses, the best man the forestry student who had introduced us. The ceremony was conducted by Werner Simonson, the High Court Judge turned Anglican vicar, who spoke firmly about what Christian marriage was about. The church was filled with our relatives and friends; my school friend, about to become a nun, was there. So was Jane, who's wedding we went to a few months later, though not Veronica and Marianne. There is a photograph of me with Lotte, my grandmother and Roger's grandmother, both of them powerful personalities, both tiny, sitting on a bench in the garden of the hotel where the reception was held, me between them, looming large in my long dress and grinning cheerfully.

My parents had not seen each other or spoken since they'd separated some months earlier. My aunt Ilse, kindness personified as usual, made sure my mother was all right and with friends and family. As I walked up the path to the church and then to the altar on my father's arm and he turned to sit in the front pew next to my mother, in her blue flowered dress and matching hat, I had a brief moment of worry at how they must be feeling. But it didn't last. I was happy and moved, proud of my new husband, surrounded by people in my old and new life. And though we had the visible proof that day that marriages don't always survive, we drew no conclusions for ourselves and were astonishingly optimistic about ours.

If the occasion was difficult for my parents, it was even harder for Roger's parents. They hadn't seen each other for twenty years and Roger's mother had been traumatised by the divorce. There were some rictus smiles from both ex-couples, some tension in the air from time to time. But they seemed to deal with it and I was absorbed in my own feelings, enjoying being the centre of attention.

At the reception, my father read an awkward but touching poem he had written – a family tradition for important occasions – about Roger and me, with references to Roger's political inclinations and our meeting in Oxford. It was politely affectionate, though in reality he never really understood Roger, his intensities and reticences, or why I loved him. We cut the cake, I changed into my linen suit and pointy hat, confetti was thrown and we set off on our brief honeymoon to the Cotswolds. It was all quietly traditional.

And I was marrying a goy, a Welshman, in some ways an insider, in some ways a route to assimilation.

⁂

A few weeks earlier I'd visited a birth control clinic in London, taking Roger with me as the required proof that I was engaged to be married and was duly taught how to fit a cap and handed one in its round blue tin to take away. The night of our wedding, in a small hotel near Oxford, penetration, painful, deeply satisfying (Freud says sexual intercourse is an act of the greatest aggression resulting in the greatest intimacy) finally took place. With hindsight of course, our route to penetration, given the sexual revolution of the 1960s that followed, seemed bizarre.

Roger had persuaded me to have a much longer honeymoon in Libya. He'd been offered a six-week contract to work with the UN in Tripoli and because he'd become increasingly interested in working in the Middle East he was keen to go. I was apprehensive about the territory, having never been outside Europe, but as a Fifties girl, I accepted without question that I would go where his work took him. So a few weeks after our wedding I had my first encounter with the Middle East, in a Libya before the discovery

Roger in Cyrene, Libya, 1960

of oil, before Gaddafi, a country of extreme poverty, ruled by King Idris.

Our temporary home was a sparsely furnished flat in a modern house, blinds drawn against the sun, in a suburb on the edge of Tripoli. I felt homesick and lost at the beginning, strange surroundings, not enough to do, few people I knew. But we settled in, Roger and I did things together as much as his work allowed and we were watched over by a charming older couple from the UN, he Roger's boss, who looked after us rather as they would their own children, feeding us regularly on their scorpion-filled terrace in their lovely old house in Old Tripoli, taking us to feasts put on by Libyan colleagues, where saying no to more food was impossible and where once I thought I'd literally explode with overeating.

We walked down the road to the local shops to buy vegetables and meat, passing children in the streets with faces covered in flies and wearing rags. I had never seen such poverty. In our dark gloomy kitchen I cooked stews and roasted chickens. It was not exactly what I'd envisioned as the beginning of married life and it wasn't easy to turn this place into anything as comfortable as a home. But slowly I began to appreciate the hot, untidy landscapes, the scruffy streets, the children's curiosity about us, the way people dealt with their poverty-stricken lives, their friendliness. I even got used to being asked constantly by the women I met (who made me wonderful sweet tea, sometimes with nuts in it) whether I was pregnant. 'No? Well when are you going to start your family?'.

Libya was undiscovered territory in 1960 and we began to explore. We wandered round Leptis Magna, the magnificent Roman ruins near Tripoli, with no one else in sight, taking a swim in the sea, returning to picnic under the columns. On a visit to a farming project in Benghazi, we drove 400 miles along an endless road on the edge of the scrub desert, stopping overnight at a guest house, cockroaches floating in the water running down the corridor from the lavatory overflows.

Back on the road, we saw a structure in the far distance. As we got nearer it became clearer – an arch, in the middle of nowhere, built by Mussolini when the Italians had so brutally occupied Libya. We stopped for tea in a crumbling hotel near Appollonia and Cyrene, the ancient Greek city, where there were ten waiters in white aprons serving a handful of guests, and finally reached Benghazi that evening.

It was a strange six weeks, without the props of my life, my friends, work, familiar surroundings. I was intensely aware of em-barking on a new and unfamiliar life, with this new husband who

I found quite mysterious and fascinating, who had his own view of how things were and for whom the Middle East was important. We travelled well together. And by the end of our time, I had developed my own attachment to the territory and, in particular, to the Arab people and their gentle generosity.

We returned to Oxford in October, where Roger was beginning a new life as a research fellow at St Antony's College, the most cosmopolitan of the graduate colleges in the university specializing in international relations, economics, politics and history of various regions of the world. Roger was attached to its Middle East Centre. We rented a small furnished college flat and I set about finding work.

16

WORK

I T WAS AN exceptionally cold grey November day in 1960 when I bought a copy of the *Oxford Mail* as usual and went to a café to sift through the jobs advertised. There was one for a social worker at Littlemore Hospital, a large Victorian mental hospital on the edge of the city. It had recently been taken over by an enlightened South African psychiatrist, Dr Mandelbrot, who was making important and on the whole humane changes – unlocking the wards, turning them into mixed wards for men and women and generally trying to turn this grim institution into a more open place.

I applied and got the job. On my first day I drove our battered blue Austin car into the car park, walked through the nearest door and found myself in one of those long dark corridors. As I walked towards the entrance hall I passed an elderly man pacing up and down, unkempt, anguished, muttering to himself, in a world of his own. I was to meet him so many times, pacing this corridor, one of the few people in the hospital still suffering with third degree syphilis.

I made enquiries about the social work department and eventually found my supervisor, a middle-aged German, friendly enough but abrupt and seemingly at a loss about what to talk to me about or what he should give me to do. His first assignment for me was to go and see a man who had just tried to kill himself. I was completely at a loss about how to handle this; tentatively I went to his small room, off a huge ward, where he was lying on the bed, face to the wall. I tried to talk to him. He was miserable and silent. I felt helpless. I touched his arm, talked as gently and carefully as I could and then left. I was of no help to him. I was a complete novice and had no idea what I should be doing.

Gradually, I was given more patients to see, some in the hospital, most of them discharged and back at home. My supervision was minimal and what there was I didn't find helpful. It was a young Canadian woman, also just starting her career in social work, who became a lifeline for me. By coincidence she had started work on the same day. We talked endlessly about the patients we saw and tried together to work out our theories and approaches. It was to her I admitted that an important reason I was working in a mental hospital was to test myself, to see whether I was mentally ill. There was no shortage of isolated symptoms that I could identify with – rituals, ruminations, anxiety. But somehow, somewhere, I knew that I was not ill, not out of control, not mad – not yet anyway.

I was pensive about the institution I was working in – a place of confinement, where the mad were seen as separate and different, the 'other', something that Foucault was writing about at the time, seeing the modern medical treatment of the mentally ill as just as controlling and cruel in its way as earlier treatments. But I also remembered my mother's sense of being somewhere safe, a haven, away from a life with family that she wasn't able to cope with.

Slowly, painstakingly, through my encounters with the patients, reading and talking with friends and colleagues, I began to learn a bit about how to support people and help them to help themselves in their difficult lives. My experience with my mother helped, though the patient population of Littlemore was largely working class, so most of the people I saw had to deal with poverty as well as mental fragility. I became absorbed in the causes and effects of mental illness, its connection with social realities and inherited traits.

I drove all over Oxfordshire and the Cotswolds, double de-clutching my way round winding roads in our ancient car, trying to support people in their depressions and fears. I was twenty-four years old. I'd had some training in social work but not much. I'd read some Freud and other psychoanalysts on my course and R. D. Laing and David Cooper. I'd experienced my mother's mental states. I believed that material well-being, or lack of it, was bound to be a factor in mental health, though I also believed that childhood experiences and life circumstances played a large part in emotional conflicts. I was also very inexperienced.

Many of the people I saw were suffering from depression. I tried to build up their confidence, help solve practical problems, find out about their feelings about their families and help them grapple with them. And I listened. Many of the people I saw lived solitary lives, either alone, or with families who didn't communicate much. They often lived in grim circumstances – in the back streets of those pretty Cotswold towns where the houses were dank and dark and smelt of poverty. I was often glad to get away. I was surprised at the relief they showed when I paid attention to them. And relieved that occasionally I could help.

This was a period when social work was itself in something of a crisis, keen to establish its claim to professionalism, as it always recurrently is and doing it by acquiring a sort of sub-Freudian set of ideas and language. One version of this was to interpret any request for material help in psychological terms. There was, on the whole, little sympathy for anger or feelings of helplessness on a patient's part because of poverty, difficult material circumstances, difficult spouses or children. We were taught that it would be a mistake to take such expressions at face value, that they were surface difficulties substituting for the real problem, their deepest feelings. I and my Canadian colleague found ourselves out of sympathy with the ethos.

And sometimes I broke the rules. Mrs K, living near Oxford, had been treated for depression, Her husband had murdered an elderly woman in Ireland after a fit of drinking. I saw her regularly and she talked to me about her marriage, about what she was feeling about her husband and about the Catholic Church she belonged to but found somewhat lacking in the support she needed. She needed to go and visit him. She had very little money. I gave her the money for the fare. I told no one.

It was also a tumultuous time for mental health institutions

– for doctors and nurses as well as patients. Attitudes to mental health were changing fast. Mandelbrot, as well as opening the wards, employed a psychiatrist who'd worked in a prison and was interested in therapeutic communities. The central philosophy of such communities was that patients are active participants in their own and each other's mental health treatment and that they share responsibility for the daily running of the community with the staff.

That was the theory. I found it attractive enough. But I was shocked by the way it was put into practice by this doctor. He held daily, public meetings for the patients, about fifty of them crowded into a large ward, who were encouraged to express their feelings in these large forums. There was something distinctly bullying about the manner in which the doctor insisted that everything a patient wanted to say had to be said in front of a large number of people. Private talks with doctors were discouraged. I had no objection to group therapy as such, but these meetings were not simply that. To me, they felt like a kind of demand for public confession. I could see the distress on some of the patients' faces. I found the meetings, the manner of the doctor in charge and the effect on the patients increasingly repellent and eventually stopped going to them, switching my allegiance and working with a psychiatrist in the hospital who did not share these ideas and who I admired greatly not just for his psychiatric knowledge but for his humanity.

Our one-bedroom college flat was sparsely but comfortably furnished, student-like, full of books, my upright piano against one wall, the John Piper print we'd been given as a wedding present over the mantelpiece. The kitchen was tiny, filled with crockery and pots and pans, all wedding presents. We often had family and friends to stay, including my mother. She'd recently been taking typing lessons in the rather progressive hospital in Epsom and they had placed her in an office in the local town to do some sheltered work. At first it was fine; then, gradually, her stories became more and more fantastical and paranoid – people hiding behind desks, throwing things at her. It took us a while to realize that she was deteriorating mentally. It turned out she'd stopped taking her medication. I felt a wave of sympathy for her – she was out in the world, she was working in an office, something she'd never done in her life and she wanted to be like everyone else, normal without the medication that kept her stable. Back on medication, she recovered, but the job didn't work out.

My sister, now a seventeen-year-old, doing A levels, later training as a nurse, was in love with a student at Oxford who she would later marry. She came often, reporting on what was going on at home with my father, with Miss Berenz. I still had strong protective instincts about her.

Roger had quickly become well established at St Antony's College, which attracted interesting graduates from all over the world. I was proud of his work and his modesty about it. St Antony's was much less formal and pompous than many Oxford colleges and above all had women as well as men as students. I enjoyed our life there, loved meeting the Middle Easterners who congregated at the Centre – they were warm and funny and full of energy and I became increasingly interested in Roger's work and the Middle East. We ate and drank in the buttery, went to jolly dances and had supper parties for our friends.

I was still full of insecurities, needed reassurances and would go over evenings with Roger – had I said idiotic things? had I made a fool of myself? did I antagonize x or irritate y? Extraordinarily, it didn't dawn on me till later that these were the sort of questions my mother constantly asked me and which I found so demanding and irritating!

Roger and I continued to be movie addicts, listened to chamber music, to Elvis, Charles Aznavour, Georges Brassens, Frank Sinatra, Dave Brubeck. We often read the same novels and talked about them endlessly – Iris Murdoch, Margaret Drabble, Doris Lessing. We went to the opera and to the theatre, hearing Lenny Bruce, the stand-up comedian and satirist and my first encounter with the issue of free speech in the short-lived Establishment club in London; drinking coffee with friends at the equally shortlived Partisan coffee house set up in Soho by the Universities and *Left Review* editors, Raphael Samuel, Stuart Hall and Eric Hobsbawm.

Early in the first term of this new life, Roger bumped into Mike Hammond, someone he had known as an undergraduate and invited him back for supper. He was an American Rhodes scholar, had been a medical student with me, though I didn't remember him, had given up medicine and was trying to work out what he wanted to do with his life, living in a dank basement flat in the Iffley Road. On his first visit we sat up till 3.00 in the morning, the three of us, talking about everything under the sun. He was quietly utterly charismatic, passionate about music, interested at that moment in Nietzsche, in medicine, in what was wrong with the Catholic Church. We talked and argued and laughed. We listened to music and to Elaine May and Mike Nichols on our 78 vinyls. We talked about the American election and listened to Mort Sahl ('Vote No and keep the White House empty for another five years.') And this stocky, quiet man with his pock-marked face and deep chuckle became part of our lives. It was the beginning of a strange relationship between the three of us, which continued for two years, Mike often coming three times a week, the conversation always different but the talk, the arguments always going on deep into the night, always intense.

It was partly Mike's directness, his total engagement with whatever was happening and with me, that made such an impact. There was no caution, no arms-length talk, no watchfulness and I found that enormously seductive. The conversations encouraged me to explore things because I was being encouraged, and I felt I was learning about things as I'd never quite learnt them before. I found myself rather childishly identifying with Truffaut's film *Jules et Jim*, a tragic romantic triangle – two men, their friendship and their obsession with a passionate woman – and a moving med-itation on freedom, loyalty and love. Mike was to have a profound effect on both our lives.

※

In the summer of 1961, Roger and I went to Florence for a holiday. I'd been through a bad patch of anxiety. I came across a short story by Margaret Drabble about a young married couple on holiday together and the tensions between them. She seemed to catch the kind of troubled feelings that can occur in young marriages. Something about the story and my own resolve, made me determined to try and deal better with my great need for reassurance.

We took with us Mary McCarthy's *The Stones of Florence*, one of the great guide books. We called on my great-grandfather Grelling's daughter from his second marriage, Annemarie, a warm handsome woman who lived with her family in a small palazzo in the centre of Florence. Lunch was served by waiters in white gloves.

And quite apart from the wonders of what we saw, it began to seem possible that I could sometimes divert myself from rising anxiety, from the black holes. I could, I thought, decide to be happy – or perhaps rather to let myself be happy, and worry less about what might be, whether things were all right – and live in the moment more. It was something of a breakthrough. I stopped trying so hard to fit in. I began to recognize some advantages in a sense of displacement.

It wasn't just my work in the hospital that made mental illness such a particular preoccupation for me at that time. In the autumn of 1961, a year after Roger and I got married, my mother came out of hospital for what turned out to be the last time. She had been treated by a sympathetic psychiatrist at the hospital in Epsom where she'd been an in-patient for several years. He helped her to see that in some ways her relationship with my father had made it harder for her to survive in the outside world and thought that she'd be more able to do so now that she had separated from him. Or at least that is how I interpreted my conversations with him and my mother's subsequent actions.

She decided to come and live in Oxford, where she would be close to me. I accepted this as inevitable and necessary. It also filled me with apprehension. My father fully supported her financially and would go on doing so, but there was no other contact between them. Though my brother and sister saw my mother regularly, it was me she rang continually to get reassurances about her daily life and her feelings. I knew she would rely on me to make her life outside hospital possible – and I suspected my brother and sister were relieved about that.

My mother moved into a small hotel in the Banbury Road with a friendly manager. Considering that she'd been in mental hospitals over a period of eight years, and the institutionalization this inevitably induces, she coped well. She came to our flat every day for tea. I was often tense and irritated with her, but I knew I had to spend this time with her, talk to her, help her live in the world again. And, as ever, my aunt Ilse came up with practical help and warm support.

After a few weeks, we found a flat for Fips to rent – the top floor of a large North Oxford Victorian house, very light, with large rooms. She and I scoured the antique and junk shops for furniture. She had kept a strong sense of what she liked and together we turned this place into a comfortable home for her. It was a huge and brave enterprise on her part and I didn't feel proud of my irritation with her needs and dependencies. But she established a way of life and with support began to feel some confidence. What helped me get through was the knowledge that the situation would not go on forever. I felt my mother was managing. And Roger and I were beginning to make plans to live in Cairo for a year.

❧

The summer before we left for Egypt something else happened. Mike, our American friend, was on the point of leaving to go back to America. On his last weekend in Oxford, Roger had gone to see a friend and so I was alone in seeing him off. In the course of saying goodbye to each other at the station Mike and I acknowledged, suddenly and painfully, that we had developed strong feelings for each other. Looking back, I realized that of course there had been earlier signs, Mike sometimes edgy and evasive with me, and we had both avoided addressing them. I got on the train with him to London, where he was staying with friends; we tried and failed to part when he got on the tube, we walked around Hampstead for hours, talking, occasionally hugging and kissing, falling silent, overwhelmed with our feelings, devastated at what we'd done, at what it might mean. It was a chaotic and frightening day

I had no experience or ability to deal with all this and was, in my naivety, completely taken by surprise. I loved my husband, but I found I loved someone else too. Having once been fascinated by Roger partly because of his qualities of holding back, I found myself responding fiercely to Mike's expressiveness and openness, to someone who was not emotionally withdrawn.

That evening, I went back to Oxford in a daze and when Roger came back, in my confusion and turmoil, I told him what had happened. Did he want to hear it? I suppose I had always felt that we should be truthful with each other and I think he felt the same. I don't think I was capable of concealing this. He was devastated, the more so because he knew and in his own way loved this man too. He could see only too clearly what there was between us because of his own feelings for both of us.

I can't say I coped with any of it well. I was agonized and self-obsessed about it and I went to Egypt later that summer unsure of what to do with these powerful feelings, both of us recurrently miserable, our marriage somehow on hold.

Years later, Roger said to me that he had felt on probation. Certainly our emotional life was not resolved in Cairo. But travel to exotic places was something that Roger had brought into my life and bound us together. We were good at it. And there was something about Egypt, being the extraordinary and complicated place it was, which gradually took us over and we managed to embark on our life there with energy, often bound to each other by similar reactions to difficult or absurd or exhilarating situations. It was more growing up together and though there were evasions and tensions between us, we were also, without saying it, united in thinking this new world we were in was there to be discovered.

17

EGYPT

THOUGH I WAS full of confusion about Roger and Mike, I'd begun to understand a bit better the ways I was negotiating my way in the world. There is an inevitable double life the second-generation immigrant lives and I suppose that I was accustomed to living this, to accommodating contradictory ideas, to things not fitting. I began to recognise the things that mattered to me – friendships above all, being part of things, love, work, sex, politics. I still felt easily abandoned emotionally, but had begun to deal better with my sadness. Family was there in the background and I wrote to my parents from Egypt regularly, though not with great intimacy and it was also a relief to be away from them. My father had begun to see Annemarie, the friend of my parents from Germany, who was now divorced. She made him happy and I was glad – as far as I knew this was the first time he'd been involved with a woman since my mother went into hospital. I was in touch with my sister, but not very much – though I did confide in her about Mike – and even less with my brother, who was working as an electronic engineer.

❧

The road from the airport into Cairo was lined with eucalyptus trees. We arrived at dusk on a hot day in September 1962, the dry heat still evident in the evening air, the landscape dusty. We were met by a young driver in a United Nations car who took us through the suburb of Heliopolis, and eventually along 26th July Street (named in honour of the Egyptian Revolution) across the Nile to the island of Zamalek. Roger tried to ask him in Arabic about the officer's club we passed – was it the one where the junior officers had first challenged the now deposed monarch? But he couldn't make himself understood. He'd been learning Modern Literary Arabic, good for reading government documents but not so good for ordinary conversation.

Roger was writing his thesis on cotton and the economy of Egypt in the nineteenth century and needed to look at papers in Egyptian archives and libraries. He'd applied for work as a teaching assistant in English language at the American University in Cairo. In the spring of 1962 the university had written to him to say that they could offer me a similar post, that we would need both salaries to live on – $3,000 for the year, eight hours teaching a week. I said yes, with the confidence of youth. I knew nothing about teaching English. I worked full time at Littlemore hospital right up to when we left and did very little preparation for the job.

My first impression of Cairo was that I wouldn't survive the noise. The principle was that drivers kept their hands permanently on the hooter. This was truly a city that never sleeps, the main street in Zamalek buzzing night and day with people and cars, buses full to overflowing, extra passengers clinging on to the outside of the battered vehicles as best they could. After a week I stopped noticing the noise.

Empty flats attracted cockroaches and I reeled from a sink-full of them when we were flat hunting. We found a spacious duplex apartment in a modern tower building in Zamalek, an island in the middle of the Nile with tree-lined roads and handsome houses, round the corner from the noisy main road, forty dollars a month.

On our second day we went in search of the American University, housed in an old tobacco factory. Coming in from the noisy streets, we found the beautiful central courtyard at the University, filled with bougainvillea, hibiscus, jacaranda, a haven of calm.

For the first and only time in our life, Roger and I were sharing an office. We were joined by Margot. A tall, elegant American graduate, high cheekbones and a raucous laugh, she was taking history courses and studying Arabic and considering marrying an Egyptian, Ali, she had met at university in America. She was negotiating all sorts of cultural matters – with him, with the country itself. Ali, who taught at the Institute for Public Administration, was quiet and calm and on the whole amazingly tolerant, given the vast cultural stumbling blocks between them – not to speak of the religious ones, he a practicing Muslim, she from a Catholic family. She had made it her business to discover a lot about Islam, about Egyptian history and particularly about the lives and habits of Egyptian women. She'd also, to my delight, discovered how to make the right mix to remove body hair, from legs, arms, upper lip, with home-made wax and tried to teach me how to do it, though I never quite managed it.

Was it my time in Egypt when I began to think about women's position, their lives as handmaidens to men's lives, the barriers to their freedoms? I'm not sure – I was slow to understand how fundamental feminist ideas were to seeing the way the world worked, though here, staring me in the face, were so many different ways in which women's lives were restricted.

Our pupils were friendly and polite and rarely challenging. The students in our undergraduate classes, coming from all over the Arab world, were mostly traditional in their outlook. For the girls, marriage was almost universally their goal. Our male students were adamant that they didn't want their wives to work.

I was a reticent teacher, inexperienced and shy. I taught my classes English grammar and sentence construction and we had regular conversation classes. One day I surprised myself by deciding the discussion would be about the morality of cutting off people's hands as a punishment for stealing. I had several Saudi Arabian students in my class and this was a punishment in their country. It was a measure of my naivety that I decided to take this on. As it turned out, the conversation was lively and I didn't experience any great hostility from the Saudis, though they fiercely disagreed with me. They were polite because I was their teacher and I suspect they were unconcerned about my views because, as a woman, my opinions were not very important.

Between lessons we sat in that magical sun-filled, flower-filled courtyard for hours, reading, drinking tea, talking to colleagues and to the friends we made in the course of the year. Some of these were graduate students, many Egyptian but some from Greece and other Arab countries, hardly any of them Muslims. The university had been founded by missionaries and became a place where children of the old privileged classes tended to go. They were brought up with European culture and were in a sense living in two worlds; when Nasser introduced a new period of modernization and socialist reform, as well as staunch advocacy of Pan-Arabism, our closer friends, most of them women, had been much affected, becoming more aware of themselves as Arabs. They had spoken English and especially French fluently to each other; now they talked about making the Arabic language much more part of their lives. They were intensely curious, lively, warm and candid and deeply engaged in their studies and their changing worlds. I was struck by how forceful they were, how confident of their opinions, how courageous, though it wasn't easy to be a woman with aspirations in this society, nor one who wanted certain degrees of freedom.

And, as we soon learnt, there was plenty of drama in their lives. One of them, the daughter of a father high up in the military, was about to elope with an Englishman, a fellow student. Another told me of her experience of clitoridectomy, something that the women in her family all expected, the pain and shock of it, the consequences for her sense of herself, her sexuality, learning to live with it.

Roger and I and Margot quickly bonded, not least over some of the absurdities and irritations from some of the more small-minded and bossy Americans at the university, who had never lived abroad before. Roger kept a file of the more ridiculous memos we were sent. One advised us not to give our post to the bawwabs (doormen) in case they removed the stamps for re-selling. Their lack of sensitivity to the people they were living among could be breathtaking. But there were also Americans teaching there with strong connections with the Arab world, some married to Egyptians, some of Arab origin, some anthropologists with deep knowledge and affection for the country.

Nadia, a Coptic Christian and member of the English Department, made contact with us in our first week. She devoted much of her fierce energy to supporting her only daughter, by then eleven years old, who'd been born with a large inoperable tumour on her face, stopping at nothing to find the right school and every possible support for the wellbeing of her child in a country where disability was often swept under the carpet. She showed us how things worked at the university, where things were in the city, introduced us to people and tirelessly demonstrated that quite extraordinary hospitality for which Arabs are famous and which over the year made a deep and lasting impact on us. On our second meeting I admired a tee-shirt she was wearing and the next day it was on my desk.

By the time we came, Nasser had established a major programme of reform – for women's rights, for workers, for the transfer of wealth from rich to poor. But there was a cost to some of our friends who came from ancien-régime families. They lost much of their property but also many of their rights as citizens and this despite the fact that they were often sympathetic to the egalitarian aims of the regime.

And there were plenty of reminders that we were living in an authoritarian state. Nasser's presidency was in some ways a golden age of culture, in theatre, film, poetry, radio, literature, music, comedy, producing singers such as Umm Kulthum, with her unmistakable rich contralto voice, whose monthly concerts were well known for their capacity to clear the streets of some of the world's most populous cities as people rushed home to tune in, and writers Naguib Mahfouz, a Nobel Prize winner, and Tawfik el-Hakim. But intellectual and cultural life was closely monitored and censored. For foreigners like us, life in Egypt was easy and delightful and though we were also being watched we were small fry and of little interest to the government. Our phone was tapped; when we picked up the handpiece, there was a loud whirring sound from the East German tape recorder. Our mail was looked at and occasionally censored – I was careful what I said when I wrote home. We were aware that the Mukhabarat, the secret police, eavesdropped on conversations, so were careful about what we said to friends in cafés such as the famous Groppi. But as foreigners we only had to be careful. For Egyptians these issues were serious matters of survival or the risk of being sent to the dreadful Tora prison in southwest Cairo.

Roger and I developed a daily routine for work, walking up the main street, first encountering the small boy who had registered where we live and knew he'd get some money from us every morning, across the Qasr El Nil Bridge, the mist coming off the Nile at the beginning of a fresh Cairo day. And then to Tahrir Square, a traffic nightmare of old cars, buses and donkey carts and into the university.

Lunch was back at home, at about 2.00 p.m, usually soup or stew, prepared by our maid. At first we had resisted having a maid, finding the idea of having a domestic servant alien and difficult. But we'd been strongly advised to hire someone, helpful for us, people said, and giving a wage to someone who needed it. So eventually we found an older woman, a mother of two, who was motherly to me and made most of the decisions about her work without my having to instruct her.

After lunch, the siesta. I loved lying in our bedroom with the hot sun coming through the window, making love and going into a deep sleep; followed by starting again in the early evening, when we usually went out. I loved this double start to the day, the afternoons in our apartment, the long evenings.

And we had a busy social life, occasionally parties and formal dinners revolving around the United Nations and the embassy, but much more of it informal evenings, with much jollity, often ending rolling up the rugs and dancing, with friends, Egyptian and American – artists, archeologists, academics, architects: I first met Ahdaf Soueif, the distinguished Egyptian writer, at her parents' house when she was eight years old. And always the warmth and generosity – I could respond to this life much more easily than our social life in Oxford, felt, ironically, more at home, more part of things here, perhaps because I wasn't trying to be an insider.

We ate out in restaurants with sawdust on the floor and waiters with long white aprons, went to the movies, the audience talking all the way through and by the end the floor covered in popcorn, to the opera, most memorably *Boris Goudonov*, in the handsome opera house built by the Khedive in 1869 and destroyed by a fire in 1971.

Teaching English took only part of our day. Roger went to his libraries (encountering a blind librarian in the first one he worked in!). I decided to enrol in a sculpture class. Our teacher was an elderly, beautiful American sculptor from Lake Forest, Sylvia Judson. I could not have been more encouraged and her enthusiasm for my work meant that what started as no more than a hobby became a bit of an obsession. I knew I'd never be a great sculptor, but it occupied my hands and mind a good deal for several years.

I also decided, uncharacteristically, to perform in the university's annual show, that year a musical, *The Boy Friend* by Sandy Wilson. I was one of the Perfect Young Ladies. I'd never danced on stage before. With the help of a brilliant New York choreographer we learned how to dance in harmony, how to jump backwards up on to our partner's shoulder. But though there were plenty of Egyptians acting in the show, it had a distinct touch of the kind of ex-pat life we regarded as slightly ridiculous.

Each week, we got to know Cairo more. We walked for hours, in the wide streets of the nineteenth and early twentieth century city. Once I was frightened – when, thoroughly lost, we were followed by a small group of teenagers which grew larger and larger, chanting loudly and more and more threateningly that we were Israelis; we headed as fast as we could to a main road.

In the old Fatimid city we often ended up in Fishawi's, the old café hidden in a narrow street of the medieval Khan el-Khalili, the Grand Bazaar, filled with old men smoking their hookahs. We bought corn on the cob roasted on coals at street corners and in small cafés we ate bowls of foul mudammus, fava beans, the staple diet of Egyptians. I began to be fascinated by Islamic art and took a course on it at the university. Probably the most important influence came from George, an American historian of Islamic architecture and archaeology who had lived in Cairo for many years. Ebullient, sturdy, never failing to speak his mind, he was from a large Catholic American family and gay, finding in Cairo the kind of freedom, especially sexual freedom, he didn't have in America. A few weeks after we arrived, he turned up, red-faced and jovial, at our flat early one evening without warning, sat down on the sofa and asked us whether we'd like to hear his diaries about his time in Egypt. Without waiting for an answer, he proceeded, with great flamboyance, to read to us. Soon he became a regular visitor and a close friend. He adored Roger and liked me well enough. He hinted at extraordinary sexual adventures in Egypt. He knew and described the city with the intensity of love.

He taught Roger and I about focus on patterns and Arabic calligraphy rather than on figures, the pleasures of artistic balance, of pattern and control, of reticence and subdued colour. So gradually the massive, high vaulted Mamluk mosque of Sultan Hassan, built over three years from 1356 'without even a single day of idleness', became something we grew to love. It was George who took us on

a tour of the old city wall and its gates. He introduced us to the
City of the Dead, an astonishing Arabic necropolis and cemetery,
below the forbidding Mokattam Hills, four miles long, a dense
grid of tombs and mausoleums. Here people lived and worked
among the dead, some to be near their ancestors, some forced there
because of pressure of space and demolitions in the city; others
still had come in from the countryside looking for work. The
poorest lived in the slum, Garbage City, where the Coptic rubbish
collectors, the Zabaleen, processed the city's garbage.

⁂

Roger's work on the production and economic influence of Egyptian cotton, the world's strongest and silkiest, meant we spent days
too in the Nile Delta, north of Cairo, where the cotton was grown.
We stayed with Mahmoud, a dear eccentric friend, a Chaucer
scholar, tall and fleshy with a self-deprecating sense of humour
and a fine sense of the ridiculous. We sat in his charming but
run-down ezba in the evenings, the gas lamps drawing hundreds of
mosquitos into the dusty rooms while he told us of his anguished
efforts to return the goose which a student had given him for a
bribe; and of his uncle who managed to marry two English chorus
girls, Aunty Flora and Aunt Doris, each owning fields on the
family estate until they were expropriated in 1952.

On our first trip to Alexandria, he walked us along the layers
of promenades above the Mediterranean, to tiny restaurants on
the beach where I managed with difficulty, as a badge of honour,
to gulp down small live shellfish. We toured King Farouk's former

With Roger in Upper Egypt, 1963

palace – full of kitsch furniture and lighting, its vast bedrooms magnificent in their vulgarity and bright colours. And in his guided tour of his beloved city Mahmoud explained to us, with considerable indignation, why he so disliked Lawrence Durrell's attempt, in the *Alexandria Quartet* (which I had just read with some compulsion and much pleasure) to turn Alexandria into a city fed more or less entirely by his own imagination where foreigners led a golden life that had nothing to do with the reality of the mostly Arabic-speaking Egyptian population.

Back in Cairo, people came to stay: my Oxford friend Marianne's parents; Roger's sister; John Cairncross, clever, charming, translator of Racine, who turned out to be a spy, the famous Fifth Man, with Philby, Burgess, MacLean and Blunt, though we knew nothing about it at the time.

In February, Roger and I went on a trip down the Nile from

Cairo, first to Luxor before going on to Aswan. We travelled in a small boat which stopped first at the elegant Cataract Hotel, then moved across Lake Nasser and down the Nile towards the Sudanese border.

It was 1963 and the Aswan Dam was in the process of being constructed; the villagers living on this part of the Nile had been moved to new housing in Aswan. As we chugged slowly down-river, what we saw was village after village of beautiful painted houses, ghostly, abandoned and already half drowned. At dawn we reached the Temple of Abu Simbel, at that time still on its original site, guarded by the huge statues of Ramesses II, watching as the sun's rays entered the central hall to light up its entire length.

I was nervous about being Jewish. My memory of our time in Egypt is of Jewishness and Israel being taboo subjects except with the closest friends. For Jews in Egypt this was a difficult time. The year before we came the anti-Jewish and anti-Israeli propaganda campaigns had intensified in the Arabic, French and English-language press as well as Radio Cairo. About 7,000 Jews remained living in Egypt, most of them Sephardic, mostly white-collar workers. Nasser's pan-Arab ambitions, which were part of the general struggle against European imperialism and colonialism, the creation of the state of Israel and the wars that followed made the position of the Jews in Egypt precarious. They were on the one hand often seen, like other minorities, as pro-Western collab-orators and sympathizers with European imperialists, not part of the Egyptian people. But after 1948 they were also seen as agents of Israel and working against the interests of Egypt. So the Jews were hit hard by the punitive measures brought in by Nasser.

We were the only British people at the American University and I was conscious of how differently from our American colleagues we responded to this society – more careful in our judgements, less confident about being right, less outgoing. I felt this even more about Roger than about myself (in some ways I didn't really think of myself as British). I was protective on his behalf and also anxious about what I saw as some people's reactions to his rather understated and withheld responses. And particularly so about the Suez crisis, which was only six years earlier and for which Roger and I felt a good deal of shame.

And this was the first time I had lived away from England for any length of time. In the first weeks I had periods of serious homesickness. I realized how heavily I relied on the structures of my life – our house, our families and friends, my work. Here I had to create new ones in unfamiliar territory. One way was to bury myself in novels. I read Olivia Manning's *Balkan Trilogy* – a portrait of a young, rather naive couple, Guy and Harriet Pringle, living in Romania at the time of the advance of the Germans in 1939. It's a novel about war, about exile, about ex-pat life and its more feverish ways and about a young marriage and its complexities and difficulties, Guy wantonly gregarious and extrovert, Harriet more withdrawn and also more observant, coming to terms with having to share her husband with a wide circle of friends and acquaintances and trying not to feel abandoned.

I loved and admired this novel, but I was also comforted by it.

Not in any simple way, because the couple were not simply like us – Guy on the surface might have been more like me, Harriet like Roger, but Harriet was a woman and a wife – but because we were a young couple living abroad in an unfamiliar country, partly amongst ex-pats and we were trying to understand what was going on around us and what was going on in our relationship. Olivia Manning saw me through some of those early weeks of homesickness and bewilderment.

Gradually, inevitably, I learnt to pick up on the marvellous and maddening details of living in Egypt – the kindness of strangers, the suspicions and conspiracy theories, the gap between appearance and reality, the need for Egyptians to please even if there was no hope of fulfilling the promises; and then the pressures to conform, for young men through certain kinds of masculinity, 'manning up', underpinning the powerful patriarchy in the country and for women, the usual expectations of femininity, sexuality, motherhood, supporting the man's identity rather than making one of her own, often disguised in my eyes at least by a vitality and outspokenness in the women I met that was new to me. Egypt left an indelible mark on me, not least by the women I met there.

So many discoveries for me in Egypt. I observed up close the significance of nationalism and the effects of colonialism. I learned how Arabs felt they were seen in the scheme of things. And I made deep friendships which lasted for decades, mostly with women and through them began to learn more about the place of women in the world.

And the struggles with my own nature went on, exacerbated

by living in a strange place and by the uncertainties of our marriage. I think even then I felt it inevitable that I would live with endless doubt. I longed for certainties, but thought there weren't any - except that love and work were the things that mattered. And being an outsider here - in a startlingly different culture, as a Jew in an Arab country - was somehow less painful and more interesting - perhaps because the outsiderness was so obvious and that I had no desire to belong to the society, only to understand it.

How to make sense of it all and live with less introspection and anxiety? In general I found it hard to stop thinking and hugely appreciated the things - good conversation, friendships, swimming, sex - that made the thoughts stop going round and round in my head.

18

AMERICA, 1963

FOR ME, PART of early marriage was the sense that adventures would be an ordinary part of life. The year in Egypt was our first time living abroad, but not the last. In my twenties we lived out of Britain on and off for nearly a decade.

I relished the discovery of other countries. But I often stumbled into experiences and responses without a clear idea about what they meant. They went into some deep storage and later, often much later, crystallised into some kind of meaning. I had no plans or particular ambitions for my life and there were a lot of things I didn't understand.

In the autumn of 1963, we set off again, this time for America. Roger was going to Columbia University to finish his thesis.

Though I hadn't contacted him at all, the situation with Mike had not gone away and hung over us. I felt it would be resolved, one way or another, by my seeing him again.

We decided to go by sea and boarded a German boat in Southampton which took eight days to reach New York. Not a comfortable journey – too slow for me and a feeling of being trapped with passengers I didn't feel drawn to. On the last night there was a disconcerting cabaret put on by the mostly German passengers, doing hysterical imitations of Hitler in ways that were not reassuring. We watched it for a few minutes and then fled.

At 6.00 a.m. on a magical early morning we arrived in New York harbour, still looking much like the harbour I knew from Marlon Brando's On the Waterfront, collected our luggage and hired a cab, making our way to Roger's father's duplex flat in West 33rd Street, where he lived with Roger's stepmother and two young sons. We stayed with them for a week or two until we found a friend's sunny flat in Bank Street in Greenwich Village. For an exhilarating few weeks we ate in small Italian restaurants, went to jazz clubs, walking through Washington Square past the chess players every day. I found a potter who threw enormous pots, baked them in her own gas oven and tried to teach me to centre huge lumps of clay on the wheel. I never quite managed it. When our friend came back we found a flat in Riverside Drive, within easy distance of Columbia University. It was tiny – room for a table and two chairs in the living room, the double bed filled the bedroom – and quite dark, but with a view of the East river which we never tired of, the advertisements on the far shore flickering as it grew dark. Outside, the parkway, originally planned according to the English gardening ideal, ran alongside the Hudson from 72nd to 125th street, filled with walkers and runners and parents pushing prams.

And so, like many before me, I fell in love with the city. The outspoken waitress in the overcrowded small cafe on Broadway where we often had breakfast, shouting the orders for eggs to be cooked 'easy over' and 'sunny side up', seemed to me to think herself to be entirely equal to those she served in a way that was never true in England. That of course turned out to be an illusion, but there was something here which was liberating. We had come from an England where the shadings of class were still part of our lives, everyone's lives, where trying new things was not encouraged (the astonishing stream of accomplished pop music, speaking of ordinary experiences with knowledge, rebellious precision and brilliant wit had only just begun), where being a man, preferably with a first class degree from Balliol, was still supremely advantageous, where the sexual revolution was just beginning but not yet the feminist revolution.

In America there seemed to be a prospect of things freshly imagined, new possibilities of belief. I was allowed to try things out, to experiment without having to be brilliant at something, to find out what I liked.

I found work in Raymond Loewy and William Snaith, a design and market research firm based in one of the tall glass skyscrapers in Park Avenue. I became part of a team doing market research on the state of Duke University's women's college and why it wasn't working for its students. They used something called Henry's Thematic Apperception Test; two columns of questions, one about the student, one about the college and the relationship between the two. The idea was that if the two sides didn't coincide enough, then the student and institutional aspirations were too disparate and the institution wouldn't work well. It seemed rather crude to me.

The team liked me for my British background and especially my accent. My boss was charming, a clever man who treated me well and was full of interesting ideas about marketing. Each day that I went through the glitzy glass doors and up in the smart lifts I encountered a hot-house of gossip and competitiveness. It was the first (and last) time I've worked in a company where two warring colleagues threatened each other with violence.

We had some happy family times with Roger's family, found wonderful free concerts in churches on Riverside Drive, went to the movies in the art deco cinemas all over Manhattan. Our friends were mostly writers and academics and people on the political left. And politically there was plenty of drama. 1963 was the year of Martin Luther King's 'I have a dream' speech, the year of the Harlem riots, the death of DuBois, the historian and civil rights activist, the year Betty Friedan's *The Feminine Mystique* was published.

On November 22, I was sitting on a Greyhound bus on my way to meet Roger who had gone to Harvard ahead of me. The driver stopped at the turnpike, turned round and said curtly: 'President's been shot.' The fifteen people on the bus put their papers down for about twenty seconds and then went back to their reading. No one said anything or engaged in conversation. I was shocked. But the lack of response from my fellow passengers somehow made my own responses muted. I reached Cambridge and walked into Harvard Yard, where people were sitting in huddled groups, many of them sobbing. The day, apart from its terrible drama, was something of a revelation about Kennedy's popularity in the US, which in the country as a whole had not been huge. I was conscious of how highly he was thought of amongst liberal people in Britain. And in a place like Harvard there was devastation. That evening, I sat round a dinner table with ten friends. Emotions ran high and in the heat of these everyone was convinced that Johnson would be a disastrous president. In the stunned state we were all in, we weren't exactly making shrewd political judgements. A few weeks later Roger heard a powerful speech made by Malcolm X in Greenwich Village, after he'd remarked on Kennedy's assassination that it was a case of 'chickens coming home to roost.'

Early in the new year I visited Mike in Milwaukee, our first contact since we'd parted in London the previous summer. He picked me up from the train station in Chicago and we went to his apartment and talked. It was clear that our feelings for each other hadn't gone away. But we still didn't become lovers and neither of us felt able to do anything about what we felt because of our guilt about Roger. We wandered around Milwaukee art galleries, took walks around the lake, I listened to him conducting his young orchestra – by this time he'd decided to become a musician – we ate in huge gloomy Milwaukee restaurants with waitresses in bunny costumes, both of us in a state of bewilderment and confusion. Two days later he took me back to the train station at Chicago and we repeated what we had done in London – I got on the train and then just as it was leaving, got off again. We drove back to his apartment in silence and that night we finally became lovers. There was a sense of relief and of anticlimax. Curiously, I thought at the time this somehow settled things, that we'd broken the taboo, we'd had sex and the world hadn't either collapsed or become transformed, that I was now more able to commit myself to Roger. That was the mood I was in when I went back to New York. I see from letters I sent to my sister (using rather high-flown language) that I was partly elated about loving two men, though also filled with anxiety. I was very preoccupied with trying to work it out and at one point went to talk to the poet Muriel Rukeyser, whom I hardly knew, about it. But my visit to Mike had strengthened his feelings and then mine. We talked on the phone and despite our attempts at resolution, we got in deeper; it became an increasingly passionate affair. I went on a few greyhound bus journeys to Milwaukee to visit him. On these brief visits, we touched each other constantly. I was so overwhelmed by feeling that I never had an orgasm when we made love. It didn't matter.

Roger decided at one point to go and talk with him. We were all flailing about, trying to find clarity, solutions, resolutions.

In the summer of 1964, Roger went back to England for an interview for a fellowship at St Antony's College in Oxford. It coincided with my sister's wedding and there are touching photos of Roger and my sister embracing when he got there. We didn't have enough money for me to go too.

There was a moment that summer, at the end of our year in America, when I wondered whether I was going to stay with Mike.

I recognised the same in him. But I couldn't do it. There was still love between Roger and me and though I wasn't sure of our future, I also found it impossible to betray him by leaving in this way; and I thought it would destroy any chance of Mike and I being happy.

So I went home to England with Roger, on a cargo boat from Newport News in Virginia. It was an extraordinary trip, with a cargo of coal and twelve passengers, including a beautiful young man of eighteen, looking like Marlon Brando, who everyone fell in love with, men and women alike. He befriended us and we saw him on to the train at Antwerp, waving him goodbye on his journey to Barcelona to discover Europe and pursue his fantasies about Ava Gardner and Ernest Hemingway.

19

TURMOIL AND RESOLUTION

ONCE BACK IN Oxford, where Roger now had his permanent fellowship at St Antony's College, I decided to go somewhere on my own.

I was full of guilt. And I was frightened.

But I was also conscious of a certain freedom: I was not trying to be good and that was a relief. I'd needed to be good for so long – over my mother, over trying to fulfil my parents' expectations, in trying to oversee my sister's life at home (though I'm not sure she needed me), in wanting to be part of a perfect couple. I was ashamed of my chaos and of hurting Roger, but I was also dimly aware of doors opening, of weights falling off my shoulders. After this, being good never quite had the same hold on me again.

I felt too that my mother was coping with living alone. In one sense she never stopped being '*das mutiges madchen*' and I admired her for that. She was at some level very determined, though it was so often masked by anxiety. She had joined the local orchestra in Oxford, playing, as she ruefully said, on the last desk. By that time too she was going every day to Oxfam to stuff envelopes and generally help with sending material out. The Oxfam people had the greatest affection for her. She met the Queen there once and told her that she too was from Germany. She was without any sense of grandiosity, inviting Sir Oliver Franks and his wife to supper at her flat and serving the mousse she had bought for us all in the plastic bowl it came in from Budgens. She went on posh package holidays, to Norway, to Switzerland and always made some friends. She remained beautiful and, even in the worst of times, never stopped dressing smartly. She sometimes wore lipstick and she always powdered her face. Otherwise no make-up. All her life, even when she was living in Oxford, she continued to go regularly to Harrods to have the hair removed from her upper lip. At times of great stress she would buy unbelievably expensive handbags.

❧

I set off to London to stay with Jane, my friend from Oxford and to find a job. Before I went I explained to my mother why I was going. I also told my grandmother Lotte, asking her not to pass on the news to my father – I wanted to do this myself. She couldn't contain herself and by the time I got to London he had already made enquiries about me from Jane, demanding to see her, to find out what was going on. She found him very authoritarian; he made it clear that he was worried about my state of mind and not pleased with the way my life was going; she felt that he was indicating that I might be heading for my mother's mental troubles. He and I were already in a period of monumental arguments about politics. He disliked my radicalism, I his conservatism. I was aware that I disappointed him. Not only was I involved in left-wing politics, but my adult life was turning out not to be orderly in the way he wanted it to be and I could see that he didn't think I was fulfilling his hopes or what in his eyes was my potential. It was not until much later, when we created and ran a successful publishing company, Virago, that this changed – when I suspect that he was pleased above all that I was a chip off the old block, a good businesswoman. But for now he was unsupportive and unhelpful.

For six months after his meeting with Jane, I made no contact with him.

I found work as an au pair with a South African woman living with her three children in a large house in North London. She was deeply involved in anti-apartheid politics, warm, very emotional and wanting to be friends. I enjoyed our friendship, the buzz of politics in the house, the children. I picked the children up every day from school – two girls and the eldest, a boy, and gave them tea. The life was absorbing and distracting without being too demanding, which was just what I needed. My employer was part of swinging London: I was still pretty innocent and easily amazed by what went on – George Melly doing his party trick with his penis between his legs at her Christmas party, her lover drunkenly trying to get into my bed late one night.

Roger came to see me from time to time, tense meetings which made neither of us happy. I had a brief affair with a beautiful man who drove a van and wrote television scripts. He was sleeping with quite a few women. One day he rang me to say that he'd contracted gonorrhoea and he'd made a list of the women he'd been sleeping with in two columns, one where they might have become infected, the other not. I was, he told me, in the safe column. But I was taking no chances and spent an uncomfortable afternoon in the sexual diseases clinic of St George's Hospital, just to make sure.

Mike and I wrote to each other: and as time went on it became clearer that we were not going to live together.

Gradually, as I became absorbed in this London life and focused less on impossible personal conundrums, I began to relax more and after about nine months I began to allow myself to respond to the feelings I still had for Roger. I eventually went to see him in Oxford and we talked. I said I wanted to try and get back together. He had by then embarked on a new relationship, but decided he too wanted to try. This was the late spring of 1965.

So, with a mixture of apprehension and optimism, I moved into Roger's flat in Banbury Road. By then he was happily established at St Antony's and deeply involved in the Middle East Centre there. He had also become friends, through campaigning for the Labour Party in the 1964 election, with Bob Sutcliffe, a left-wing economics don at Jesus College, who became an important part of our lives.

I enrolled in part-time sculpture and pottery classes at the

Oxford Poly, much encouraged by my sculptor teacher, less so by the pottery teacher. We decided to stop renting, bought a town house in Headington behind the football ground and I turned the garage into a studio. I became obsessed with sculpting, getting up in the middle of meals to go on working on a piece. I went to lectures, college suppers, dances, we cooked meals for Oxford friends and our London friends and relatives came to stay at weekends. I stopped agonizing about what I should do about Mike, I'd made a decision to live with Roger; and we were happier together than we'd been for a long time.

⚘

We wanted to have a child. When the months passed and I didn't get pregnant, we started having tests. Roger's sperm count was all right, a relief to him and also, I realized, to me. The problem seemed to lie with me, but though there were some small physiological problems there were no obvious large ones.

It is such a particular feeling. You can't do this most ordinary of things, this thing that happens to people all the time, whether they want it or not. I thought about little else, while always trying to protect myself against the next disappointment. My friends had many children. So did my sister and brother. Pregnant women became the most beautiful in the world and the most envied – especially my friends. The sense of being an outsider to this world of motherhood was overwhelming. The battles with my body became a large feature of my life.

My gynaecological history turned out to be one of a certain

amount of chaos mixed with black comedy. Tests for infertility in the mid-Sixties were poorly developed and crude and most doctors were uninterested in the problem, though even then it was known that one in ten couples had difficulty conceiving. Robert Winston recalls that when he told a colleague in the 1960s that he wanted to start a fertility clinic, his fellow doctors warned him he'd be starting a 'futility clinic.' Women struggling to conceive sat in the same waiting rooms as pregnant women. Early on, doctors made various suggestions to me. Perhaps we made love too fast? Did I know about fertile periods? Was I tense? In cubicles with curtains as walls, I was asked whether I had orgasms; I was slapped genially on the thigh by young male doctors who said: 'We'll get you pregnant'. For one of the tests, Roger and I had to make love at six in the morning, rather heroically succeeding on all but one occasion, when we were reprimanded for failing. Each month, I would hold my breath in a state of excitement and tension, as I waited for the first drops of blood and prayed they wouldn't come.

And always this sense that I was not a proper woman. We went on having tests: I had several D & Cs, we tried everything that was available – which at that time was not very much. I learnt to be robust and even raucous about my body: I was determined not to go under. I longed for a child, I wanted to be a mother and I was also aware that I was not doing what was expected of me.

It was a lonely business, even though it was shared with Roger; we made jokes about it, united in our sadness. But being infertile took its toll, on our relationship as well as other things (Roger had two children with his second wife).

With hindsight, I don't think I ever felt confident that I would get pregnant. I wonder now whether I was afraid of passing on my mother's illness, or that I feared that pregnancy would make it more likely that I would go mad.

For about eighteen months we tried to conceive and then in late 1966 embarked on trying to adopt a child. It was something we both wanted to do. The process was long but we were lucky – we had two sympathetic social workers from Oxford Council who were exceptionally subtle and helpful. They paid us many visits and talked about who we were, about our families, what we wanted for ourselves and our child. They asked whether we wanted a boy or a girl. Implicit in the adoption procedure seemed to be a notion of trying to match a child to its potential parents, though we were surprised to be asked whether we had a preference about hair colour. It was then still possible to adopt a baby, something that became more difficult soon after. And that's what we wanted, a baby as young as possible.

In some ways we were not ideal candidates for adopting: our parents were both divorced, which statistically made us less likely to stay together. There was my mother's illness: I lay awake at night trying to work out ways to talk about it which would min-imize it. But in the end I told them how it was, straightforwardly and truthfully and, miraculously, it didn't stop them believing we were suitable parents. Given the process (which in later decades became even more complicated and prolonged, with a good deal of inappropriate political correctness thrown in) we were able to talk to them with unusual candour. I recall telling them in one conversation that I thought it was hard to predict how life and relationships would turn out.

On March 3rd 1967 we got a letter from Oxford Children's Department to say we were accepted as adoptive parents. All we had to do now was wait for a baby to be born.

20

LEBANON

S O THE WAITING begins, the longing for a child, sometimes physically painful, increasing as time passes. The adoption process is underway. We continue to try and conceive. And
meanwhile we are making plans to go to the Lebanon.

Roger wants to spend a year improving his Arabic. He receives
a grant with which we buy a pale blue Volkswagen station wagon;
we are going to pile into it enough possessions for a year and drive
from Oxford to Beirut.

On June 5th 1967 the Six-Day War breaks out between Israel
and the neighbouring states of Egypt, Jordan and Syria. After a
period of high tension, Israel launches surprise bombing raids
against Egyptian airfields and engages in aerial clashes over Syria.
Syrian artillery attacks on Israeli settlements on the border are
followed by Israeli responses against Syrians in the Golan Heights.
The Egyptians finally impose a naval blockade on Eilat in Israel

and order the UN buffer force to leave the Sinai Peninsula. Within six days Israel has won a decisive land war and taken control of the Gaza Strip and the Sinai Peninsula from Egypt, the West Bank and East Jerusalem from Jordan and, as its final offensive, the Golan Heights from Syria. A ceasefire is signed on June 11th.

We're not clear how this war, whose political importance will turn out to be so huge and will lay the foundation for so many future conflicts, is going to affect our year. We have some contacts in Lebanon, but not many. We have few certainties about where we're going or where we will live. We're aiming for Shemlan, a village high in the mountains above Beirut, where there is an Arabic school. It's famous in the region as the 'spy school'; it's where the foreign office send their people to learn the language.

We set off from Oxford one sunny morning in late July, taking with us our burly and genial friend, John Parker, a historian who grew up in Alexandria and who wants a holiday and to come with us as far as Greece. He is a gifted linguist – after each border crossing he effortlessly breaks into whatever is required – French, German, Serbo-Croat, Greek, Arabic. We stay in small hotels or set up our tents on campsites.

On the motorway to the south of Germany we pass the sign to Dachau. Strange to see this name in such a mundane, ordinary setting and I remember my stomach lurching when it appeared. I felt distinctly uncomfortable in Bavaria. Munich, a city full of fine pictures and churches and old ladies with surgical boots (*What were you doing in the war?* I found myself thinking), loomed large in Hitler's rise to power. In the post-war chaos after 1918, the city and its rowdy beer halls offered the failed Austrian painter and returned soldier a receptive audience for his politics.

The drive onwards into Austria and former Yugoslavia (this was Tito's time, the country not yet broken up) was magnificent, the kind of terrain I had learned to love from those Swiss holidays with my parents – jagged high mountains, dark forests interspersed with green meadows. It was very hot, the sky cloudless and no wind.

Reaching Belgrade, we first put up our tents in a large campsite on the edge of the city, then went in search of supper, finding a restaurant in one of those streets lined with tall plane trees in the city's nineteenth century quarter. The tables set in the garden between the gravel paths were filled with people deep in conversation, utterly relaxed, smoking, drinking. Huge trays of hearty food were delivered to the tables by waiters in large white aprons. It felt like a haven of peace and hospitality, an idyll of European urban life on a hot summer's evening, the buzz of conversation, the smell of roasted meat, the sun slowly setting over the roofs and trees. It has stayed in my mind's eye forever. The next time I saw Belgrade – at the beginning of the Balkan wars of the 1990s – the atmosphere was utterly changed, grim and charged with menace, the streets and cafés filled with soldiers hung with weaponry.

That night we were woken by the sound of prolonged loud tapping. It was 2.00 a.m. and as we poked our heads out of the tent we saw a large party of Albanians putting up their tents – a comic sight. Next morning, we embarked on the daunting journey down the motorway running down the centre of the country. It was a three-way highway built up of large concrete rectangles loosely joined together, jammed with cars and heavy lorries: we knew that there were reputedly more accidents here than on any other road in Europe. And sure enough, soon after we set off, Roger driving, we saw one immediately in front of us – a car hit the side of a huge lorry and crumpled like the piece of thin metal it was. Everyone drove on, avoiding the wreckage.

I looked around me. I thought – here I am in a world I don't begin to understand, a German Jewish woman grounded in my own particular history – an exiled family, an ill mother, a woman trying to belong, going to live in an Arab country which is at war. I have a moment of panic and it passes – mostly I feel oddly secure on this journey.

Roger and John Parker said we should find some food, so at one point we turned off this hot, relentless highway, with flatness as far as the eye could see, the only visible crop endless fields of maize, to try and find some food. Instantly we were in a village with mud roads, no shop, nothing in sight for us to buy. Women in black sat in their doorways, staring at us. We got back on the road and survived on water and chocolate. Eventually we reached Skopje, still in the throes of being rebuilt after the earthquake in 1963 which destroyed 80 percent of the city, relieved to find a bed and a meal.

The next border we crossed was into northern Greece, heading towards Meteora ('suspended in the air') country, one of the largest complexes of Eastern Orthodox monasteries. The six monasteries were dramatically perched on sandstone rock pillars, on the edge of the Plain of Thessaly near the Pindus Mountains – only about four or five monks living in each, full of wonderful frescoes and with marvellous views over the countryside. In the nunnery they complained about the length of my skirt so I walked with my knees bent.

Earlier that year, on April 21st 1967, a group of Greek right-wing army officers had seized power in a coup d'état. It was a speedy coup. Preparing lists in advance, they had arrested politicians and other leading authority figures as well as ordinary citizens suspected of left-wing sympathies, over 10,000 people in total. Eleven articles of the Greek constitution were immediately suspended. This meant that anyone could be arrested without a warrant at any time and brought before a military court. The colonels called the coup a 'revolution to save the nation.' Long-standing political freedoms were instantly suppressed. Torture became a regular and deliberate practice. The right of assembly was revoked and surveillance on citizens became a fact of life. By the time we were there that summer Greece had become a police state. The official justification was that a 'communist conspiracy' had infiltrated all Greek institutions and that drastic action was needed to protect the country from a communist takeover. Anti-communism was the defining characteristic of the Junta.

As we travelled along the rough roads, very few of them tarmacked, there were notices every few miles abusing communists, which John translated for us.

The sun began to set. We turned into a roadside restaurant, empty except for us and a small local band. We ordered our lamb kebabs and rice and suddenly the band broke into the most famous tune by Mikis Theodorakis - a defiant gesture, as Theodorakis, the most famous living Greek composer, was an enemy of the

Junta, had been imprisoned by them and his music banned. The band were showing us, their only audience, that some Greeks hated the Junta. We showed as best we could our appreciation for their courage.

It was a rough, hot journey down to Piraeus, where John finally left us to return to England. He'd been a great companion. We hugged him and invited him to come and stay with us in Lebanon. We put our car and ourselves on to the boat going to Beirut harbour. Our plan had been to drive to Lebanon via Turkey and Syria. But the Syrians were banning the British from coming into the country after the Six-Day War. So we sailed to Beirut harbour from Piraeus, a restful and beautiful journey, arriving in heat so saturated with moisture that I wondered whether I could put one foot in front of the other.

The customs official lingered over my Jewish maiden name for a while, but we got through and set off for the mountains, through the buzzing city by the Mediterranean and up the wide Damascus Road. It was dusk by the time we turned off to Souk El Gharb, high above Beirut, following the signs to Shemlan. It was also misty and the road was exceptionally winding and narrow in places. Roger drove and I tried not to scream as I looked down into the steep gorge below.

We arrived in Shemlan, the mist cleared and we found Cliff House, a local restaurant serving chicken cooked on charcoal, with lemon squeezed on top. I'd never tasted anything so wonderful. That night we stayed at the Melcom Hotel, run by Armenians, just above the village.

The place we found to live in was a small summer house, teetering on the edge of the mountain, owned by a sweet-natured elderly woman, Milady. There was cold running water, a tin bath and one oil-drip stove for the whole house in what turned out to be a very cold winter – Shemlan was on the snowline. But for now the weather was still warm and we had a small vine-covered terrace with a long view down to the city and the sea.

It was all remarkably easy considering we'd arrived in a place we didn't know, a car full of possessions to see us through the next year with nowhere to live. But I felt safe with Roger in this new territory and any emotional territory where there were difficulties between us was once again overridden by the excitement of setting up our new life, which we did with some ease. More growing up together, more companionship.

I suffered from my usual homesickness and spent the first three or four weeks reading nineteenth century English novels on the terrace, finding particular comfort in *Middlemarch*, an England that seemed comprehensible and deeply rooted in things I at least partially understood – class, marriage, love, ambition. Roger set up his Arabic lessons and we located a Palestinian family in the village who we had a contact for. They invited us to tea and talked about the Six-Day War. They were, of course, devastated by it. It was a terrible war for Arabs – Arab casualties were far greater than Israeli – and in particular for Palestinians. Israel's territory grew by a factor of three, including around one million Arabs now under Israel's direct control in the newly captured territories.

Unsurprisingly, our year in the Lebanon was dominated by the aftermath of this war. It was everywhere – in conversations, in the newspapers, in political debate, in people's anguish. We spent time with Lebanese, Palestinians, British and Americans and befriended several journalists. It was five years since Kim Philby had defected from this city to Russia and he was still a hot topic of conversation. I could never fully share the indignation of people who thought his actions had simply been acts of betrayal.

At weekends we went down to Beirut to swim in the sea; we ate in small restaurants on the beach. With autumn came sudden storms, with rain and hail the size of ping pong balls.

The city was cosmopolitan, glamorous in parts – our friend Patrick Seale's apartment (destroyed in the civil war) at the time one of the most beautiful places imaginable, close to the famous Hotel St. Georges, built on the rocks with the sea beating against the living room wall. When the spring came, stalls sprouted up on every street corner where freshly picked oranges were squeezed. People were immensely hospitable and lively; after supper at friends' houses the carpets were regularly rolled back, the music put on and the dancing began.

Two or three times a week we drove down to Beirut from our mountain retreat, on small winding roads, through the large Druze village (where people always looked at us with suspicion) – a hazardous business in winter when under pressure from ice and snow chunks of tarmac broke away over the edge of the mountain. I took some courses at the American University, sculpture, Islamic

Roger and me with friends on our balcony in Beirut, 1968

art. Roger attended lectures and seminars on Middle East history and politics.

In November I went to see a charming gynaecologist to see if he could help with pregnancy and had a D & C in the hospital in Beirut. As ever, hope sprang up that this time I might conceive. I recovered in our little mountain house, wearing three sweaters to bed; by now it was snowing up there and the drip oil stove didn't do much to heat the place. Friends came from England for Christmas and on Boxing Day we went down to the sea to swim and on the same day drove up to the cedars of Lebanon, where it was snowing.

On Sundays we regularly went to Biblos and Sidon, or the Bekaa Valley, walked in the mountains near Joun, where Lady Hester Stanhope lived at the end of her life in an abandoned monastery known as Dahr el Sitt – beautiful country and at this particular moment relatively peaceful: the terrible civil war started seven years later. But even in our time there were regular political dramas which usually involved guns and violence.

We spent our last month in a flat in Beirut and decided we would go to Israel on our way home. This involved getting a second passport, going to Cyprus and leaving the car there, ready to pick it up for our return journey to England.

Roger's father had an Israeli colleague in Cyprus who invited us to dinner the day before we went to Israel. It was a pleasant enough evening until the conversation turned to the Arabs. Some of them are my best friends, our host said. Then he began to tell us about atrocities the Arabs had committed. Roger tried to stop him: 'We can all exchange atrocity stories but where does that get us?' But the man didn't stop; it was like a compulsion. I felt more and more uncomfortable and then suddenly, on Roger's initiative, we got up and left in mid-meal, angry and outraged. It was my first direct encounter with this kind of Israeli attitude to Arabs.

Next day we flew to Tel Aviv, drove to Jerusalem where we stayed first at the American Colony Hotel and then in the YMCA, a lovely old building near the Damascus Gate, our room next to a café which blared out Tom Jones singing 'The Green, Green Grass of Home' much of the evening. I lay there with a splitting sinus headache and wished we were back in our Lebanese mountain retreat.

A friendly British journalist on the *Jerusalem Post* confirmed what we had already observed – that the effect of the Six-Day War was to produce as much paranoia in Israel as it did in the Lebanon. Here it was a siege mentality we encountered. It was a momentous moment in the history of that part of the world and analyzing it is hugely complicated; but there was no doubt about the hardening of attitudes in Israel.

Our journalist friend took us on a drive around Jerusalem with his family; on the way back we passed some Arab villages on the hillsides and the children started chanting a song in Hebrew. Their parents sharply told them to stop. They were embarrassed. We asked why; the words of the song, it turns out, learned at school, were utterly contemptuous of Arabs.

Driving down to Tel Aviv the next day, we heard the news of Bobby Kennedy's assassination on the taxi radio. Two days later we returned to Cyprus to pick up our car for the journey home. The boat took us to Mersin on the south coast of Turkey. The Turks had just built the spectacular coastal road along the Mediterranean; we sped along, hardly a car in sight, small fishing villages still intact with the occasional Crusader castle jutting out into the sea, northwards to Istanbul and making our last stop in Turkey at Edirne, an assertively Eastern city, a last glimpse of the culture we'd become so familiar with over this past year. At the Bulgarian border, the guards opened the boot and rattled our trunk, presumably to see if there was a person in it - they didn't bother to open it. And then on, slowly, to England, stopping in Vienna which felt to us dauntingly monumental and authoritarian - not much sign at that time of Freud's presence and to my somewhat jaundiced eye too many bierkellers with the men dressed in lederhosen and their raucous laughter. The sun shone out of a cloudless sky and we drove and camped and sometimes stayed in hotels, gradually getting acclimatized to being back in the landscapes and the cities of Europe. I was happy to see them again.

꙰

And so, in the late summer of 1968, our travels and living abroad ended. On our second day back in Oxford our friend Bob Sutcliffe came to see us. He was excited; he told us that everyone he knew had moved leftwards and that we might find ourselves cut off if we didn't 'catch up.' We were still absorbed in our Middle Eastern world and his news left us rather cold. But 1968 had already been a momentous year in Europe and the US and there were many events which more or less passed us by in our mountain retreat in the Lebanon (no 24-hour news in those days): the Prague Spring in January, the short-lived attempt to bring democratic socialism to Czechoslovakia under the grip of the Soviet Union, ending with Soviet tanks in the streets; in January too, the Tet offensive in Vietnam, a series of surprise attacks by the Vietcong and North Vietnamese; although the offensive was a military defeat for the communists, it had a profound effect on the prestige of the US government. Then in May, the student protests in France, starting with a series of strikes and occupations, involving eleven million workers for a continuous two weeks and resulting in the largest general strike ever which for a time brought the economy of France to a virtual standstill and almost brought de Gaulle's government down. There was fear of revolution. But the violence on the streets evaporated quickly, workers went back to their jobs and in the June elections the Gaullist party emerged stronger than before.

For some it demonstrated that events of this kind don't lead to lasting radical change unless other profound political changes take place. In all kinds of ways it was an important moment for the left.

In 1968 and 1969 we watched our TV screens as campuses worldwide became battlegrounds for social change, television hugely influential in forming the political identity of this generation. We watched the bombing of Vietnam and the Biafran war. In America we saw Black Power gaining influence, the civil rights movement moving to the northern cities; the German student movement, the SDS, formed an extra parliamentary opposition against the authoritarianism of its government; people of the Third World, in Asia, Africa, Latin America, affirmed their solidarity against imperialism. In Argentina the student protests were joined by labour unions. In Japan the highly politicized students union Zengakuren developed. And international solidarity became a feature of radicalization.

For us, the impact of all these events had been overshadowed in Lebanon by the traumatic effects of the 1967 Six-Day War. Now, as we settled back to life in England, we became aware of these political landscapes we had missed and of new ones – feminism, human rights, the gay liberation movement.

21

KATE

B Y THE AUTUMN of 1968, Roger was back at St Antony's. I wasn't certain what I wanted to do, half waiting for a baby to arrive. I didn't want to go back to social work. I took a temporary job at the Oxford Modern Art Gallery.

On a routine visit to my friendly dentist, he noticed a small lump on my upper gum and asked me what it was. I have no idea, I said, and he told me I should have it checked at the hospital, adding I should make the appointment quickly. I was alarmed and went to the doctor the next day. A week later I was called to the Churchill Hospital and examined. I was told that I needed an operation to take the lump out. No one seemed quite sure what it was, but they knew they wanted to operate soon. By then I was frightened and, in tears, rang Roger. I was sure I had cancer.

Two days later I went into hospital. I was in a ward with six other people, everyone waiting to have an operation on their face.

One young girl's mouth had been severely bitten by her horse. There's something about the face going wrong which is exceptionally threatening and we all felt it; the face looks on to the world and is looked at by the world.

It turned out I had a myxoma, a soft tissue mass in this case located in the gum. It was very rare in this position – only six people could be found in the medical literature. Myxomas are the basis of myxomatosis in rabbits. This one was quietly eating my mouth away. It didn't metastasise but it required the upper jaw to be taken out to make sure it didn't spread. The doctors were reticent, the more so because it was so rare, which made it more frightening for them as well as for me. I confidently thought that, as an ex-medical student, I'd easily be able to get information from them, forgetting that the moment you become a patient you also become helpless and dependent. Roger spoke out for me impressively: 'You may think you're watching her, but she's watching you. It's a relationship like any other.' he said at one uninformative meeting with the silver-haired surgeon.

The next day they took out my left upper jaw. When I came round from the anaesthetic, the doctor and nurses and Roger were at my bedside. A nurse began to pull the bandage from my mouth. The doctor asked me a question. I tried to answer. They had somehow forgotten to explain that after the bandage was removed I would sound as if I had a cleft palate. I could barely make myself understood. I thought quite simply: My life's come to an end, I'll never be able to make myself understood again. It was some time before they told me they would make a plate which would solve the problem.

I lived on liquids for several days. My mother, concerned and anxious, came to visit me. My father reacted coolly, outwardly at least, to the whole thing. I was hurt but not surprised – he seemed on the whole to deal with bad news by denying its badness. He didn't come to see me, though he made it clear he expected Roger to keep him informed about what was going on.

I was put in a ward on my own and the doctors placed a radium plate in my mouth for a week, to make sure the myxoma had been totally removed. My visitors could stand behind a protective screen if they chose to. It was a measure of my paranoid mood that I silently tested my friends and family; those that didn't stand behind the screen loved me more than those who did.

Making the permanent plate – the next stage – was a process so painful that the two consultants doing it were almost as traumatized as I was. It went on for about three hours. They couldn't use an analgesic because they needed me to feel where the plate touched. Tears poured down my cheeks, constantly and involuntarily, as they built the plate, step by step and tried fitting it in my mouth. I remember these two men, looking desperate, forced, unwillingly but necessarily, into doing something that caused me such pain.

For months, on and off, there was a good deal of pain – the after-effects of the operation and then the occasional infection. The fact that my face was involved, that the surgery and aftercare involved so much touching and fiddling around with my face and my mouth, was disturbing; it made me edgy and irritable and I felt invaded. Roger was very supportive and my mother and my friends were too. But the sense of loss around my face and my voice and the feel of this foreign body – the plate – in my mouth was something I had to deal with alone.

And then there was the shock. It had happened so quickly. I felt numb and lost, tired, not able to work. I thought about how my looks were affected – by the metal clasps on my teeth to hold the plate, by the red patches that came up on my left cheek when it was cold and when I cried. It took me a long time to take everything in. I don't think I had any idea until much later quite how much confidence I lost in that time.

After some weeks, I started doing some editorial work on Roger's PhD thesis to keep myself occupied. I decided to ask my publishing friend Peter Carson to send me freelance work and discovered I enjoyed it – copy editing, proof reading, indexing. I didn't know it at the time, but this was the small kernel of the beginning of my publishing life.

So the year went on, with a lot of painkillers and resting and a sense of aimlessness. And a lot of time to think.

It was the late '60s and the world around me had been changing. By now the Pill had become available to young women, to all women, which led to new sexual expectations for women and particularly for men who now took for granted women's sexual availability. In 1964 Mary Quant had started selling miniskirts on a large scale from her shop in Chelsea and I, like so many of my contemporaries, went and bought them and enjoyed the liberation of eight inches of leg showing above the knee. I became aware of myself as a sexual person in a way that was new to me. I loved the music and the words to the music; we collected all the Beatles' vinyls, the Beach Boys, the Mammas and the Papas, the Rolling Stones and played them endlessly.

These were some of the visible signs of what was also a revolution in expectations. They went deep. Roger and I had grown up in a time of social conservatism, with a particular set of beliefs and expectations we were, or so I thought, comfortable with. I accepted the idea that marriage involved the woman supporting the man's working life, fitting her own work and life around it. But now new ideas about women, about sex, about marriage, about work, about women's independence began to make their mark.

I already felt in some sort of limbo – we'd been away for a year, I felt away from things; I had no regular work because of the operation and its after-effects; the fear of mental illness had receded but hadn't entirely gone; and we were waiting for a baby whose arrival we couldn't control.

The longing for a child remained the most powerful feeling. But there were others – a sense of uncertainty about how to place myself in the world, a desire to find a life that was mine though I didn't know what it might be, or how to look for it, how to talk about it. The condition of marriage itself might have contributed to that. With hindsight, always easy, I may have accepted the traditional role of the wife less than I thought, though I had thought of myself as happily compliant and wanting to fit in with the rules. I wanted to be a helpmeet to my husband. I'd always had fantasies of being a support to a brilliant man. Now I had a feeling of constraint, of having desires I didn't properly understand. And I suppose it was horribly predictable that, at a time when my confidence was low, I would respond to someone who found me attractive.

I started an affair with a literary agent in London, whom I'd met in Paris a few weeks after the operation. Roger and I had bumped into our friend Patrick Seale and Eleanor Philby, wife of Kim Philby, in Les Deux Magots, and he was with them. We all spent an evening together. He was a Marxist, half French, an alcoholic. I started seeing him in London and he soon wanted me to leave Roger and live with him. I didn't love him but I was fascinated by him and by his world. We had meals in smart restaurants, he talked to me about publishing, I watched him at work with his authors, he took me to parties where I met interesting writers. I became aware, late developer that I was, that my unease about not having a life of my own was partly to do with not having found work that I loved. I began to think publishing might be that work. He was my entry into it.

I told Roger about the affair; for all its difficulties, I still felt it was better than lying to him. He knew when I went to London that I was seeing and sleeping with the literary agent. He didn't like it but he didn't try and stop me. As in other things about my life, he thought the decision was mine alone – something I never found easy. He knew I wasn't in love with the literary agent. But it was a strange and dangerous situation.

After a few months Roger told me that he'd begun to have an affair too, with a woman in Oxford who was very much in love with him. I didn't feel particularly threatened by this, didn't feel I would lose him and perhaps was relieved that I wasn't the only one having an affair. After Mike I had always felt I was the wilful one in the marriage, the naughty one, and I didn't particularly like it.

At one point in the autumn of 1969, Roger sat me down and asked me whether I still wanted to live with him, still wanted to go ahead with adopting a child with him. I said yes with complete conviction.

But I did want to go on seeing the literary agent. He was intellectually seductive and I was excited by the life he was introducing me to.

And so, emerging from the gloom of illness, of living in something of a vacuum, I went to London regularly. I liked being on the move, found it soothing and reassuring – no man's land. And I wanted both worlds, for very different reasons. I thought I could manage it all.

❧

In January 1970 we heard from the social workers that there was a possibility that a child might be born that we could adopt. At the end of February, the first women's liberation conference in Britain, the first, that is, of the second wave women's movement of the 1970s, was held in Ruskin College, Oxford. On the weekend of the conference, a friend came to stay and asked me whether I wanted to come with her to Ruskin. I remember thinking – this isn't for me; interesting but not something that's any part of my life. I was a socialist, very much absorbed in international politics. I'd never read *The Second Sex* right through, had only dipped into Betty Friedan's *The Feminist Mystique.* I'd read some fiction – by Doris Lessing, Margaret Drabble and others – which touched on women's lives in particular ways which would later become more explicit. I was aware, but only dimly, of what was going on in late sixties America in feminist politics. I had kept my close women friends from college and we talked a lot. But I knew very little about feminism.

Our friend came back from the Ruskin women's liberation conference; she was excited. It was the first gathering of this kind in Britain, hundreds of women from all parts of the country, expressing very divergent views, sometimes very personal, on women's lives and what was needed to improve them, to give them more autonomy, more possibility of work, more space in the culture. There were mixed reports of the conference – some said the sharp exchanges were very sharp, others that a good deal of warmth was present. There were contentious proposals and a sense that things were being said that marked something new. It was the official birth of the women's liberation movement in Britain.

On March 3rd our daughter Kate was born. We picked her up from the hospital on March 12th. She had been born by Caesarian, hurriedly, as her biological mother's placenta had come away suddenly. She was smooth-skinned and exceptionally beautiful. We took a yellow Babygro to the hospital, dressed her in it and brought her home. She slept for long periods in the first few days, so much so that we rang the hospital to check that everything was all right. My longing for a child was instantly, amazingly satisfied by her arrival.

We were the last of the generation in Britain to be able to adopt a child early, within the first six weeks of life, though we asked and were granted, permission to have the baby even earlier. So Kate, when she arrived, came to us at nine days old, together with a large teddy bear from her biological mother, later called Simon by Kate. She was a child I loved so immediately that it felt as if I'd been waiting for her all my life. Everything else disappeared; we were totally absorbed in this new person. So at the time Ruskin barely registered.

My mother came over to see the new baby. She was happy for us and, much to my pleasure, responded warmly to Kate, keen to be involved, always pleased to see her. Did I think about her feelings as a mother in relation to my becoming a mother? I don't remember such thoughts and we certainly didn't talk about it; perhaps I couldn't relate my feelings of connection and love for Kate to what she might have felt and was rather sad about that. My father, who lived in London, took longer to come and I felt, perhaps unfairly, that he was nervous and wary of adoption.

Kate was born into a world of a new Tory government. It was the time of the Affluent Society, but not for everybody; there was high unemployment. There was women's liberation and gay liberation. Men wore their hair long. Shirley Conran hailed the duvet as a liberating object in housework. There was student unrest. Underground newspapers flourished. Friends took LSD – not me, I was much too frightened of going mad – and described some magical hallucinations and also some terrifying ones. It was a world where there seemed to be no limits – experiments with drugs, with sex, with politics, with living, were in the air. Anything seemed possible. We were overtaken by a huge wave of possibilities, seemingly with no guidelines. Boundaries were there to be pushed, everything was tested. In a sense, the assumption of the stable family was beginning to come to an end. There were experiments and accidents and not much control except things one might impose on oneself. I wasn't very good at that, often led by my body, driven by sexual feelings, leaping into affairs without thinking of the consequences.

⚘

For me Kate's arrival was as if a long emotional drought was over and I could respond to this person I seemed to have been waiting for for years.

Up to now I'd always tended to feel anxiety about the people I loved, to brood on it easily, to allow doubts to creep in. Not now. No anxieties, no doubts, I loved her, no qualifications. She also happened to be an enchanting child, everything I'd – we'd both – fantasised about – lively, sturdy, responsive, calm, beautiful. The feelings I'd had about not quite being a proper woman more or less disappeared. We sat with her endlessly, held her, fed her, walked with her, me proudly pushing her pram in the University Parks wearing a mini skirt. We took her everywhere, to friends and relatives, out to supper. Roger shared the feeding, the changing, the bottle-washing. We put her on cushions in strange houses and she went straight to sleep. She was the easiest child.

If I had fantasies of what kind of a mother I wanted to be, they included the usual things – making her feel utterly safe, warm, protected – but also giving her a sense of space, of not imposing my needs on her. I truly didn't want to be a needy mother. I was frightened of not being able to give her a sense of inner certainty, something I'd not been good at myself. Very young, she seemed to have a strong sense of her self, of what she wanted. I hoped I could confirm this feeling in her.

As for adoption, I was always reluctant to take away certainties – focusing on what's not there rather than the obvious love between us. Blood ties are real enough but also overrated in my view.

I always thought that I would do some work. I felt some discomfort with myself for needing this, but knew that it was part of me. I feared that I'd feel isolated alone with a child, that I would brood without some contact with the outside world.

And there were things I hadn't resolved, about myself, about the black holes, about the kind of isolation I felt from time to time, with the thought that nobody but me ever felt this way.

Some weeks after Kate was born I began occasionally going to London again, taking her with me in the car, staying with the literary agent. Why didn't I stop seeing him? Roger knew about my visits and didn't ask me to stop – that was not his way. And perhaps we were both so overwhelmed by Kate's arrival we didn't address the oddness of it, the risks.

Writing it down, it's hard with hindsight to see how I could have thought this was a manageable life, or one that I could live with any sort of integrity. But that's not what it felt like at the time. I was committed to my marriage and my child and I liked the excitement of the life I was learning about in London. Being someone who lived with a lot of doubt especially about emotional matters, I was, in my own way, trying to make sense of things, tunnelling on with my life.

In the autumn of 1970, Roger took a year's sabbatical and we rented a flat in Islington. I went on seeing the literary agent.

The literary agent was unhappy. He had failed to persuade me to live with him and he knew that with Kate's arrival that was the end of the matter. He began an affair with the woman who'd been in love with Roger – they both had their reasons for doing this. We stopped seeing each other. I, who'd felt in charge of things, that I could manage and juggle this life I was leading, now, disconcertingly felt devastated and out of control.

I was driven by compulsive feelings which I didn't understand. I wrote endless notes and letters, most of which I didn't send. I drove round and round London, past the literary agent's house. One night I threw a brick through his window – I went with a friend and felt better afterwards!

I was at home with a child I loved. I could respond to her, I could function in an everyday sort of way. And in other ways I found myself out of control, compulsive, on the verge of madness – that old black hole that I feared. And I couldn't really talk to Roger We found each other unreachable. I understood his emotional reticence, his distance, his hurt, but I couldn't cope with it.

I was also aware of something else – contradictory, selfish, shameful, necessary, clear – of being greedy for life, wanting to take it on in some new way, wanting it to be different, a feeling intensified by my pleasure in having a child. I had a vague and unformed sense that I wanted to break out of being a wife, to be more independent, to take part more fully in the world of work, to be part of changing things.

Perhaps by then too much had happened between me and

Roger. Something broke in me. I told Roger I wanted to be on my own. The thought of dealing with life on my own with Kate, of having to earn a living, was not in the least daunting to me. I was cocooned in my own feelings. Roger was angry and miserable but I suspect felt impotent. I behaved with ruthlessness. I knew that I would be depriving Roger of daily life with Kate. I knew how enormous that was. I wasn't proud of it. But though I felt very guilty, it didn't stop me.

Roger is the only person I've lived with full time. When I left our marriage, I began to live with men without living with them full time. Gradually, I recognised that I wanted to be in a loving relationship but also needed time and space to myself. I was not the only woman who felt this at this time, though for me it seemed to have added relevance because of my relationship with my mother – about being so conscious of her neediness when she was in the house. I still have a version of needing space – difficulty when there are other people in the room, worrying about whether they're all right, bored, what they need, whether I'm doing or saying the right or wrong things.

So, for good or ill, for the rest of my life I have lived with men but not all the time. There's a price to pay of course, as with everything. Perhaps I chose a certain sort of freedom rather than safety, often enough happily.

And so it was that in the summer of 1971, I stayed in London with Kate while Roger returned to Oxford.

22

THE ONLY GAME IN TOWN

IN 1926, THREE years before Virginia Woolf wrote *A Room of One's Own*, Sylvia Townsend Warner published *Lolly Willowes*, an elegant and enchanting novel with a feminist strand and a dark heart. It was one of Virago's early Modern Classics. Lolly Willowes, sent 'as if she were a piece of family property forgotten in the will', to live with her brother and his family after the death of her father, is 'so useful and obliging' until she finds her senses dulled and her mind 'groping after something that eluded her experience.' She says 'women have such vivid imaginations and lead such dull lives. Their pleasure in life is so soon over; they are so dependent upon others and their dependence so soon becomes a nuisance.' Lolly Willowes sells her soul to the devil and becomes a witch – a solution not open to most. But the sentiments are familiar to women of my generation.

My first proper encounter with the women's movement came

in early 1971. A woman whose child went to the same baby minder as Kate told me she was going to a women's meeting in Dalston. I was interested. I went with her. The house, close to Ridley Road market where I regularly drove after the movies to pick up a smoked salmon and cream cheese bagel at midnight, belonged to Sheila Rowbotham, already beginning to make her name as a feminist historian. We crowded into her semi-basement living room, women of all ages and all kinds of experiences of life. The discussion that evening was about work and children. I'd never heard anything quite like it – thoughtful, informed debate with a sense of urgency, certainty and possibility of change in the air. And they were listening to each other.

I went again the following week, again a crowded room, too many people. We needed to divide into smaller groups. I found myself part of a group of twelve who agreed to meet in a tall, four-storey house belonging to one of our members near the Arsenal football stadium. And so the Arsenal group was formed and we met every week for the next five years and irregularly for another two, trudging up the stairs, settling into the room with overflowing bookshelves, posters on the walls, sitting in comfortable slightly battered sofas and chairs, or cushions on the floor, starting the evening with news and gossip about our lives and moving on to the chosen theme. And quite quickly feminism and the women's movement became a regular part of my life.

When Juliet Mitchell wrote *Woman's Estate* in 1971, she observed that when the suffragettes burnt down houses, assaulted members of Parliament, planted bombs and cut telegraph wires in the first decade of the 20th century, they were imprisoned, forcibly fed, beaten up, but their most militant organisation, the WSPU, was left untouched. Nobody thought it necessary to smash the organization. Mitchell says: 'It is sometimes necessary to shut women up, but their political organizations are never to be taken too seriously'.

Something not dissimilar happened in the early seventies. In its organizations and its ideas, the women's liberation movement was revolutionary. It could also make revolutionary statements in public without anyone quite noticing.

Iconoclastic, with its impulses reaching well beyond its membership, under its name women's liberation created crèches, publishing houses, magazines, rape crisis centres, law centres. Women's liberation, some of whose members carried legacies of war, empire and migration, set up peace camps and anti-racist organisations and developed its four – and then six – founding demands. It made its political presence felt on the whole through conversation and actions by small groups. It was a grass roots movement rooted in daily lives and the particularities of women's lives.

The media was colourful in its reporting of women's liberation. Bra burning was at the forefront of the images (though it never happened); women were referred to as girls – 'thank you, boy', Germaine Greer, once retorted on television after the presenter had thanked the 'girls', three women in their twenties and thirties. Impertinently personal questions were asked 'Has anyone ever asked you to marry him?' Ludovic Kennedy once asked Carmen Callil in a television interview: 'Not on bended knee' came the answer, quick as a flash. Male interviewers were smiling or sneering, patronizing or bemused, nervous or benignly tolerant. But there was a sense too that most of them saw women as essentially unserious and therefore unthreatening. Yet, as its slogan 'the personal is political' hinted early on, it was a movement that was to make a huge impact.

Historically, movements for women's rights have had a tendency to wax and wane. Women have at regular intervals rediscovered themselves – their strengths and capabilities, their political will. They haven't always found it easy to communicate these efforts. Each generation seems to need to reinvent its rebellion. We were no exception. This women's liberation movement came out of a time of student protest, Black Power and draft resistance in the US, sectarian socialist groups, earlier women's groups, Third World resistance.

The 1970s women's movement made me understand how much it was a man's world I was growing up in; women were by definition outsiders. I had my own reasons for sensing I didn't belong, but I was not alone. I was eventually drawn to feminism partly because of my own inner conflicts – barely understood ambitions and desires for independence on the one hand and the desire for love and commitment, the pull of loyalty to family traditions on the other – and partly because of observed social injustices, sexism in the workplace, restrictions on what women could do, violence perpetrated against women, restraints on women's right to control their bodies – the list was long.

And there were many feminisms – something that the wider world didn't always understand – with some fierce disagreements between them as well as overlaps. Probably the main division in the early seventies was between those who believed that sexual difference was the primary problem, that male power was deeper and more damaging to women than capitalist exploitation and class differences; and socialist feminists, who believed that women had to analyse their particular subordination in a society where capitalism and class were the root cause of exploitation of both women and men.

Writing about this now, I'm struck by how difficult it is to describe and explain the times we lived through. The more you experience the more you realize how circumstantial values and ethics are. We were living in our particular moment.

For many of us, the 1970s women's movement was something of a utopian moment, with, as Barbara Taylor puts it 'its courage and confusions, its open-hearted visions and myopias.' We were trying to change the rules, wanted equal opportunities and chances, wanted to live freely and also unselfishly, combining and balancing collective struggles and personal desires. Our lives were busy, filled with meetings, arguments about ideas, about how to live in an egalitarian way; they were filled with romances, intense friendships, children. We thought the future was full of promise and hope and belonged to us; but we also regularly bumped up against the present, the real world – inequalities of class and race and money, domesticity, jealousy, rivalries, our conflicting desires about independence and love, confusions about men, about work and children.

We believed passionately in what we were fighting for, we had our regrettable share of moralism. We were not always right, of course, though we often were – about some of our basic demands such as equal pay, available nursery places, a woman's right to choose what happens to her body and much more. There were women who felt that they were excluded from the movement – often because they felt it didn't address their particular concerns. But the truth was there weren't many of us who called ourselves feminist at that time – far more women rejected the description. And perhaps not without reason. It could be an uncomfortable label, mocked and stereotyped, a signal for scorn and aggression in some milieus, not to be taken seriously. For me, my sense of being an outsider was in some ways exacerbated by declaring myself a feminist. But the opposite was also true – I felt at home in a group of people who looked at the world in a way I could make sense of. I felt elated by it, felt I belonged. For a while, feminism seemed to me the only game in town, just as socialism had illuminated the world for me in the 1960s, seemed at the time a sort of mini enlightenment about so many things – class, race, religion. Now I defined myself as a socialist feminist.

The politics of the time raised the question of collective identity. Women were finding themselves torn: between domesticity and independence; between familial ties and freedom; between a longing for connection and a yearning for solitude. Changed consciousness was considered a necessary part of political change. Women had been too much silenced; what followed was the need to 'find a voice'. If women spoke out, it was thought, they would find themselves and then find themselves together. Many of the early journals and books of this women's movement included personal testimony, autobiography, diaries. The idea was that by speaking out about their lives, their desires, their pains, women would throw off their sense of oppression. The shared experience of collective oppression was important and necessary. It was not by any means the same thing as establishing an individual identity – a much more complicated process. And some women were much more oppressed than others. Yet what these personal testimonies did reflect was how diverse and different experiences could make some sort of collective sense. Women were isolated from each other – another focus of the second wave movement. What followed from that was that many problems were seen as 'personal' to them, or the result of conflicts between individual men and women, rather than inbuilt forms of oppression reflecting common conditions faced by all women.

Out of this came the idea of consciousness raising groups, which, like many ideas of the women's movement, came from America. Consciousness raising was a way of trying to reach a better understanding of women's oppression by bringing them together to talk about their lives without the presence of men. The idea was that out of this would come political consciousness. Most consciousness raising groups followed a roughly similar pattern – a weekly meeting with a small group of women, usually in the house of one of the members, with no formal leader for the discussion and with a spoken or unspoken assumption that every woman would have a chance to speak. Behind all this lay the notion that our feelings tell us something from which we can learn, that they are expressing something that can be political and that they can lead to actions to change things.

Consciousness raising of some kind has been part of every utopian and idealist political movement and has always produced arguments about which comes first – changing the outside world or the inner life. There was a good deal of misunderstanding and disparagement of consciousness raising, both at the time of this women's movement and later. Perhaps it was sometimes more a form of therapy than a raising of political consciousness. Perhaps the emphasis on personal experience meant that political and philosophical ideas were bypassed. But in its various versions it offered solidarity and was an important method by which women understood women's condition. It embraced the notion that every voice counts, which meant fierce arguments about the expression of difference.

We didn't think of the Arsenal group primarily as a consciousness raising group, although we did talk about our lives and in particular about our family backgrounds – Orthodox Jewish, working class East London, Communist, north of England middle class, Austrian and German Jewish, upper class English. For most of its life the group of ten or twelve women met in the same house every week. There was some coming and going– people left because they didn't like it (too cerebral, not enough working at grassroots), because they moved, because they wanted to be involved in different activities; and new people came. We were almost all university educated, almost all self-declared socialists, mostly though not all middle class, in our twenties and thirties. We were on the whole privileged women, though one working class woman brought her mother to meetings, whose life had been far from privileged. We were white. We were heterosexual. In

*Mark Karlin, me, Caroline Bond, Hermione Harris
on Women's Liberation march, 1975*

1971, when the group was formed, four of us already had children.

What did we do? We spent time analysing what we were thinking and reading and had some provocative conversations about Simone de Beauvoir's *The Second Sex* and her novels, Engels, Bebel, Valerie Solanas, Juliet Mitchell, Doris Lessing and *The Golden Notebook*, Oliver Sacks and *Awakenings*.

We were active in campaigns, over abortion, family allowances, women in trade unions, training for girls, against wages for housework. Some of the group were involved in supporting the night cleaners battle for rights at work, one woman worked in campaigns around race. We talked about love, about make-up, families, music, jealousy. One astonishing evening we discussed rape and by the end discovered that, out of the eleven of us, seven had experienced either rape or attempted rape.

Several of the group were writers. We collaborated to put out Shrew, the magazine published by the Women's Liberation Workshop and put together by existing local groups. We talked to other women's groups, occasionally men's groups, and to groups in schools. We invited people to speak to us on particular subjects – anthropologists, economists, trade unionists, men as well as women. We wanted to understand more about what lay behind the decisions we made about our lives, our children's lives and if necessary to challenge things.

We probably didn't talk enough to feminists with whom we disagreed – on wages for housework, for instance, or on sex workers, on attitudes to childcare. There was periodically unease about what kind of group we were trying to be. Though we identified with some of the ideas coming out of the movement, we were also aware that we had a good deal more freedom in our lives than many, indeed most other women, by virtue of class, race, education. Some in the group were irritated by the lack of personal talk and on one occasion a woman who'd just had a baby was appalled that the group barely addressed this at all.

On the whole we avoided talking in depth about our personal feelings, occasionally bizarrely so. As a group we were quite anxious about the personal – about being intrusive, about being exposed. Our reticence about our private lives came partly because of who we were and partly because quite a few women in the group knew each other's men. That on the whole ruled out personal talk about sex and relationships, though there were plenty of general discussions about both. For most of us, the intimacy of female friendship was in our lives before the women's movement and it wasn't primarily this that we were looking for. As it turned out we had much more intimate conversations when we met in twos and threes. I remember a conversation with one of the group about sado-masochist sexual feelings and the contradictions and confusions this engendered – and how relieved I felt at having had it.

So the group acted both as a group and as a series of more intimate friendships, many of which survive to this day. There was disapproval between members of the group from time to time – certain behaviour or ideas were seen as 'unsupportive' of other women, 'reactionary', 'elitist', all those words we used in those days. On the whole, though, we got through the tensions by talking about them.

For me, our discussions about work and motherhood were hugely important. It was a subject which filled most of us with passion, guilt, confusion. In a TUC study done in 1963, of women in full time and part time work, it became clear that a large majority, whether middle or working class, with children and without, wanted to work. Yet the issue of who looked after our children loomed over this and still does.

I had my own history about the need to work. I had seen my mother's life, without work, full of brooding and preoccupation and was frightened by it and determined to avoid the same fate. And with that came an often-ambivalent struggle to keep an attachment to the mother who needed me, who exasperated me, who in some ways looked to me for some of her unmet desires, who I also understood. Keeping boundaries between us was a struggle.

I'm not sure I could have done it without the existence of the women's movement at that time, which helped me to see that a daughter doesn't have to reproduce a mother's life.

Later I became aware of all this in my own life as a mother; what I wanted (easy to say) was to be a strong mother for Kate, to give her the intimacy and safety she needed and yet not be needy, cloying, give her space to go her own way, follow her own desires, for her not to need to watch my life as I had my mother's. Work was part of what I needed and I worked in a very absorbing job. We knew we couldn't 'have it all', even then. I had to find the compromises that were possible and live with the seesaw of guilt about Kate – never feeling good about not being there at teatime, ringing her instead, keeping her awake in the evenings so that I could spend time with her, always worrying that it wasn't enough.

With Kate, aged 8, in London 1978. © *Nina Kellgren*

And perhaps it wasn't. She has spent a lot of her life as a mother being at home with her children. We've always been close.

❧

The scene is a miner's holiday camp in Skegness, a seaside town on the east coast. It's October 1971 and the second national women's liberation conference is just beginning. I have left Kate, who is now eighteen months old, in Oxford with Roger and arrived with friends from the Arsenal group in a building with bright lights and several large halls, where I register and am assigned a small bedroom with thin walls upstairs. I jerk awake in the night to the sound of a baby crying and though I felt completely safe leaving her with Roger, I also feel awful at being away from her.

One of the halls is filled with tables covered in pamphlets, books and badges, representing countless women's groups and political organisations – a scene which is to become deeply familiar to me over the course of the seventies. The place is filled with hundreds of women, greeting each other, hugging, talking loudly. There is an air of anticipation. Most of us are wearing slightly fading clothes, long skirts, jeans or velvet trousers, shawls and scarves – 'the picturesquely dowdy manner of the movement', as Elizabeth Wilson once described it. I feel excited.

There were in fact three conferences that weekend at the holiday camp – the women's liberation movement, the Trotskyist International Socialists and a section of the National Union of Miners. The first night we heard rumours of a racy cabaret with stripping put on for the NUM. In the halls there were friendly exchanges with the miners, some of whom expressed disapproval of what we were doing, others showing rather baffled interest.

The women's liberation movement at this point was a loosely knit national organization of local women's groups. At the time of the Skegness conference it had been captured by a group of Maoists, some of them men. They had strong views about what our politics should be and they saw themselves as in charge. They had organized the conference as a series of plenaries and workshops and lectured the audience whenever they could, usually on the principles of Marxism-Leninism. Most of us were exasperated and irritated and bored at their interventions.

Apart from the domination of their dogmatic views, they were a problem in other ways. The women's movement was for women only. There was a growing sense of rebellion in the air and some anger. On the second day a gay women's liberation group went up on stage, took over the microphone from the Maoists and made impassioned speeches about what the women's movement really meant to women, suggesting we talk about the things we cared about – sexuality, childcare, lesbianism, the family, work – and do it in the small groups that represented such an important part of how the movement operated. It was a triumph from the platform, eloquent and coherent and the first time that gay women had addressed heterosexual women publicly with their version of what liberation might be. At the final plenary session, the Maoists denounced the lesbians as 'bourgeois decadents'. By this time we'd had enough. There was shouting and weeping and some very loud arguments. Eventually, after some physical tussles, the small group of Maoists – astonishing that such a small group could cause such disruption – were driven from the platform and led from the hall by the caretaker, the leader shouting all the while that we understood nothing about socialism or historical truth. We were exhausted, but triumphant.

23

PUBLISHING AND POLITICS

IN THE SPRING of 1971, I was embedded in motherhood, living in a flat in Highgate with Kate, taking her regularly to a small nursery group, to tea with friends (once catastrophically to a friend whose child had measles and Kate caught it. I can still see her lying in her cot, stoical and unusually quiet, covered in spots). I still marvelled at the pleasure I took in looking at her, watching her, touching her, at her changing self, at her robust attitude to the world. And without question, being a mother made me feel in some way or another that I 'belonged'.

I took her to see Roger in Oxford every weekend, he bringing her back on Monday – something we did for eleven years. I was still filled with guilt about her not being with him full time. He was an attentive father, reliable, with a capacity to play which I admired. I had wanted him to be the father of my child and I was right – he was a good father. He kept a diary of Kate's doings and sayings. As for views on her upbringing, I rarely felt this was a problem, that mostly we shared the same attitudes, sometimes without much need for discussion and where we didn't, we resolved things amicably.

I took some time to recover from the bruising encounter with the literary agent and my own chaotic emotions at that time. But now I began to have an affair with Stuart Holland, an economist working at Sussex University. He was keen to marry me, buy a house, live a conventional domestic life. I was not in the least ready for that, still attached to Roger and also to the new freedoms of living without a husband. I never felt the slightest fear at the prospect of living alone with Kate financially and emotionally Roger was very much part of her life. I missed seeing Roger's mother but Roger took Kate to see her regularly, as he did to my mother in Oxford. My mother came to visit in London and I went to Oxford to see her. We had Christmases together – often difficult for me, but much helped by Kate's presence, which was always upbeat. My mother once took her plate out of her mouth and left it on the table at Christmas lunch. Kate and I giggled. She and Kate had deep affection for each other.

My father we visited in Putney, rather more formal visits, visits which for me always had a shadow of the life I should in his eyes have lived – a more conventional wife, mother, more certainties, more what he would see as order.

In April, I wrote twenty letters to publishers asking for editorial work. I got three replies, including one from Chatto & Windus, where I went for an interview with Nora Smallwood, the grand dame of publishing and Ian Parsons in their labyrinthine building in King William IV Street. They were pleasant enough but not particularly accommodating about my having a child. Roger meanwhile had been to see Frank Cass, an academic publisher and while there asked about work on my behalf. They offered me a part-time editorial job, just what I wanted and so it was that I began work that summer with the genial, if sometimes ruthless, Frank Cass, a man who had never been to university and who loved books. I drove Kate in my battered white Renault to our wonderful baby minder, Madeleine Carter, in the mornings, parked my car in Bloomsbury and settled down to editorial work in one of the tall terraced houses by the British Museum. They were not smart offices; they were full of piles of paper and enthusiasm. I had a lot to learn; my colleagues were friendly and began to teach me some of the basics of publishing. Many of the new books on the Cass list were academic, often converted theses, often but not always interesting. I was given a good deal of freedom to work on them as I wished. The habit of the company seemed to be to do very little editorial work on these theses and I tended to follow this - not always a good thing, but at that stage, though I was a good reader, I was an inexperienced editor.

By the time I joined the firm, they were also publishing a Jewish list (Frank and I agreed to disagree about Israel), a reprints list, a literary and history list and a long list of journals, some academic, some literary and more military journals than anyone else in the business. His journals were earning Cass an international reputation. Their editor was a tall gangly Englishman called Jim Muir, now a formidable BBC Middle East Correspondent.

I began to edit a series of travel reprints and invited the well-known travel writer James Morris to come and talk to me. I got a reply saying he couldn't come but someone called Jan Morris could. I thought no more about the coincidence of the name. On the allotted day a shy woman with the shadow of a shaved beard on her face came up the stairs, wearing a brown tweed jacket and skirt. Jan Morris. We had a fascinating conversation about travel writing. It was only some weeks later that the news of James Morris's sex change was made public.

Authors were welcome in the offices. Tambimuttu, the editor of *Poetry London* was a frequent visitor. *The Goon Show* team dropped in regularly when we later started a showbiz list and put together their scripts.

I learnt a great deal about reprints and later took the idea of re-covering out of print classics to Virago. Cass started them when he was running a small bookshop and someone asked for an obscure volume about sixteenth and seventeenth century British industry. He thought – if one man wants it, perhaps others do too. In 1960, he reprinted a book of African history which sold well. Then President Kennedy decided that black studies had to be taught in every American university. By then Cass had about 300 titles on the subject and he found a market. He reissued important books on the Middle East, on social history, on travel, on the history of science; *Science at the Crossroads*, a particular gem, was one of my first books – an exchange published in the 1930s between Soviet Marxist and western liberal scientists. I spent many happy hours reading for possible reprints across the road in the reading room of the British Museum.

I had discovered work I loved. I had pleasant colleagues, I was able to work part time so that I could spend time with Kate – something that became infinitely harder later. And I was in the thick of the new political life of the early 1970s. I felt at home in this new world.

For a while I lived communally in Camden Town, in a house in Gloucester Crescent owned by Dinah, my friend from Brixton days. She lived there with her husband and her twins, various friends and intermittently her father, who had spent some years in mental hospitals. She was in a number of women's groups and from time to time went off for the weekend with encounter groups, from where she reported wild confrontations and once an occasion where they all peed together as a sign of solidarity. She was much bolder than me about drugs.

Dinah was a talented writer and her first novel was published by Barrie and Jenkins. Her husband Frank, an American actor who came over with the Second City theatre group, was also trying to write. I was horrified to discover from various publishing friends that he had sent to them his written account of our commune with our real names left in and had reported on matters of great privacy. It almost broke our friendship.

It was something of a haven, this household; Dinah and Frank were old friends and I found it strangely comforting to watch Dinah with her father, who was very hard to reach in his particular mental state. A shambling old man, he sat at the large kitchen table and she talked to him patiently, about what he'd like to do that day, what to eat. He would occasionally burst into rambling, partially coherent reminiscences of his life in Africa as an executive in a multinational company. Dinah was more loving and less irritable with him than I was with my mother and I wanted to emulate her. She and I talked a lot about the effects of having a mad parent, the protectiveness we felt, the irritations, the longings to be mothered or fathered. Fiction was one way she dealt with her feelings about it. He appeared in her novels as the father she was trying to find, to reach, to hunt down as the person she wanted him to be. She eventually went to live in the ashram in Poonah with the Baghwan, changing her name to Pankerjee. We stayed in touch for many years.

Stuart, the economist visited from time to time. I was still dealing with my complicated feelings for Roger. I was appreciating space of my own, began to recognize that it was quite difficult for me to attend to more than one person I loved at a time. Having a child exacerbated those feelings. At this moment a communal household suited me – I liked the casual, rather chaotic way of living, people coming and going, the children playing with each other, meals cooked for anyone who happened to be in.

But I was also looking for a place of my own. It was 1972, the height of one of the great housing crises, when prices could double overnight and there was a huge demand for any property that had a roof on it in London. I spent evenings after work driving round north London with Kate in the back of the car, discovering, memorising the streets I liked. Eventually, with a loan of £4,000 from my father (which he turned into a gift) for the deposit, some money from the sale of our house in Oxford and an uncomfortable conversation with a patronizing bank manager who suggested that I should lead a more conventional life, I got a mortgage and moved into a three-storey terraced house in Tufnell Park. It's the house I've had ever since, with my daughter, with lovers, with lodgers who became friends and with my grandfather's grand piano that originally made its way from Nazi Germany in 1938.

In my new home the pattern of life continued – work at Frank Cass till the early afternoon, picking up Kate from Madeleine, whose vitality and love for the children she was caring for was palpable and enormously reassuring to a working mother. She seemed to get energy from being with the children, she had the endearing trait of telling me as much as she could about Kate's day with her and she adored Kate. I shared my house with three lodgers, partly as a way of surviving financially. This didn't work particularly well for me. Two of them got on with their own separate lives. The third, a warm and friendly teacher, a committed socialist, had a strong desire to live communally; he wanted to share the household tasks but also to be part of Kate's life. I didn't want that. I took Kate to see Roger in Oxford every weekend; he was a devoted father. I had a lover who came regularly and was deeply fond of Kate. And the truth was that though I knew of many friends who were living communally, I wasn't very good at it long term or very attracted to its propositions – joint decisions about everything. For a while we muddled through, because we were fond of each other, but it became obvious that I wanted to live with my daughter and my intermittent lover and so the teacher rather angrily left and the people living downstairs continued to live their separate lives and occasionally baby-sat.

✿

Politics became a larger part of my life – the regular meetings of our women's group, the marches in central London – over nursery places, abortion rights, equal pay. There were other demonstrations too. In the summer of 1972, five dockers were held in Pentonville Prison, a show of strength by the Heath government to demonstrate their determination to curb the power of the unions by the 'rule of law.' There were demonstrations outside the prison gates and one balmy evening, a huge full moon looking down, I took Kate in her buggy and joined the crowd, wanting her to be part of our times.

✿

I saw a good deal of Bob Sutcliffe in the Seventies. We met regularly at the British Museum, across the road from my office and one day over a cup of tea he introduced me to Hugh Brody, a film maker and anthropologist who became one of my closest friends. We soon discovered that we had in common an assimilated Jewish childhood (though his parents sent him to Hebrew classes and celebrated Jewish holidays, no conversion to Anglicanism for them, for which I rather envied him.) That bond has remained and we regularly exchange deeply comforting acknowledgements of feelings about belonging and not belonging that we had thought we had in isolation and turned out to be shared.

Bob had joined a Trotskyist group – something we often argued over – and come out as gay. He was in the thick of revolutionary politics and economics. From 1972 to 1975 many of the textbook certainties and conventional economic orthodoxies were beginning to crumble as inflation jumped from eight to 27 percent, unemployment doubled and earnest debates raged about whether parliamentary democracy would survive. In 1972, *British Capitalism, Workers and the Profit Squeeze*, written by Bob and his friend Andrew Glyn, both distinguished economists, was published as a Penguin Special. The book cost 55p and became a cult classic. It argued that the profits squeeze would not only lead to reduced working class living standards as wages were cut but would also imperil the survival of capitalism. In these exhilarating times, the arguments were persuasive and unlikely things such as the end of capitalism seemed possible, though there were plenty who were sceptical of their thesis and their basic belief that 'working class leaders must adopt a new attitude to wage demands: they must realize that wage claims are becoming the political weapons in a battle in which the existence of capitalism is at stake.'

Stuart was, meanwhile, a strong believer in the parliamentary road to socialism. He was much influenced by Tony Benn and would come home in the evenings extolling the virtues of Benn's Marxism. Feminism wasn't part of Stuart's thinking. I was often cooking a meal or painting the house when he arrived, neither of which he did much of. We argued a good deal about that and other matters. He felt I didn't give him enough attention, or space in the house – 'one drawer in your chest of drawers for my things'

– and that was true. I found it hard to cope with someone who had such a class chip on his shoulder, lived without doubt, was so sure he was right about everything. But there was also tenderness between us. And we shared a love of music – he was a very good singer – and he loved Kate.

Meanwhile, there were the conflicts and splits and confusions in the women's movement as well as the exhilaration and excitement of trying, and sometimes succeeding, in making more sense of our world and even changing it however slightly – becoming a bit more visible in the work place, in politics, in the media, in academe, though it was a slow business. And there were many smaller, more personal meetings of friends over kitchen tables, long conversations into the night about how things were and how they might be. 'Too much talk, mum, too much talk', my daughter said. It may well have helped to instil in her doubts about the efficacy of words. In the women's movement we were intoxicated by them.

At the end of 1972 I begin to think about moving to a more general publishing house. Dinah had just published her second novel with Barrie & Jenkins. She suggested I went to see her editor, Christopher MacLehose. The offices were in a handsome building on Highbury Fields and this tall dark man with the deepest voice and a charming smile appeared and we talked about many things, on most of which we disagreed, especially politics. To my amazement, he hired me. And so I started as a part-time editor in this small trade company, most famous for publishing P. G. Wodehouse.

On my first day I was led to the office I was to share with Patricia Parkin, who'd just broken her leg falling down the area at the front of the building during a publication party. She became probably the most important influence on my life as an editor. Trained in one of the prestigious and gruelling trainee copy editing jobs at Penguin's Ed2 division at Harmondsworth, her expertise was astonishing. There was nothing she didn't know, no rule of the famous Penguin house rules book she lent me that she hadn't internalized. Above all, she was one of the great nurturers of authors, especially novelists, great and small. They all knew how lucky they were to have her as their editor. George Macdonald Fraser named a character after her. Fay Weldon said she edited 'without you really noticing, very subtle in how she made you change things or see things you might be doing wrong.' She edited the first twenty-four books of Barbara Taylor Bradford. Allan Sillitoe said she was the best editor he ever had. She represented, as Patrick Gale said, 'an endangered species: a fiction editor without ambition.' She had no desire to rise in status, to be more managerial, believing that it would take her away from her beloved manuscripts, on which she worked with her blue pencil and a quiet passion.

I needed this paragon. Though I had absorbed a good deal about publishing as a whole at Frank Cass and how to support authors through the publication process, I hadn't learnt much about the art of on-the-page editing. The first book I was in charge of at Barrie & Jenkins got a review in the *New Statesman* which began: 'This is the worst edited book I have ever read.' (Amongst other things I had made a mistake with the early pages which meant every index entry was one page out.) I was of course utterly mortified. But Patricia, who wasn't just clever and competent but also kind – by then we had become friends – taught me what I had to do next time. I learnt the Penguin guide more or less by heart, understood the details of preliminary pages at the beginning of books, the accepted spellings and house style (not the *Guardian* but *The Times*). By the end of her patient lessons I had become a competent copy editor.

Led by Christopher, the four of us in the editorial department met weekly. These meetings were a joy – friendly, surprising, informative, professional. We found each other stimulating and good company; there were few tensions and we seemed to appreciate the very different perspectives of the other three. That first year at Barrie & Jenkins was one of the happiest of my working life.

The fourth member of the editorial team was John Knowler, an immensely talented and interesting man. We talked a lot – about books but also about politics and he knew I was a feminist. There were hardly any feminists in publishing at the time, but one of them was Carmen Callil, a good friend of his (I always thought he was in love with her). Australian, born in Melbourne, her father was Lebanese, her mother Irish. She was educated in Catholic boarding schools. She read English at Melbourne University and left Australia for England the day she graduated, where amongst other things she worked for the alternative magazine *Ink* and eventually set up her own PR company. In 1973 she had the brilliant idea of starting a feminist publishing house; Rosie Boycott and Marsha Rowe were on her first board, but after a short while went off to found *Spare Rib*, the feminist magazine. John told me that Carmen was looking for someone to work with her on the list and suggested we met. I'd already had a short encounter with this small, curly-haired, hugely energetic woman, with an enviably small waist, at the Xerox machine in Barrie & Jenkins where she was doing some freelance publicity work. I introduced myself, saying I had seen her occasionally at Frank Cass's, where I had worked. 'You poor thing', she said and turned on her heel and walked away.

A few weeks later she suggested we had lunch in Chelsea, and she told me how she'd been working so far, first with Rosie and Marsha and then with another woman which hadn't worked out. She was also running her own PR company, with the support of Harriet Spicer, who came to the job straight from university and worked on Virago too.

Carmen had already commissioned some interesting titles – including Angela Carter's *The Sadeian Woman* and the autobiography of Mary Stott, the Women's Page editor of the *Guardian*. I told her about my working life and my connections with the women's movement, the writers I knew. We talked about our personal lives, about Kate, who by then was four years old. I agreed to do some part-time work on the list. I felt a buzz of excitement at the prospect.

24

VIRAGO - BEGINNINGS

I N MY FILES from the early days of Virago are stories by
women who were writing in the 1960s and early '70s. One is
from Mary Gordon, the American novelist and essayist. 'Once', she
says, 'I was told a story by a famous writer. "I will tell you what
women writers are like," he said. The year was 1971. The women's
movement had made men nervous; it had made a lot of women
write. "Women writers are like a female bear who goes into a cave
to hibernate. The male bear shoves a pine cone up her ass, because
he knows if she shits all winter, she'll stink up the cave. In the
spring, the pressure of all that built-up shit makes her expel the
pine cone and she shits a winter's worth all over the walls of the
cave." That's what women writers are like, said the famous writer.
He told the story with such geniality; he looked as if he were
giving me a wonderful gift. I felt I ought to smile; everyone knows
there's no bore like a feminist with no sense of humour. I did not

write for two months after that . . . I should not have smiled. But he was a famous writer and spoke with geniality. And in truth I did not have the courage for clear rage. There is no seduction like that of being thought a good girl.'

The wish to write has marked every feminist movement, but the 1970s women's movement was to a remarkable extent a writer's movement and writing and politics (new feminist politics) became inextricably connected.

In the early Fifties many employers still operated a 'marriage bar.' The benefit rates for married women were set at a lower level than those for men. As late as the sixties and even seventies a woman had to have her husband's permission to sign a mortgage or hire purchase agreement.

Simone de Beauvoir compared women's oppression to that of Jews, Blacks in the US, colonized nations, but saw sexism as uniquely different because women live eyeball to eyeball with and often love their oppressors. She described housework as 'holding away death but also refusing life.' Her answers were sometimes simple, sometimes judgemental (high heels 'doom women to impotence') but she knew the contradictions of her position, understood that women were half victims, half accomplices. Her basic position was that women must be treated as full human beings, as men are.

In the Britain of the late 1960s women were fighting for equal pay, for affordable nurseries, for rights in the workplace. And there were the beginnings of a women's movement. A few books were published which paved the way for feminist thought and scholarship – Hannah Gavron's *The Captive Housewife*, Sheila

Rowbotham's *Hidden from History*, Juliet Mitchell's *Women: The Longest Revolution* and Betty Friedan's *The Feminine Mystique*, Margaret Drabble's and Doris Lessing's remarkable fiction. But these were still exceptions.

One of the things the feminism of the '70s did was to make a virtue of these so called 'female' territories. For me, who felt an outsider and wanted to belong, there came a gradual dawning that 51 percent of the population felt themselves outsiders, that there was something to be said for starting in the margins, that 'belonging' wasn't nearly as interesting as I'd thought (though it still seemed comforting) and that maybe the point was to try and create insiderness from the outside.

What we wanted was for Virago to be a publishing house which broke silences, brought women's lives centre stage, expressed ideas of the women's movement in a male-dominated culture. In a world of many feminisms, we believed, like one of our early authors, Dora Russell, 'in the value of women as women, not just as companions of men'; we argued not just for equality of rights but for the very essence of what women represent to count in politics and society – hoping to change the balance in a small way. We set about doing this by looking at what women were doing and writing and thinking at that time, the early days of the second wave women's movement, at writers with new ways of looking at the world, searching for originality by writers of talent, old and new, who wrote with intensity, made new connections, had startling insights, made us laugh, shocked us, remembering Brigid Brophy, 'A society that is not free to be outraged is not free to change.'

We had other explicit aims too – we would not just print books but sell them, as widely as possible, to people who shared our views and hopefully to those who didn't, to women and men, to young and old. Anyone can print a book, it's selling it to people that's difficult. We paid particular attention to our covers. We discussed not just the merits of the writing but the audience we might reach with it. We were not interested in publishing only for the converted. Virago's history was all about trying to occupy the margins and the centre simultaneously. We believed we could create an inspirational, financially-viable list. We were part of rebellious times. There was optimism and energy in the air. We wanted to change the world.

It's hard to remember how disturbing and unmarketable feminism was to many people in the early Seventies. To some the name Virago, chosen by Carmen and Rosie Boycott, was a problem at first: hardly anyone knew the original meaning – a man-like or heroic woman – or saw the irony. Anthony Burgess had particular problems with us. Here he is in 1981 reviewing the remarkable stream of consciousness novel *Pilgrimage* by Dorothy Richardson; 'by no stretch of usage can "virago" be made not to signify a shrew, a scold, an ill-tempered woman . . . It is an unlovely and aggressive name, even for a militant feminist organization and it presides awkwardly over the reissue of a great *roman fleuve* which is too important to be associated with chauvinist sows.' We read the review out to each other in the office, enraged, falling about laughing, not entirely surprised. Then in 1978 Fay Weldon wrote in the *TLS* that 'the solid substance of their list and the very feel of their books has all but changed the connotation of the word. Say Virago to me now and I visualize an industrious and intelligent lady in her middle years.'

In 1974, still working at Barrie & Jenkins, I began reading manuscripts and proposals for the Virago list and editing some of the books that had been commissioned. It meant jolly evenings in Carmen's flat in Smith Street in Chelsea with plenty of wine and giggles. There was already a lot to read. Women had heard about Virago and came up the stairs with ideas, manuscripts, opinions, often strong ones, and offers of help. The historian Barbara Taylor remembers meeting us there: 'there was a little room which represented the entire offices of Virago. I remember being investigated by some very white, intimidating cats. The enterprise seemed grandiose, fantastic, almost as fantastic as my own hopes of writing a book for them to publish.' One day a tall, rangy American with long frizzy hair and a face of strange beauty staggered up the stairs balancing an enormous manuscript. Merlin Stone had written about the goddess religion; she had done years of detailed research, travelled all over the Middle East and was utterly committed and somewhat mystical about her work, passionate in her hatred of the Judeo-Christian tradition and what it had done to the goddesses. Carmen and I read it and were fascinated. It needed a lot of work and we eventually published it in Britain as *The Paradise Papers*; in the US they called it *When God Was A Woman*. Years later Merlin returned to see us. She had meanwhile met and married an English working-class man, much younger than her and taken him off to live on a small wild island off the West coast of Canada. He had gone off hunting in their first winter: there was a heavy snowstorm and he didn't come back. He was found eventually, dead. Merlin was convinced that she was responsible; the goddesses in her book usually had their young consorts killed and she felt that she had done this to her young husband. She was inconsolable.

Meanwhile, as I was becoming absorbed in the Virago list in my spare time, bad things were going on at Barrie & Jenkins. A consortium took it over and moved in, one that seemed exceptionally interventionist, often ignorant about how publishing worked, not very interested in books and very interested in money. They fired Christopher MacLehose, John Knowler resigned and only Patricia and I remained. I was part time and they didn't have any interest in me or my books. So I too decided to resign. In early 1975, I began to do freelance editorial work and to scout for two Scandinavian publishers. I didn't make much money, but it didn't seem to matter. I was surviving financially, helped by renting out rooms in my house. The three of us, Carmen, Harriet and I, offered our mortgages as guarantees for the company. One day, encouraged by Stuart, who was concerned about something I didn't much think about – that I had no financial participation in Virago – I put a £50 note in an envelope, sat opposite Carmen at my kitchen table and said I'd like to have half of the Virago shares. She didn't look pleased, but she agreed.

When she began commissioning the very early books, Carmen had turned to Quartet Books, one of the clients of her PR firm, for handling production, distribution and sales for Virago. They were a genial quartet of men, friends of Carmen's, sympathetic to radical ideas, supportive of the enterprise and when I joined Virago in 1974, I began to go with Carmen to the weekly editorial meetings in their offices in Goodge Street where we presented the books we wanted to publish. Our fold-over first catalogue, emerald green – we sweated over the copy, as we always did – said 'The first mass market publishers for 52 percent of the population – women. An exciting new imprint for both sexes in a changing world.'

I turned out to love publishing and I never stopped thinking how lucky I was to be working on books I loved, where passion and political beliefs were expressed and which encouraged new and often contentious perspectives.

In the early days Carmen and I visited some of our authors together. We'd been introduced to Rebecca West by Jill Craigie, the film maker, who was working on the suffragettes. Somewhat apprehensively because we knew of her reputation for forceful opinions and disdain, we went to see her in her West London flat; most of her writing at that point was out of print. She was the most direct person I've ever met, her fierce brown eyes undimmed by age. Her mind was quick and sharp; she would dismiss people in half a sentence – 'Virginia Woolf said I had hairy arms; there was no such thing in my family . . .' She was brisk, welcoming to us and friendly, moving slowly, crippled by arthritis. It was the beginning of a long relationship where we put her novels into the Classics, her journalism into the non-fiction Classics and I became her editor for her non-fiction and unpublished work, including The Young Rebecca, formidable unpublished essays from her early twenties, when she was a fierce feminist and socialist. I grew to love her. She reported back to Jill Craigie that she had liked meeting me and Carmen; 'nice gels, lesbian of course'.

Charlotte Wolff, another fierce woman, lovable but dogmatic, was the author of one of our first novels, *An Older Love*. She was a physician and psychotherapist, a refugee from Nazi Germany. She had written about lesbian love and in her seventies decided to write a novel around the subject. Charlotte was a friend of Sybil Bedford and we asked her for a quote on *An Older Love* to put on the cover. She sent us her quote in a letter, but added firmly that she was doing this for someone who was a friend and not for Virago: she did not approve, she said, of the quote on the inside covers of all our early books from Sheila Rowbotham, which said that Virago is a feminist publishing company and 'It is only when women start to organize in large numbers that we become a political force and begin to move towards the possibility of a truly democratic society in which every human being can be brave, responsible, thinking and diligent.' Sybil Bedford did not, in other words, approve of the Virago enterprise. Two years after the publication of Charlotte Wolff's book, she sent us two of her novels asking if we would include them in the Virago Modern Classics (we did). She had been won over.

Our first list announced Angela Carter's *The Sadeian Woman*, her study of de Sade, his equation of sexuality with power and his vision of a woman who exists in perfect freedom; *Fathers and Daughters* by Cathy Porter, demonstrating the vital role of women in revolutionary changes in nineteenth century Russia; *Is This Your Life?* looked at how women are seen in the media. *The British Women's Directory*, collecting grass roots and mainstream information about all aspects of women's lives, was conceived, argued over and edited for weeks round my kitchen table, discussion of the contents alternating with discussion of our lives and loves. *My Secret Garden* by Nancy Friday, introduced by the great journalist Jill Tweedie, was a bestseller from America about women's sexual fantasies, something women were not supposed to have. Our printer's reader (they had them in those days) scrawled in heavy green ink in the margin of the proofs on page 18 'I can't bear to read any more of this!'

At the press conference in 1975 to launch this first Virago list, eleven books in all, a journalist at the back of the room asked how we were going to find enough books for a second list. Nothing could have demonstrated more clearly the gap between those who felt the growing excitement of change in the air and those who were baffled by it or were simply unaware it was going on. The fact is that things were changing. Women were changing. And women were writing. The least of our problems at Virago was finding books.

The office had meanwhile moved from Smith Street to Carmen's new flat in Chelsea. She gave up her long black dining table in the daytime to Virago. At the end of each day we polished the table to recover its sheen. Harriet Spicer, Carmen's assistant at her publicity company, began to take up Virago work, mainly in production. Each day I took Kate to her primary school in North London, rushing off as soon as I'd settled her, trying to deflect the disapproving looks that working mothers still got in those days, and crossed London in my battered white Renault - so battered that one winter's day the bonnet fell off at a traffic light - arriving in faraway Cheyne Place to find Harriet and Carmen wrapping books to send to the press with such speed and dexterity that I was overwhelmed with admiration and feelings of inadequacy. I was a typical working mother, always a little out of breath, a little late, just about keeping on top of things, mind grappling with the split between the life I'd left – getting Kate ready for school, breakfast, worries about whether she was all right – and the life I was going to, piles of manuscripts, attention to detail, phone calls, giant electric typewriters. In those early Virago days I felt like a creature from another universe. The feeling soon passed.

It was in this flat that we launched the first Virago book with a party, in the autumn of 1975. It was Mary Chamberlain's oral history of a Cambridgeshire village, *Fenwomen*. We were nervous but it was a glamorous, well-attended event. The book got a lot of good press coverage and a hostile article in *The News of the World* centre-fold, 'Why Mary sold a village's love secrets' accusing Mary of exposing stories about the women's sex lives. It was taken up by the *Cambridge Evening News*. Mary bravely decided to deal with it by holding a public meeting in Cambridge, refuting the accusations. And Virago had taken its first step into the public world.

It soon became clear to us that an imprint was not enough. We wanted more freedom, Mary Wollstonecraft's voice in our ears 'Independence I will ever secure by contracting my wants, though I were to live on a barren heath.' We were on a barren heath – we had no money. Carmen read up on cash flow and business plans and in late 1976, over cucumber sandwiches and tea at the Ritz, I first met Bob Gavron, with his mop of white curly hair and big smile and his fierce business mind – very emphatic on cash flow and bottom lines. We showed him the business plan. He ran the St Ives Group of printing companies: together with Paul Hamlyn, the publisher, his and Carmen's friend, he guaranteed a bank overdraft of £25,000. My uncle Ernst Grunfeld, who owned the family firm, believed in me (though I'm not sure he believed in the feminist enterprise) enough to loan us £10,000. Alison Weir, a friend from Egyptian days, gave us £5,000. Carmen, who had already put money into the company, put in £1,500 and somehow we got enough together to make an independent company viable. Harriet bought some of my shares. At the beginning of 1976, the three of us launched the independent Virago Press publishing list, Carmen as managing director, me as editorial director, Harriet as production director.

Our new independence had an immediate effect – ideas came bursting out from likely and unlikely sources and fed on each other. We approached authors and they led us to more authors. Through our connections, we set up an advisory group of thirty or forty: historians, journalists, teachers, novelists, academics, including Angela Carter, Germaine Greer, the historian Sally Alexander and the literary historian Elaine Showalter. They were wonderfully creative, suggesting books, writing introductions, helping to promote titles in the press, in schools and universities, to spread the word about what we were doing.

I'd meanwhile become friends with historians and teachers who were part of the History Workshop movement of the 1970s, led by Raphael Samuel, wild hair and smiling face, head filled with ideas, who gathered people together in his house in Spitalfields. Through these friendships came one of our early projects – books on the history of the nineteenth and twentieth centuries from women's perspectives, history from below, social history, the history of everyday life, with roots deep in the marginal groups of British society, countering the intellectual and political conservatism of the dominant historical profession of that time. I had reason to bless my experience of publishing reprints at Frank Cass.

These vivid histories, classics of their kind, out of print for decades, had an immediate impact on the teaching of history and the humanities in universities and further education colleges. *Life as We Have Known It* with its memorable voices of working-class women and a surprising and moving introduction by Virginia Woolf, was our first independent publication and sold 10,000 copies very quickly. Maternity, a poignant and heartbreaking collection by the same group of women, the Women's Co-operative Guild, did likewise. *Round About a Pound a Week* touched an instant nerve in the difficult economic circumstances of the late 1970s and was reviewed in the *Mail on Sunday*, unusual territory for Virago books. *Testament of Youth* by Vera Brittain, her moving and painful autobiography of the First World War, suggested by Rosalind Delmar the feminist historian, sold hundreds of thousands of copies, particularly after the six-part television dramatization instigated through Carmen's TV connections. We reissued first-hand accounts of the suffragette movement by Emmeline and Sylvia Pankhurst, encouraged by Jill Craigie, who toiled up the stairs to our offices many times and regaled us with ideas and possibilities and left us photos from her wonderful collection of suffragette memorabilia.

Though early on WHSmith's wouldn't stock our books (our friends and supporters led a campaign asking for Virago books in their shops which was ultimately successful), it was obvious from the sales figures that we were choosing books that resonated with readers. It was partly individual titles, partly the list as a whole. In the early days of Virago booksellers often told us that people came in to ask for the latest Virago book. Of course not everything sold well and there were always books we published which we knew wouldn't sell in large quantities. I loved the moment in the week when the sales figures arrived almost more than any other. We knew that to achieve what we wanted to, we had above all to survive. Carmen was something of a genius at building publicity and over the years her skills rubbed off on everyone who worked at Virago. In the first year we never used the word 'feminist' on the cover of our books – we believed that enough bookshops at the time were conservative and would be put off by the word.

So there we were, the three of us; no secretaries, we did our own typing on oversized rented electric typewriters. We employed an outside sales team and a (male) accountant, otherwise we covered everything ourselves. We saved on everything, re-using envelopes, only second-class stamps, never taking taxis. Carmen and I were war babies and Harriet, fifteen years younger, was at home with this austerity culture. It never occurred to us to think the enterprise wouldn't work. We never stinted on sending out free copies of the books for publicity, believing that word of mouth was a crucial part of getting news of Virago books out to the world. We grew from publishing eleven books in our first year with a staff of three to nearly forty in our third (by 1993 we were publishing nearly one hundred with a staff of nineteen). We were profitable. We didn't pay ourselves much. We gave our authors small advances and made sure the royalties went out on time.

And what pleasure our authors gave me! I've never got over the feeling of how lucky I was to be working with these people, with their talent and originality, their courage and humour. I still miss the long phone calls with Angela Carter, about everything under the sun, politics, friends, the state of feminism, writing, the misunderstandings about political correctness – with her piercing intelligence and humour. Long hours spent at home working with so many authors, Cathy Porter, Mary Chamberlain, Denise Riley just a few of them, lunches with Dora Russell, with Carolyn Steedman, with Maya Angelou, parties to launch our books. And everything imbued with the strong sense that we were working together, doing something that, with each book singly and with the list cumulatively, was shifting things, shifting women more centre stage.

Towards the end of 1977 we decided we needed an office and Carmen needed her flat back. We found a large room at the top of a tall building at 5 Wardour Street – 'a one room walk-up at a dubious address in Soho', as Margaret Atwood, the hugely talented novelist, poet and renaissance woman, one of our most loyal and bestselling authors later described it – a long haul up those dark, scruffy linoleum-lined stairs, past the hairdresser and the men's drinking club, to that large fourth floor room, two long tables for desks, the electric typewriters, filing cabinets, a small kitchen and lavatory across the passage and a roof top fire escape staircase where we sometimes teetered to eat our sandwiches on hot days. We shared the cleaning of the office between us, so every third

Margaret Atwood. Photo by George Whiteside, 2006

weekend it was my turn. Sometimes I had Kate with me and she would draw pictures and make Xerox copies of her hands, while I anxiously polished the desks and the phones and swept the carpet, aware that Carmen and Harriet's standards were high, higher than I had for my own house, and that cleaning was not my best thing.

That year Alexandra Pringle joined us. She was a friend of my neighbour Peter Townsend, who ran the magazine, *Art Monthly*, where Alexandra was working. I met her over the garden fence and eventually lured her to Virago. It was not an easy switch for her – she was interested in the art world and was having a lovely, relaxed time, as she later recalled, spending hours in pubs with her painter friends. Virago was a shock to the system, where relaxation was not the order of the day and she sometimes felt like a slave. She turned out to be a wonderful editor and became a close friend. Lennie Goodings, from Canada, joined us about six months later, as a publicity assistant to Carmen. It was the five of us who became the core of the next phase of Virago, a phase that lasted more than a decade.

With Virago in Soho, I started my working day with coffee at Patisserie Valerie, often with Bill Webb, who by then was dividing his life between his wife and me. I walked down the scrubbed early morning Soho streets to the seedy entrance of the tall grey building and up the brown lino stairs to the fourth floor and our one-room office. This is now 1977. By lunchtime Wardour Street was seething with people, the basement sex shows open, the flocks of starlings beginning to gather in Leicester Square.

Many people braved those stairs – writers, designers, agents,

Directors of Virago Press: from left, Harriet Spicer, Ursula Owen, Lennie Goodings, Alexandra Pringle, Carmen Callil at 15th birthday celebration, July 5th 1988. © Susan Greenhill

journalists, foreign publishers, friends – for meetings, sandwich lunches, for parties with check table cloths covering the desks and a wind-up gramophone playing Cole Porter. We walked up and down many times a day, taking an author to lunch at a local Chinese, taking the postbag at 5.30 p.m, meeting an agent or a journalist for a drink.

Virago gave me a lot of confidence and taught me many lessons. One was that there was no point in trying to be liked by everyone. As a young woman, wanting to belong, I would go to great lengths to resolve misunderstandings, for fear I would be disliked. I realized fairly quickly that I couldn't do this job with that attitude.

We also inevitably had our internal conflicts, some of them private, some more public. It was an invitation for sceptics to say that we quarrelled because we were women, 'and of course we all know women can't work together.' There's nothing to do with such a statement but shrug. We knew that any enterprise with passion behind it is bound to run into every kind of human feeling – love, hate, ambition, fear, competitiveness, envy among them. But it wasn't always comfortable.

Unquestionably we had a passionate common purpose. For all of us, Virago was always the 'other person in the room' when we talked and argued. An American publisher once told me how, walking into the Virago office, she had never felt such a sense of people completely focused, heads down, committed to and driven by what they were doing. It was not easy to work at Virago if you weren't driven, or if you thought slowly, or needed a lot of time to consider before making decisions, or felt oppressed by an ethos of speediness. But it was also a wonderful place to work, with an extraordinary sense of energy coming from everyone, each in their different ways; where passion, excitement and commitment, affection and support was plentiful, despite difficulties and conflicts.

In 1974, our first year of working together, Carmen and I had sat in each other's houses talking about our lives, about books, about feminism, reporting on manuscripts, laughing, sometimes drinking, a lot. When proofs of the famous *Hite Report* on female sexuality were sent to us, reporting on how 70 percent of women didn't have orgasms through in-out, thrusting intercourse, but had them easily with clitoral stimulation, we read it together with much drink and hilarity and, rightly or wrongly, decided to turn it down. We didn't always agree on books, but we respected each other's work and taste and I think this was the strength of that early list. I admired the breadth of Carmen's reading, her energy, her capacity to take on large enterprises – the wonderful four volume edited diaries of Beatrice Webb was her idea. She trusted my editorial capacities and knew the value of my contacts for the list.

By the time the list was launched in 1975 our relationship had already changed. No doubt the reality of the enterprise brought out in both of us characteristics which had been shrouded earlier. I thought she was too easily dismissive of people, she thought that I was too politically correct. When we met people together, I was quite often silenced by her. She was the begetter of the idea, the star of the enterprise, the person the press knew and wrote about. I didn't always find that easy, but my real difficulty was Carmen's need to marginalize my contribution, the insistence on using the word 'I', not 'we', the fairly constant pressure, as I saw it, for me to remain in a box of her making, not too visible to the world. To put it crudely, she thought I wanted too much, to have too much of a share in things, I thought she wanted everything, didn't really want to share at all.

Looking back, I felt something else. She had a certain power over me. She was sometimes a colleague, a protagonist, sometimes an opponent and, when we were in conflict, in my heart I felt that she was better than me, freer than me, bolder. I could easily lose faith in my abilities; she could frighten me. Even when I kept my end up, I didn't feel I fought well enough, felt that she had more tools than me. It took me a long time to discover my strengths (partly by discovering my weaknesses).

For some months I trudged up those stairs in Wardour Street every morning with gloom in my heart, still excited by the enterprise but daunted by the sense that I had to fight my corner so hard, that there was this tension to be dealt with, that it made me miserable. Several times I thought of giving up, but was encouraged by the few people I talked with to keep going: 'It's yours too,' they said. It didn't feel like it.

But we did manage to work together and it was not all tension. We were reasonably friendly and sometimes affectionate. But I think we were afraid of each other. Harriet was not – and was a genial presence. Carmen and I now normally kept our private lives to ourselves, though twice when we were alone in the office, working late, she showed me intimate letters. There were stories circulating about our 'quarrel', around our competitiveness and disagreements, many exaggerated and inaccurate. But though we had some good times together, were bonded by what we were doing, we never recovered our earlier easiness and it didn't get better. With hindsight, it was probably a mistake for her to share the enterprise with an equal.

I had my own needs and eventually I grew up and learnt to create my own territory.

25

MEANWHILE, FAMILY

B ILL WAS BY this time part of my life. He'd met my family, I'd met his. We all coped with this reasonably well at least on the surface. My mother liked him a lot, accepted him and never asked questions about how we lived. My father was more wary, sometimes patriarchal in the way he spoke to Bill, dealing with another quiet and intense Englishman who he couldn't really understand.

I went to see my mother in Oxford regularly at weekends on my own, staying one night but finding it difficult to stay longer – affection interrupted by irritability and with a longing to be listened to (I never seemed to give up on this) set in after a day. I usually drove her to the Randolph Hotel and we ate a four course Sunday lunch together, which she loved. She was pleased when I visited but on the whole impressively undemanding when I didn't.

Sometimes Bill and I went together; on one occasion, in the

early eighties, visiting when she'd had what seemed like a relapse into psychosis. Deeply withdrawn, she came to lunch with us in a local restaurant. She was completely silent and seemed full of anger. When the bill came she flung her purse down on the table. All our attempts to coax her out of the mood, get her to talk, failed. When later we walked by the river in Port Meadow, she refused to walk with us, shaking off our arms. We got back in the car and I, who was in my mid-forties, heard myself burst into tears and say: 'What have I done?' She said nothing, but it was a revelation to me about how I felt about her and had done for years – that it was my job to make her better and I was continually failing.

Over the course of that evening, when we went to the opera, she gradually relaxed and engaged in conversation a bit. I talked to Ruth and Peter about her condition, which they'd also noticed, but though we all encouraged her to go and see the doctor, she didn't go. My impression was that she'd do anything to avoid going back into medical care and hospital and who could blame her? And after about six months she emerged from this period of withdrawal and paranoid feelings and went back to a fairly stable state. She never went back to such a psychotic state again.

I was doing the usual balancing acts of a working mother, feeling guilty about either Kate or work. The time I had with Kate when Bill wasn't with me was good for us both. She had by now gone to secondary school, having had a term with Roger when she was twelve, in a huge school in Berkeley, California, where he was teaching. I went to California so that we could both be with her in her first days there. She loved it – this vast place with its concrete playground, looking like the school in *Blackboard Jungle*, the children there hugely diverse, the teaching excellent. She was offered drugs in the playground and learned how to turn them down! She loved America and would have liked to stay; coming back to Camden was a disappointment to her. She was a sparky girl, witty and mischievous – definitely not wanting to be defined in middle-class ways, making a point of not being defined as belonging to any particular group, some of her friends wanting to go to university, others uninterested in this route and often outsiders. She, like many middle class children at the time, introduced glottal stops into her language – she on a big scale. I loved her company and enjoyed her friends, she had birthday parties in strange places like swimming pools and I regularly made a birthday cake in the shape of a train, with Swiss rolls and icing sugar. She seemed not to mind that it was the same one every year.

In a piece on mothers and daughters in the *Observer* (we agreed to censor each other if we didn't like what was being said) Kate, who was fourteen at the time, ended her comments:

'My dad's a historian and I hate history. My mum's a publisher and I hate books. Reading – it's so quiet I have to have the radio on!'

(She did read and later became very proud of Virago. Those are the books of mine she wants to inherit. Her daughter Natalia said to me when she was ten: 'Mum says you made history!')

At the stage where adolescents are searching for their way of being in the world, Kate was becoming more aware of her origins and the complications of being adopted, leaving her at

With daughter Kate, on holiday in France, 1986

times turbulent and confrontational. I often confronted her back till Bill one day suggested I didn't have to do that – something of a surprise to me. We occasionally had noisy rows, though we made up quickly. It was often poignantly clear that she wanted to please me and Roger, for us to be proud of her. We were, enormously – as much as anything for having her own opinions, going her own way. It became clear very early that she had a magic touch with young children, who gathered round her spontaneously. And quite early in her teens she knew she wanted to be a teacher.

Back in England, she met my friends and authors, who often came to the house. Some of them were quite famous, but Kate was unmoved by that, sniffing out, as her generation did, any inauthenticity and egotism. She and I were close but she watched my activities in the women's movement at some careful distance, insisting on having her own independent view of things, once agreeing to talk about what it was like to be the daughter of a feminist at the ICA, where she was given rather a hard time by the large adult audience, who saw her as privileged.

26

VIRAGO - GROWING
THE LIST

A ND SO VIRAGO grew and branched in new directions. We started publishing new fiction, including translations from Russian, Swedish, Italian. Zoe Fairbairns was our first venture into what might be called feminist fiction. She had written her first novel when she was nineteen and, nearly ten years later, brought to us Benefits, a dystopian novel imagining life in Britain in the future, with a political party in power that has undone the work of feminism and returned women to the home. With its suitably chilling cover, the book made a large impact on young women and became in its own way something of a classic. Later Alexandra brought in new young novelists - Lucy Ellmann was one, Elspeth Barker another - and we published Pat Barker's early novels, discovered by Angela Carter.

We launched a series of practical health handbooks, we

Virago launch of Tatyana Tolstoya's 'On the Golden Porch', 1989, with Tatyana Tolstoya on right, Karl Miller, centre, Angela Carter left

published radical texts from America – Adrienne Rich on motherhood, Kate Millett on literature and sexual politics – and from Egypt, the memoirs of the emancipated Huda Shaarawi. In 1978 we published a sex education book, *Make it Happy*, about sex for young people without the moralising then usually associated with such a project. Jane Cousins became a close friend and stayed in my house for several months. Editing included fierce arguments late into the night – about the sexuality of children, the place of love, the age of consent. The book sold well; there were questions asked about it in parliament, and it was removed from several libraries – signs of success as far as I was concerned. *Finding a Voice* by Amrit Wilson was a landmark book about the divided cultural life lived by Asian women in Britain, told in their own voices. If women's voices had not been much heard, Asian women's voices had been even more silenced. *A Literature of Their Own*, a seminal study of 200 nineteenth and twentieth century women writers by the American academic Elaine Showalter, became a sort of bible of lost women writers.

And 1978 was the year when the Virago Modern Classics began – a library of reprinted women's fiction, novels forgotten, out of print, unavailable, the principle behind it the same as our non-fiction reprints. The series, edited by Carmen, became the most widely known part of our list. It began with *Frost in May* by Antonia White, a searing story of a Catholic girl's experience of school, and Carmen formed a close relationship with Antonia White which lasted till her death. The famous covers were created by a young designer who only a year later was killed while climbing. Carmen and Alexandra meticulously researched the pictures to go on each cover. It was one of the wonders of the series that authors who were still alive and whose books had been out of print for decades – Rosamund Lehmann, Sybil Bedford, Molly Keane, Nina Bawden, Rebecca West – saw their work revived and read and admired by a new generation of readers. Distinguished introductions were written by women (and even the occasional carefully selected man) who had often led us to the books – A. S. Byatt on Willa Cather, Victoria Glendinning on Rebecca West, Hermione Lee on Edith Wharton, Paul Foot on Olive Schreiner, Germaine Greer on Henry Handel Richardson, their passion and eloquence helping to raise the dead and make visible the disappeared.

❧

I went on marches, holding placards, the right of women to control their bodies, more day nurseries. I went regularly to Greenham

Common with Bill, who was a passionate nuclear disarmer. In the early eighties we took Grace Paley, the brilliant short story writer who'd become a dear friend, with her wild grey hair and soft Brooklyn accent and her belief that 'life is long and art is short.' She pinned badges on the women who'd been arrested that day, gave them all a hug. On another visit we tried to shake the wire fencing down, one time succeeding triumphantly despite policewomen banging our hands with their truncheons. We organized a 24-hour protest 'readathon' on the steps of St Martins in the Fields against cruise missiles, Paul Foot, Raymond Williams, Ahdaf Soueif among the writers doing their twenty minute stint. At 11.00 p.m. a group of angry homeless men arrived as Sheila Rowbotham was reading, started throwing the chairs around and calling her a cunt, at which she protested in her mild way. They felt their dilemma of homelessness was much more important than nuclear missiles. She sympathized but was indignant at being called a cunt.

Grace Paley, writer, political activist, Virago author at my London home, 1987

In 1981 we commissioned *Over Our Dead Bodies* edited by Dorothy Thompson, against nuclear bombs. Two years later, two thousand people flocked to Westminster Central Hall to celebrate the publication. During 1981, I sent the journalist Bea Campbell to follow in the footsteps of George Orwell. The result was *Wigan Pier Revisited*, a compelling account of the changes in working class life since Orwell's *The Road to Wigan Pier* came out. Around the same time the serene Janina Bauman and her daughters walked up the stairs to our office with her manuscript *Winter in the Morning*, a heart-breaking account of her adolescence in the Warsaw Ghetto.

In 1983 I read a review in a feminist magazine of a book by Maya Angelou, a Black American writer, *I Know Why the Caged Bird Sings*, a coming of age autobiography of the young Maya, about racism and trauma and how a love of literature helps her overcome them.

Intrigued, I asked to see the book when I next went to New York, read it, loved it and bought it from her editor Bob Loomis at Random House for £1,000. It turned out that Maya Angelou's friend Jessica Mitford had been trying to persuade British publishers and agents to take the book ever since it became a bestseller in the US thirteen years before. No one, it seemed, thought the story of a young black girl growing up in Stamps, Arkansas, in the 1930s would be interesting to a British public.

When we published *I Know Why the Caged Bird Sings* in 1984, we flew Maya Angelou over. I'd never met this six foot tall, deep voiced woman with the amazing chuckle before. I took her to lunch at Mon Plaisir in St Martin's Lane. She was warm

Maya Angelou at US President Bill Clinton's inauguration,
20 January 1993. Courtesy, William J. Clinton Presidential Library

and charming. She looked me in the eyes and said 'Ursula, you bought my book and I will stay with Virago for ever.' A piece of steak got stuck in my throat half way through the meal and in my spluttering embarrassment I rushed to the lavatory, choking. Maya rushed after me, banging on the door, shouting that I must come out, I could die if I shut myself away. I emerged, she banged me hard on the back and I recovered.

We printed 6,000 paperback copies of *I Know Why the Caged Bird Sings.* We got Maya on to a couple of afternoon TV shows. The 6,000 copies were gone in two weeks. We printed another 6,000 and again they went in ten days. Bestsellers aren't always predictable. It finally dawned on us that we had one on our hands. We printed 40,000. Maya performed in huge sold out venues in Lewisham, Camden, the audiences filled with young people, black and white. Middle aged white male professors went on TV to extol the book's virtues. We had parties, she cooked for us, we danced with her, she held centre stage wherever she went. She was her own 'phenomenal woman.' My three-year-old granddaughter Charlotte attended a big party at the Dorchester for her. Charlotte had never seen anyone like this tall, charismatic black woman, singing and dancing and followed her around all evening. She now has a daughter called Maya.

Some years later I stayed with Maya in North Carolina. Maya took me to her local church – the heart of the black community and as Maya explained, the place where black people could feel safe. The place was packed; I was one of six white people in the congregation. Maya performed, singing, reciting her poems 'Still I Rise', 'Phenomenal Woman,' the gospel choir sang and tears poured down everyone's cheeks, especially mine.

More people joined the company, all very talented – quiet, witty Lynn Knight, ironic Deirdre Clark. Later on Ruth Petrie, Melanie Silgado, both formidable editors and Susan Sandon, quietly authoritative in publicity. There were no longer just five of us. The atmosphere in the office was as ever brisk and hardworking, not very relaxed, sometimes very tense, with occasional weeping in the lavatory; strong friendships were formed which flourished mainly out of the office – too much tension inside it – in cafés, our houses, where guffaws of laughter were regularly heard – often about life at Virago, about ourselves, about feminism (did we think it right to shave our legs? How did we deal with jealousy in our lives?

Should we reissue *The Sheikh*, the famous desert romance with hints of racism and sexism?)

Our readers were bonded by the row of green spines on their bookshelves. The *Guardian* said 'It's not too much to say that Virago changed English reading habits for ever.' And from the beginning the Virago Modern Classics in particular, but also Virago Travellers, Virago autobiography and our other rediscovered titles produced a flood of letters from readers – comments and suggestions from friends, relatives, writers, advisors, readers, bookshops, academics, publishers – one of the most collaborative of publishing ventures.

Something like a hundred proposals for books arrived at the Virago offices each week, some full-length manuscripts, some outlines. On Fridays I piled them into bags and carried them to my car. I left the office after lunch, picked up Kate from school and drove to Paddington station, where I parked the car on the platform and caught the train to Oxford to take Kate to Roger for the weekend. He brought her back on Monday morning for school. I sometimes stayed for a brief supper, then back to London that night. It meant I didn't often have Kate at weekends and I felt the loss. But I continued to feel the need to make it up to Kate for not having her father there all the time. And I wonder sometimes whether I could have done the Virago job without those weekends. On weekdays, I often kept Kate up late so that I could see more of her. Then I would work.

This was an early issue between Carmen and me; she was worried that my having a child prevented me from getting the work done. It took some years for her to accept that our bio-logical clocks were different – she rising at the crack of dawn, me working till the small hours. Harriet once drily observed, 'the work/life balance at Virago was not impeccable.' At Virago we were hardworking, driven, excited, obsessional. There were no concessions made for children – I remember my envy when our talented Australian colleagues at McPhee and Gribble told me about their arrangements for childcare in the office. It's no accident that I was the only woman with a child at Virago for its first ten years.

Proposals came pouring in, but few of the books we published came through the letter box – most were found through contacts or word of mouth, sent by agents or suggested by friends and ad-visers. In our second year of independence I turned down a book by a man, saying we were publishers of women and was immedi-ately reported by him to the Equal Opportunities Commission, who wrote us a stern note. I learnt to be careful with my wording.

※

In the early years Carmen and I regularly drove up motorways early on Saturday mornings to large feminist conferences in Man-chester, Birmingham, Liverpool and, closer to home, London, setting up our stand, talking to women we'd never met some of whom became future authors or readers and to women of all kinds of feminist persuasions, mostly supportive ('It's so wonderful to see shelves of books by women in bookshops'), sometimes hostile ('your books are too expensive', 'not radical enough', 'should have brown paper covers'), Carmen often taking out her knitting while we manned the stand. Britain led all other countries in feminist publishing in the late Seventies and early Eighties. At one point there were eleven in Britain; no other country compared. We regularly met European and American feminist presses, especially at the Frankfurt Book Fair where we had our first, small stand – all we could afford – in 1976.

That first time we travelled by train, third class, wooden seats. Later we went by plane. On one occasion I caught a taxi with two colleagues. Sitting in the back, I rolled the window down for some air. The driver started shouting – '*Nein, nein, mach zu!*' and swinging his arm round to the back, rolled the window up again. I was outraged at his authoritarianism and I heard myself saying: 'I expect you were running one of the camps in the war.' My companions froze. Who knows whether he understood. He said nothing. And eventually I calmed down, horrified at the extent of my rage.

I loved everything about the Frankfurt Bookfair, the breathless half hour meetings, the bustle, the frankfurter buns overflowing with mustard, the parties and particularly sitting up late into the night with European and American publishers, talking about the state of the world and discovering the books being published in every corner of Europe, in Paris, Belgrade, Prague, Milan, Munich.

We had about twenty books in print by then. Two tall women in expensive sweaters and long grey leather boots came by to the stand – our first meeting with the French feminist house des femmes. They were already producing many books in the classic

European style – elegant paperbacks with subtle, small low-key illustrations on the cover. We asked them where they got the money to do so many books. One of them looked at us sharply and said: 'It is all a question of politics.' We felt suitably put in our place, though we discovered later that one of their number had a father in the oil business who was supporting them.

The feminist presses operated in very different ways. The Feminist Press in the US had one person at its head who made all the decisions about what was to be published. The Dutch press Sara was a co-operative and eleven women had to come to an agreement about each book they took on. The German presses operated in the same way. Our way of working was different. Carmen and I read manuscripts, talked to our advisors and talked to each other and to Harriet about why we wanted to publish them. It was our personal tastes which created that early list. And that tradition continued when later there were more editors commissioning books. Though Carmen and I had difficult arguments, we never argued about the books we wanted to take on, even when we didn't share each other's taste. We were both in our late thirties, we'd both read a lot and we trusted each other's judgement. We tended to publish what felt right to us. We of course made mistakes about what would sell, but we rarely did about what was worth publishing (though we did translate a disastrous novel, *Manrape*, a runaway bestseller in Sweden). And there were dramas – commissioning someone we thought was an Asian woman writing short stories for young adults, who turned out to be Toby Forward, a male curate of the Church of England. There was a huge public argument about all this: we pulped the books, the right decision, though not everyone thought so. And some sad scenes – Jennifer Dawson throwing her rejected manuscript out of the office window.

Perhaps the most magical aspect of those early days as an independent publisher was having the power to publish what we wanted. Virago was unusual as much as anything for being in control of its own money and therefore of its decision making and its destiny. There were plenty of women in publishing in the early seventies, many in publicity and rights, some in editorial, but only three in positions of real power – Olivia Gollancz, who had inherited Gollancz from her father Victor; Norah Smallwood, the doyenne of Chatto & Windus and Paula Kahn at Longmans.

We were keen to be good businesswomen as well as utopians. Our books were to be available and desirable. We kept the cover price as low as possible. In this last we were part of the early days of the B-format paperback; where it wasn't feasible to print vast quantities for a mass market, we could print a larger size paperback for these more literary books which still kept the price reasonable. These paperbacks are now commonplace, but in the early Seventies were relatively new. And the market was there for our books. In the early days we sold mainly through the more alternative and independent bookshops. That changed when our own publicity, the women's movement, the breadth of our list and customer demand took the books into the high street shops.

The bigger battle was to reach the young, especially young women. Our work to make our books part of mainstream culture included efforts to take our books into schools and universities, to make contact with teachers and examination boards, with people who set the curricula. It was an uphill struggle, not helped by the phrases that permeated the culture, used about authors from Jane Austen to Christina Stead – 'women novelists', 'female imagination', 'small domestic world'.

We had inherited a literary world where Leavis's *Great Tradition* (though he did at least include some women writers) and men's writing dominated. Second and third rank male writers were chosen for the exam syllabuses rather than women novelists who, with a few exceptions, were seen as peripheral. Even when they were admired, there was a belief that women authors wrote on a small domestic canvas, the implication being that they didn't attend to the larger matters in life: Anthony Burgess famously described Jane Austen as lacking 'strong narrative thrust', something that Mary Ellmann mocked brilliantly in *Thinking About Women*, one of our early reprints.

We rejected this view of a women's ghetto vigorously.

By the mid-Seventies new debates around women's lives, their histories, the choices available to them were beginning to filter into the educational world. Virago's early oral histories, autobiographies and diaries became essential texts for students in the humanities, arts and social sciences. Beatrice Webb's brilliant diaries, Mary Stott, the first Women's Editor of the *Guardian*, Dora Russell's educational radicalism, Storm Jameson with her passionate internationalism and, later on, Kathleen Dayus's inside view of a life lived in dire poverty – all demonstrated the scale of women's contribution to understanding social and political life, issues of war and peace, poverty and education. While often speaking in the first person singular they brought to light experience of whole social groups or classes. The autobiographical element brought new registers of experiences to their books – accounts of friendship, birth and death, children, work, abortion, loving the wrong men and the right men (these women were particularly good at examining love). The personal in their hands did not remain simply personal, but informed the political culture – one of the most important ideas coming out of the second-wave women's movement.

When Virago began in the 1970s, ideas were not much seen as women's realm and it was particularly difficult for women to make their presence felt in the intellectual world. Assisted by our advisory group, we found young authors, many of them now distinguished professors, but then not even on the lowest rungs of the academic ladder, who were writing books of great originality which challenged and in some cases dismantled established ideas, striking in their boldness, winning prestigious prizes and continuing to influence today's generation. *Landscape for A Good Woman* by Carolyn Steedman, Denise Riley's *War in the Nursery* and Barbara Taylor's *Eve and the New Jerusalem* are just three examples of such books that eventually penetrated academic syllabuses. And it was not just individual books that changed things, but the cumulative effect of many books in many genres – fiction, politics, philosophy, history – which augmented each other and encouraged a rethinking and rewriting of the culture and women's part in it. Our readers, who had continuing conversations with us, told us all about that.

Gradually the list fell into shape and grew. And trust was at the centre of this build up. Not only did we trust each other, but our readers trusted us. In the early years many booksellers told us that people came into the shop and asked for the latest Virago books. By the late Seventies people began to recognize what we represented by our name – we had become, like Penguin and Mills and Boon, a brand publisher. Our readers made us; we were married to them.

27

THERAPY

I N 1977 I turn forty. I think: I've managed not to go mad by
the age my mother first went into a mental hospital. I decide
to risk having some serious therapy.

There are perhaps other reasons why I chose this moment.
Freud and therapy were for some of us in the women's movement
mirrors of that time – when personal liberation included possibilities of loosening our anchorage to the past, exploring the self
through the medium of another person, seeing identity not as a
continuous thread but as ever-changing relationships.

People don't go into therapy unless they're driven to it – it's
not an easy process. I still felt a dread of going mad; I felt overbur-
dened and irritated by my mother's needs which were still largely
addressed to me. I still easily fell into anxiety and self-reproach.

In 1977, I also fall in love with Bill Webb, the man who introduced the adult me to Berlin. He's a good listener and understands,

because of his own circumstances, my situation with my mother. He helps me write a letter to my sister and brother. I write saying that though they are good to my mother, I was carrying too heavy a burden of looking after her needs and if they didn't help with that more, they'd have me on their hands. My brother responds helpfully, my sister more anxiously. I think she is frightened that my mother has affected my life in difficult ways and doesn't want the same to happen to her.

Bill also encourages me to talk to my father. So I take him to lunch and for the first time tell him what it had felt like to be so needed and relied upon by my mother, so involved with her troubles, and his, from the age of twelve. It is cruel of me – I gave him no warning – and he is uncomfortable, resisting some of my account. But he listens and agrees to lend me money for therapy.

I visit Nina Coltart, the brilliant psychoanalyst, who talks to me and then assigns a psychoanalytical therapist to me.

Twice a week, I arrived at the elegant grey terraced house in Wimpole Street at 8.30 in the morning, sat in the waiting room until the buzzer went and walked upstairs to Mrs Chesser's consulting room, where she was waiting at the door. I walked over to her red chaise longue, lay down and gazed at two delicate landscape water colours – hers as it turned out, she told me that much about herself when I asked, but little else. She sat behind me.

Mrs C was a gently spoken, elegant middle-aged woman. I saw her twice a week for seven years and I have only the vaguest memory of what it was like and even at the time had little sense of what my sessions with Mrs C did for my understanding of myself.

A good deal of what we talked about was triangles. Bill was

married, and with some variations we lived a life in which he
divided his life between his wife and the family and me and Kate.
We shared many things – a love of literature (he was a literary
editor), mothers who were mentally unstable, left wing politics.
It was a passionate relationship. I found 'sharing' him difficult
at times and didn't like the practical negotiations involved. But I
knew also that I needed time to myself and with Kate. As often
seemed to be the case in my relationships with men, the important
thing for me was to be present in his thoughts, to be aware that
someone was thinking lovingly about me, bearing me in mind. It
was sometimes easier than his presence.

Kate liked Bill and accepted him easily enough, though I sometimes wondered whether she had much choice in the matter. I
knew that at times she found him quite patriarchal towards her.
But crucially for me, he very quickly loved her. I felt some guilt
about his wife and family, whom I met from time to time, but not
a lot – mostly I felt it was a matter between them – and though
we both from time to time felt we couldn't manage the situation,
our relationship went on for seventeen years.

One rainy winter morning in February, in my second year of
therapy, I lay down on the couch and started talking about my
bouts of despairing anger, the rages I had felt from the age of
twelve and which went on intermittently into my adult life. I'd had
a row with Bill the evening before – perhaps unsurprisingly, the
rages were emerging more in my time with him. I shouted at him
in the middle of the night, reproducing, I realized with horror,
the shouting of my own parents in the night. I was so ashamed
and so keen for Kate not to feel what I had felt, I went to her

bedroom to reassure her, telling her what the row was about, that she needn't worry. All she wanted to do was to get back to sleep! But she found my angry outbursts really difficult, though they were rarely addressed at her.

I described how the anger burst out uncontrollably, usually an accumulation of extreme irritation, of feeling utterly misunderstood and a fear of some kind of abandonment or loss. It could be disconcerting– the suddenness of it, apparently coming from nowhere (though there's no such thing), the explosive nature of it. Dear friends who weren't even recipients of it laughed a little nervously and said – it is rather sudden, Ursula. It was almost always directed at men I loved.

Mrs C talked about feelings of abandonment coming from early childhood, but was also quite silent. Silence was difficult for me. I filled it. I wanted to know 'who I was', that I wasn't going mad, that it was okay to be in a relationship with Bill, that my anger wasn't going to devour me.

Many years later, in the Nineties, I went into therapy again with a psychoanalyst who was trained as a strict Freudian but who'd completely rejected the rules, the psychoanalytical hierarchies and internal disputes of the profession. He was eccentric, articulate, life-enhancing, old, confident and had the kind of insight and empathy which helped me to believe that I could deal with the darknesses, that they weren't surprising and that I might not be the only person in the world who experienced them.

The setting couldn't have been more different from Mrs C's. Each week he opened the door to me in his pretty house in North London, a cheery, shambling bearded figure who led me upstairs to his tiny room. Sweeping the two cats off the couch, chaotically gathering together the music lying on the music stand and on the floor, he beckoned to me to lie down and sat next to the couch in the revolving chair, pencil in hand, a few scruffy pieces of A4 on the table.

It was this 'Old Man', as I came to call him, who took on the black holes I experienced, the thought that nobody but me ever felt this way and that it was my fault, who skilfully delved into my early life, his sympathy palpable. He was probably the first person who allowed me to feel I had had a difficult childhood and that it was hard to deal with, that though my mother was to be sympathized with, I carried a considerable burden. He dug deep and, relating some of my behaviour (anger, despair, black holes) to childhood distress, convinced me, if I hadn't been before, that unresolved problems of our early years can continue to haunt us in adult life. And at the same time he held me safe. He understood my lifelong difficulty in resting in the moment, my need to think constantly about what was going on, what would happen, always trying to work out what everyone was feeling.

Often on my way to therapy I'd think – what on earth am I going to talk about? I felt I had to deliver something to him, to make my life interesting for him. I rarely remembered dreams, something I felt was a failure in itself. And it wasn't enough to be me – and slowly, through therapy, I realized that I felt this in many of my relationships.

Gradually he made me a bit less prone to apologise, or to pour everything out to people in case the 'disaster' I was experiencing would eat me up if I kept it to myself. Slowly, slowly, I sometimes found ways which allowed me to reassure myself at bad times – to internalize some sort of 'good mother' who told me it was not all my fault, I was not a total failure, that I was not the only person in the world with black holes, that I wasn't going to lose myself or my mind.

On Sunday mornings the 'Old Man' played the accordion in a café on the high street. With his delighted permission, I took my daughter and granddaughter to hear him and introduced them to him – breaking all the rules of therapy. A huge pleasure for us all. I told a friend about him and he went to see him – more breaking of the rules.

I've had therapy occasionally since he died, ostensibly to help solve a particular problem, though it often turns into more. Most recently, I sat in a chair opposite my therapist. I still hardly ever remember my dreams. I've been bolder in expressing anger. I've felt very comforted by this particular therapist's recognition of some sort of self in me, not a sharp identity, that he's uncovered. He's explored my resistance to fantasy, to free floating talk or saying something spontaneously crazy for fear it will take me to the edge. He too has been hugely helpful. And yet the edge is still what I think defines me, though I still don't necessarily recognize a particular 'self' running through my life like a thread.

I often leave the session with a powerful single line of his in my head, as I did with the 'Old Man', which beautifully clarifies something for me. Words can change lives.

28

VIRAGO'S FUTURE

I N 1982, AN announcement was made in *The Bookseller* that
Virago was to become a wholly-owned member of the Cape,
Chatto and Bodley Head (CBC) Group.

Behind this public announcement lay a history of a long, difficult year. We had been thinking about finding a larger distribution
and sales team. In 1981, the Chairman of CBC, Graham C Greene,
approached Carmen about becoming the Managing Director of
Chatto & Windus. It was a huge compliment to her and she was
very interested.

Only Carmen, I and Harriet had shares in Virago at that time.
Having talked to Carmen about his proposition, Greene turned
his attention to Harriet and me. He talked about how exciting the
prospect of Virago joining the group was – we didn't disagree –
and added, moon-face beaming, that it should be an easy thing for
us all to agree on, 'perhaps taking a week or two.' It took a year.

The conversations between Carmen, me and Harriet were quickly tense. It became clear that Carmen wanted to subsume Virago into Chatto & Windus; Harriet and I profoundly disagreed – we felt that we'd lose the hard-won and by now high profile of Virago and some of its independence. Though Carmen had the most shares, Harriet and together could outvote her. We agreed to take on a lawyer, a friend of Carmen's, to work out an agreement between the three of us.

After a few weeks it became clear that it wasn't working and Harriet and I decided we must hire our own lawyer. It was a painful situation; we all agonized and shed many tears. Bill listened to me patiently at the end of days when I worried over nuances of what we'd said to each other, wondering how we'd ever resolve seemingly impossible arguments. Harriet and I were agreed on the fundamental things, Carmen disagreed with the two of us.

The difficulties between us, especially between Carmen and me, came to the surface. They were of course partly arguments about power, about who controlled what. Virago was certainly the fourth person in the room, but we had differing views of what was good for Virago.

In the end Harriet and I couldn't bring ourselves to vote against Carmen and take over Virago, even though some people, including Faber's Matthew Evans, strongly advised that we should, that our lives would be much more difficult if we didn't. But Virago had been her idea, her initiative and we couldn't face so much blood on the floor. Some compromises were made and the final agreement, made in 1982, was that Virago would be a separate subsidiary company and fourth member of the Cape, Chatto and Bodley Head Group, now called Chatto Virago Bodley Head Cape. Carmen would remain Chair of Virago and become Publisher at Chatto & Windus.

More conflicts followed: Carmen wanted Harriet to be Managing Director of Virago, while I would be Publisher, a vague and unsatisfactory role. I refused this. Harriet and I agreed to become Joint Managing Directors. The whole was a pretty unorthodox and messy solution.

I found these conflicts difficult, unsettling; I was sometimes angry, sometimes unsure of my position, sometimes frightened of where they would end. But I now felt some ownership. And somehow bearable compromises were made. And Virago remained a separate company, which for Harriet and I was the crucial matter.

So Virago, the feminist company, the upstart, the outsider, became something of an insider – a member of the group of the most distinguished literary publishers in Britain. In a way it was what we'd always wanted – to be both outside and part of the establishment. Gradually we recovered from the year of conflict, some wounds difficult to heal. We continued to be profitable, our books were visible and regularly reviewed and were beginning to win prizes.

❧

Being part of the CVBC publishing group gave us distinct advantages in terms of profile, sales and distribution. But by 1985 there were disquieting signs, reported to us by Carmen, who represented Virago on the main board. The Group was losing money, lots of money. By 1986 the Virago board – Harriet, me, Carmen, Alexandra and Lennie, were beginning to consider buying ourselves back. Alexandra and Harriet were pregnant with their first children. We talked about the possibility of selling the company. We consulted Bob Gavron, who suggested we contact N. M. Rothschild to see if they'd support a management buyout. They sent two charming young men to see us, who liked what they saw and we started negotiations. Our reputation was high, we were part of a zeitgeist which people saw was interesting. Other publishers had begun to see that feminist books sold.

The Group was resistant to our leaving. The conversations between Graham C Greene, Tom Maschler, the two managing directors of CVBC and our board, with Bob Gavron present, were tough.

And then in the middle of these negotiations, with the news that the CVBC Group was £3 million in the red, Random House US swooped down and bought CVBC and us. It was, as Lorna Sage observed in the TLS at the time 'raining Magritte city men with umbrellas and bowler hats.' The value of our individual shares rose from about 40p per share to £7.74. I was able to buy Kate a student flat in Brighton and a magical fourteenth century house by the river in Languedoc for the family.

But we didn't want to stay in the Group, insisting on the buyback continuing, threatening to resign if they didn't allow it. These negotiations with the new owners were even tougher. In the end we won the right to leave, the shares divided between N. M. Rothschild, Bob Gavron and Random House, who continued to sell our books, retaining 10 percent.

And so to new offices in Camden Town and independence once again. It felt fine. We were, in city-speak, 'washing our own faces.' New talented people joined the company; we survived a stressful time when two directors were on maternity leave at the same time; I loved working with my colleagues, I had found my own territory and it was much easier to work without the regular tensions with Carmen.

It was the late Eighties and the world was changing. We knew there'd be a time when Rothschilds would want to be sure that they'd make their money back, to pursue an 'exit strategy.' They visited regularly, asked lots of questions, exchanged friendly banter. They had been genial owners. And gradually they began to plan their exit strategy, to put more pressure on us. In late 1989, at a dramatic meeting of the Virago board, Rothschilds made it clear that they thought that Alexandra should lead the company sooner rather than later. It was an emotional event, touching on anxieties and frailties for us all. Inevitably, whatever we individually were thinking about the future, we felt some divide-and-rule element in the negotiations and there were tears in the bathroom afterwards. And then, just as we were setting off for home, Alexandra looked at her hand and said 'I've lost my ring!.' So for the next two hours, in a state of great agitation, Alexandra and I searched through black rubbish bags in the basement of Random House for a precious ring she thought she'd lost (it turned out she'd left it at home).

In the event Hamish Hamilton offered her an editorial job soon after, which she took. Bob Gavron bought 51 percent of the shares from Rothschilds. In mid 1990 Mark Fisher, the MP for Stoke on Trent and Shadow Arts Minister, offered me the job of Cultural Policy Advisor to the Labour Party, a new job made possible by funding from Paul Hamlyn, which I took. It was time for a change. There was, after all, a world outside Virago. After seventeen years, I was leaving.

In January 1990 my father died. He'd been unwell for some years, following his prostrate operation and it was never quite clear to us, his children, what was going on. He became very withdrawn and started shuffling, a complete contrast to his ebullient energetic self. My stepmother was reluctant to talk about it. He died in hospital near the Augustinum where they lived. My stepmother rang my uncle first, as the person who was in charge of the family business, then my brother, then me and my sister. I was anxious to see him before he was cremated and though my stepmother agreed to that, she said we must make our own arrangements. Telephone calls to the crematorium resulted in his body being laid in a sort of garden shed with a curtain. It was a scene straight out of Hamlet, the gravedigger pushing us gruffly in the direction of the shed. My sister, myself and my nephew Thomas went in to see him. I was glad to have done it.

The family in England all went together in a plane to Frankfurt, Bill correcting my brother's German in his speech. Peter spoke, then I read 'Fear no more the heat o' the sun', very quietly, not much projection. Afterwards several women from the Augustinum came up to me to say that they hadn't understood a single word I'd said.

With sister Ruth (on right) at her son Nicholas's wedding, August 1997

None of us children know where my father's ashes are buried –
somehow that too was something my stepmother didn't talk about
and we didn't press her.

And then the last Virago sale.

By the end of 1990 Virago was being run by Harriet and
Lennie. In the early '90s it struggled; the market was tough, the list
and the staff numbers shrunk. Kate Gavron, me, Tim Waterstone,
Carmen were on the board. In 1992 Bob Gavron suggested Carmen
as Chair should go in and help the company out, which she did
somewhat reluctantly for a few months. Early in 1993 she wrote a
fax to the Gavrons to say she wanted to come back on the board
and make various changes, which they didn't reply to. By that

summer there was a document circulating in the press which criticized the Virago board, and said the company should be sold. By this time Bob Gavron had no stomach left for this turmoil and we all agreed to sell. I'd meanwhile been offered and taken the job of Chief Executive at *Index on Censorship*.

In the end there were two serious bidders for Virago – Bloomsbury and Little, Brown – which both presented their cases to the staff and the board. Carmen told Harriet she would not attend the meeting at which the decision would be made.

About twenty people gathered round the large table in the Random House boardroom in Vauxhall in the late spring of 1995 – staff, shareholders, Gail Rebuck representing Random House. Everyone round the table was asked for their comments about which company they thought would be best. There was much talk and some striking lack of transparency. A vote was taken. Bloomsbury won by a small majority. At this point Harriet left the room to ring Carmen, who was in her house in France. Ten minutes later, Harriet came back and said Carmen was voting for Little, Brown. That tipped the balance away from Bloomsbury and towards Little, Brown. The decision was made.

When I left the boardroom, it was dark outside. I made a phone call from a telephone box to a friend, told him the story, wept a bit and went home, feeling a mixture of relief and sadness. Relief because I was by now enthusiastically engaged in running and reviving *Index on Censorship*. Sad because some of our ideals – Virago as a collaborative concept, avoiding and defying corporate norms – didn't seem very present at this point. It wasn't the happiest way for my connection with Virago to end. But I suppose at the time it reflected its strengths and weaknesses, its energies and its conflicts. And though it has always remained at the heart of my working life, at that moment I knew I'd moved on.

29

THE VELVET REVOLUTION, PRAGUE 1989

O N T H E S H O R T walk from the airport to the bus, I, who never felt the cold, was silenced by the bitter chill of a Prague December that penetrated even my thick winter coat. Bill had met my plane in the afternoon, found a public telephone in the arrival hall of the airport and called his friend to get instructions. The bus put us down by the river near the Charles Bridge and under leaden skies we got a taxi to the flat just beyond the centre of the city, in a shabby middle-class suburb, grey blocks of flats, villas with peeling paint, piles of coal on the pavements.

The rooms in the first-floor flat were small, lit by the dim 40 watt bulbs so familiar in the Eastern Europe of the time. Plastic sheeting covered the wooden floorboards; the furniture – chairs, small settee, was in shades of brown, beige and yellow. It was a gloomy little place, with only the small balcony giving any sense of space. I felt, perhaps with my central European genes, immediately at home.

In the bedroom the two truckle beds were covered with enormous white eiderdowns. And the flat was warm, wonderfully warm and we went straight to bed and made love in one of the beds, under the eiderdown. Afterwards, Bill found the kettle in one of the wooden kitchen cupboards and made some tea and we lay in bed, drinking, talking intensely as we always did after an absence. We'd been together twelve years by then and were to be together another five.

And then, as recurrently happened, the talk turned into a quarrel. What about? About freedoms, mine and his; about divided lives; about how I chose to live with him though at times I was fighting my own divisions – needing to have time alone on the one hand and the recurrent frustration and pain about not having Bill to myself. (Though I never found the fact that a person might love someone else as well as me particularly unbearable. I had loved two people myself).

The only person I've lived with full time is Roger. When I left our marriage, I began, at first without quite realizing it, to live with men without living with them full time. Gradually I saw that though I wanted to be in a loving relationship I needed time and space to myself. For good or ill, I found myself choosing a sort of freedom as opposed to a certain kind of safety.

And when we quarrelled in Prague, I stormed out on to the street saying I was leaving, was going home on the next flight, although I knew I wouldn't, knew it would pass. And even my anger didn't keep me warm for long, so after half an hour of pacing the unfamiliar and empty streets I came back, we hugged and comforted each other and dressed to go out for the evening.

It was the day before New Year's Eve. Bill, who as well as being literary editor had continuously reported on Eastern Europe for the Guardian, had been in Prague for a week, reporting on what turned out to be the death throes of the communist regime. On November 17th, eight days after the fall of the Berlin Wall, a student protest against communist rule had been violently put down in Prague. The next day, theatres went on strike and students occupied university campuses. Within days hundreds and thousands of people were on the streets. By the end of the month, the Communist Party had agreed to hold free elections. When Bill arrived in late December the drama students had staged a sit-in; they were chased out of their building by the police, who beat them severely with truncheons as they ran up the street and tried to hide in shop entrances. It was a last futile attempt to hold on to power the communists no longer had. By the end of the month dissident playwright Václav Havel was elected president by the country's Federal Assembly and democracy was restored.

Václav Havel's party at the time, Občanské forum, had a small office in the main street between the university and the opera house. By the time I arrived in Prague, there were candles in the shop entrances lighting up the spattered blood on the glass and the office was filled with young students handing out posters, their excitement barely suppressed, as if they'd been doing this all their lives.

New Year's Eve is always a big celebration in Prague. We had left it very late, walking round Wenceslas Square on the day, calling in at every restaurant and hotel to try and book a place for supper. Everywhere was full. We managed to squeeze two places in the Europa Hotel, agreeing to share a table.

At 8.30 p.m, the square was already filling up; Havel was due to appear at midnight. The dining room at the Europa was crammed with noisy diners. We were sharing our table with a young couple – he a small squarely-built Italian from Pisa, she, Olga, a glamorous Czech woman with huge bouffant hair, black kohl round her eyes, wearing a spectacular black satin strapless dress. She went to fix her make-up every half hour or so and each time she crossed the room there were crude hoots and catcalls from the men diners. It dawned on us that she was a hotel escort. At first she was unsmiling and extremely wary, particularly with Bill, but slowly he managed to charm her into talking. The Italian turned out to be her boyfriend who visited twice a year. We talked about what was happening in Czechoslovakia, about his life as a manager of a restaurant in Pisa, we ate a traditional meal of duck, roast potatoes, red cabbage and apple sauce, drank to each other's health. Olga went on regularly fixing her make-up, the catcalls continued, but by now we were having a comradely New Year's Eve dinner and she seemed much more at ease. At 11.00 p.m. we said our goodbyes and went out into the square, now teeming with over-excited people, young and old, talking, shouting, laughing, hugging each other, friends, strangers, everyone.

We stood on small stone walls to survey the milling crowds in the long rectangular square, first staying on the edge of the crowd and then trying to make our way into the middle, embraced and embracing, the little bottles of glühwein hung round people's necks

Bill Webb with Kate, France 1986

regularly offered to us. I've never experienced such an expression of public happiness.

This was a world that Bill understood, better than me.

The Left in Britain had not been particularly concerned about censorship in the Seventies and Bill was a rare example of someone who understood why the Czechs hated the word socialism, how to them it meant repression and silencing, not liberation.

We stayed till 3.00 in the morning. Havel appeared briefly at some point, by then we'd stopped noticing the time and the cheering became ecstatic. Gradually the crowds thinned. We walked the two miles back to our tiny flat, too excited to sleep. When we got back to the square at 10.00 the next morning for breakfast, it was spotless, swept clean of the bottles and paper, as if the celebrations had never been.

January 1st was another bitterly cold day and we sat in the unheated Cathedral for two hours for a celebratory service, till we could bear the cold no longer. That night we wheedled our way into the Opera House, standing in the aisles as they performed an obscure opera by Smetana, Libuša, only performed at times of great national importance, the music uninspiring, a lot of belting out from the front of the stage. In the small single boxes above the stalls sat Václav Havel, Jiří Dienstbier, Alexander Dubček, looking dazed, fiddling with their unfamiliar ties; a strange and dreamlike sight, symbols of the extraordinary transformations of the Velvet Revolution. Czechoslovakia had rid itself of the monolith, had moved in from the cold of Soviet Communism and was soon to begin a life inside the different cold of capitalism.

30

LABOUR PARTY YEARS

O N T H E E V E N I N G of April 2nd 1992, I was in my clut-
tered living room, collecting my things together, papers,
books, preparing to drive Mark Fisher round the country as the
Shadow Arts Minister for the 1992 election, planning to go as far
north as Kendal and south down to Plymouth.

My time as the Cultural Policy Adviser to the Labour Party
began in 1990 and ended in May 1992. Labour had been in opposition for thirteen years and I, who'd had no direct experience of
parliamentary politics so far, quickly became aware of the deep
frustrations of not having executive power. It made me understand up close the lengths to which political parties will go to
gain power. Fascinating too to discover the reverence MPs were
shown, above all others, in that place, with a good deal of forelock
tugging. Their researchers, bright and ambitious, doing research
work on which MPs relied, also kept their ears and eyes open to

what was going on and talked, gossiped, speculated over lunch to each other about their respective bosses. I learned about the extraordinary constituency work that MPs do, week after week, the significance of parliamentary committees, the shifts in power inside parliament, how to fight our corner, how to collect databases, how to negotiate working with other MPs. I regularly visited a friend who was working in Neil Kinnock's kitchen cabinet and got a worm's eye view of how the leader of the opposition operated with his special advisors – in a very small space! And, having worked outside parliamentary politics till then and feeling distanced from it, I increasingly felt respect for the difficult job Neil Kinnock was doing.

My job was new – based entirely around the money given to the Shadow Arts team by Paul Hamlyn. So we were left unusually free to invent it, to do what we thought would make most impact. We wanted to take the temperature in the arts around the country.

Since 1990 we'd produced two books for Penguin, one by Mark Fisher and Richard Rogers on the future of London, another a collection of essays on cities, edited by Mark Fisher and me; we'd organized a series of lectures on the future of the arts, Liz Forgan and Robert Hewison among the speakers. Our conference about women in the arts, The Missing Culture, touched on all the ways in which women and their perspectives were marginalized in the arts and drew a huge audience; Mark had developed a dance policy, an architectural policy, a design policy, a libraries policy and we'd disseminated the information in a series of seminars and meetings. I encountered worlds unknown to me – librarians fighting to keep their buildings open, architects passionate about improving public spaces, dance schools trying to reach young people with talent but few resources – deeply moving and tireless commitment everywhere. We thought we might win the election.

That sunny April evening Mark was due to go on TV, to do battle with the Tory Secretary of State for the Arts Tim Renton. I went upstairs to have a bath, came down and opened the fridge. Mark said: 'I think I'm falling in love with you.' I said: 'Shit.'

It was a shock. I'd been looking forward to a week discovering parts of England I'd never been to, travelling with this genial, bald, round, charming and exceptionally well informed and well-liked Shadow Minister for the Arts, engaged in an exciting and unpredictable election which was raising our adrenaline levels to new heights. I didn't want this complication.

I had a nervous, sleepless night and hungrily ate toast and swigged coffee to allay tiredness before setting off next morning. The week turned out to be as revealing and exciting as I'd antici-pated. Mark drew large crowds in his meetings; poets, playwrights, painters, novelists, artists of all sorts met him in every corner of England, wanting to talk to him, telling him how much they wanted a Labour government, how much they admired his com-mitment. I hovered on the edge of the crowds, it was Mark they wanted to see and no one else would do. We stayed in hotels with high-ceilinged bedrooms, brown carpets, plum-coloured curtains, setting off on the road again after a cooked breakfast to the next venue. And by the end of the week we'd become lovers, in my case apprehensively. I was with Bill, Mark was married and I had no idea where this was going.

I drove to places and through countryside that I'd never seen – Barrow-in-Furness, Nottinghamshire, the Forest of Dean, Torquay – encountering a bewildering range of people who bundled off Mark and me to his speaking engagements – becoming aware of the mass of people who worked for the Labour Party locally, who organized these events quietly and without fuss, who felt huge affection for this party. Neither of us seemed to get tired – there's no adrenalin like election adrenalin.

On our return to Stoke, Mark's constituency, his eldest daughter joined us and we spent a few days canvassing on a tough council estate, Labour voters mainly, but some pretty disaffected ones; nobody minced their words, on the doorstep or over a cup of tea, about Labour's failures to deliver.

Back in London, a few days before election day, there was a glamorous party for the London arts community at Millbank, filled with writers, musicians, artists; there was expectancy and wild enthusiasm. Neil and Glenys Kinnock walked down a ramp with her parents to what could only be called rapturous applause. Somehow the room thought we were winning. And the polls were still putting Labour ahead, if only slightly. But there'd been the Sheffield rally, the John Smith budget and John Major's calmly confident tour of the country with his soap box. Mark and I both knew in our hearts by then that we weren't going to get in.

Back in Stoke on election night, Mark won his seat easily, with an increased majority. We sat up most of the night, Mark and I and his daughter, watching the results on TV, getting sadder. The morning after was gloriously sunny and warm. We went for a walk on the moors, not talking much, the disappointment hard to bear. And Mark and I had our complicated secret, warming us at the same time as it troubled us.

31

INDEX ON CENSORSHIP
AND THE YUGOSLAV WAR

IN 1983, DURING the Thatcher years, I commissioned a book at Virago on women gardeners by Dawn MacLeod, a formidable gardener herself. In the chapter on Vita Sackville West, she wrote a sentence praising Mrs Thatcher. When I came to edit the manuscript, I crossed the sentence out; I didn't want a Virago book out there in the world extolling Thatcher. Dawn MacLeod objected and insisted it went back in. I resisted. She took the book elsewhere.

The problems of censorship were not high on the agenda in seventies and eighties Britain. I knew something about the work of *Index on Censorship* through Bill, who knew the magazine well when it was run by the impressive George Theiner. For me it was interesting but relatively unknown territory. That was to change completely when in the spring of 1993, four years after the fall of Communism, I found myself, to my surprise, accepting the job of Chief Executive of *Index*. Surprised because I hadn't expected to be offered the job – I was not a journalist, unlike the other applicants and it was not my world. But I found myself increasingly excited at the notion of what this magazine might be – about its political and literary possibilities – in a post-communist world. Amazingly quickly, I was plunged into issues that had been no part of my life, into a world of international journalists, lawyers, activists, aid workers, people very different from the publishers and politicians I was familiar with.

I quickly discovered that the human rights world was not one where solidarity played much of a part – too much competition for funding, too many egos competing on overlapping territories. But the staff at *Index* were committed and passionate about the magazine surviving. And despite being in deep financial and circulation trouble when I arrived, we did survive and flourished.

1993 was also the year my first grandchild was born, Charlotte, followed at various intervals by three more. It is a magical relationship, being a grandparent. I was juggling a life with two men at the time, both of whom wanted to see this new baby, so I went down with each of them. Kate had had a difficult birth, but looked very happy. The baby was adorable. When she was about one, they came to live near me in London. So I saw a lot of her in her early life, taking her for walks around the neighbourhood, sitting with her in local cafés. Pushing her in her pram one evening when she was two and a half, we wandered over Hampstead Heath at sunset. Each time

Yang Lian, Chinese poet, at Index Awards Ceremony 1997. © Susan Greenhill

we climbed a hill, or turned a corner, the sun disappeared and then reappeared. Charlotte was enchanted, her eyes lighting up, shouts of pleasure each time she saw the magical sun again.

As I talked with colleagues and friends, It became clear to me that *Index* must be an arena for debate, about silencing as well as censorship, about all the unofficial, unnoticed ways in which free speech is suppressed – voices and lives that are absent, deemed unimportant, journalistic self-censorship, financial pressures, government secrecy – as well as the more obvious ways – censoring people's work, imprisonment, exile, death. We would have the best writers and the most radical ideas – something *Index* had always had.

Our themes covered everything from intolerance to widows to homosexuality to building walls. As I talked to my trusted colleague

Judith Vidal Hall we were aware that there was almost no subject where free expression wasn't relevant. Each issue concentrated on a particular country file. In our relaunched edition of 1994 we published Umberto Eco, Salman Rushdie, Ronald Harwood, Naguib Mahfouz, Dubravka Ugrešić, James Fenton, Alberto Manguel. Jon Snow offered to take a copy to Nelson Mandela just after his election as President of South Africa in 1994. He took the copy from Jon and said 'It's changed its format.' He'd been reading *Index* all those years on Robben Island.

We took on a PR firm, Colman Getty, who did well in publicizing us. It meant I had to appear on the media more than I was entirely comfortable with – *Any Questions*, *Start the Week*, *Woman's Hour*, the World Service; but I got used to it and even began to enjoy it. I was on *Newsnight* in the early '90s, discussing with Michael Ignatieff and the military historian John Keegan the possibility of bombing Saddam Hussein. Jeremy Paxman seemed much more at ease with the men than with me. I brought up Israel/Palestine but it was swept aside. When I got home, feeling I'd done badly, there was a message from Edward Said on my phone congratulating me on my part in the programme, how right I'd been to bring in Israel/Palestine etc. I felt hugely grateful for his friendship!

❧

It was a new world we were living in. The void left by communism was not necessarily being filled with democracies and thriving economies, but new states, in their search for social and economic identities, were tempted to assert these through the rise of nationalisms, xenophobia, intolerance, racism. Meanwhile, the silencing of women and minorities continued and the amplified power of the modern media raised questions about whose voices were dominating and whose suppressed.

The biggest influence on me was Ronald Dworkin, who said 'Free expression is what makes people feel human.' Though I was almost but never quite an absolutist as far as free expression was concerned – to the dismay of some in the free expression community – Dworkin's absolutism profoundly affected me. His argument – that in a democracy each citizen should have not just a vote but also a voice, was convincing:

> 'A majority decision is not fair unless everyone has had an opportunity to express their attitudes or opinions or fears or prejudices, to confirm his or her standing as a responsible agent in rather than a passive victim of collective action. It is unfair to impose a collective decision on someone who has not been allowed to contribute to the moral environment by expressing his political or social convictions or tastes or prejudices . . . The temptation may be near overwhelming to make exceptions to that principle – to declare that people have no right to pour the filth of pornography or race-hatred into the culture in which we all must live. But we cannot do that without forfeiting our moral title to force such people to bow to the collective judgements that make their way into the statute books.'
>
> (from *Index on Censorship*, May/June, 1994)

What Dworkin taught me was that it's easy to be in favour of free expression if you agree with what's being said. What's difficult is listening to, not silencing, opinions which are alien, unsettling, which one may dislike or even hate. People may not say what you want them to say or live the way you want them to live. But they have to have their voice.

My friend Hugh Brody in his work with indigenous people went further: he was convinced that it is at the margins that we find the meaning of the centre - where we hear particular stories about huge things, about the possibilities of change, of visibility for the invisible, of re-entering history.

Dworkin was a very active member of the council at *Index* and gave me endless encouragement and support. He wrote a much quoted article in our relaunched magazine in May 1994, 'The New Map of Censorship', in which he introduced the idea that freedom of expression as a fundamental human right was being challenged not only by freedom's 'old enemies' but also new ones, who claimed to speak for justice, not tyranny, who pointed to the need to protect people, if necessary by censoring, from hate speech and racial hatred in particular.

Hate speech is speech which attacks a person or group on the basis of gender, colour, ethnic origin, religion, race, disability or sexual orientation. The debate about hate speech and whether it should be censored was one that continued throughout my fourteen years at *Index*. For me it was the one problematic issue as far as censorship was concerned. The absolutists argued that dialogue and democracy are more effective in understanding the anatomy of hate than silencing. In theory I agreed, but in the face of too much twentieth century history they perhaps required us to believe too simply in the power of democracy and decency and rationality. At the end of the twentieth century we were faced once again with an outburst of hatred and destruction based on racial and religious differences which all but destroyed former Yugoslavia, at least temporarily – hate speech as propaganda, as a calculated and systematic use of lies, hate speech sowing fear and violence.

I arrived at *Index* two years into the Yugoslav wars, a series of ethnically-based wars and insurgencies which lasted till 2001 and accompanied the break-up of the Yugoslav state.

In December 1995, the highly contentious Dayton Peace Agreement was signed which brought to an end the fighting between Serbs, Croats and Bosnians, creating an independent Bosnian state divided between two entities, the Muslim-Croat Federation and the Serb-held area, Republika Srpska.

I had been to Serbia with Bill at the beginning of the war, my first encounter with war up close. I was not brave about it and it was frightening to see the military men wandering around town, drinking in the hotels, hung about with medals and weapons. But I was determined to overcome at least some of my fears.

It was the grimmest of wars. The Nobel prize winning author Ivo Andrić reflects in his novel, *The Bridge Over the Drina*, written during Hitler's war, on what had happened to his world after August 1914:

'People were divided up into the persecuted and those who persecuted them. That wild beast which lives in man and does not dare to show itself until the barriers of law and custom have been removed, was now set free. The signals were given, the impediments eliminated . . . Violence and plunder were tacitly permitted, even killing, on condition that they could be perpetrated in the name of higher interests, under set slogans and on a limited number of people, of a definite name and persuasion'.

I was fascinated by it all; we published a lot in *Index* about it and I went there several times – to Belgrade, to Sarajevo, hitching a lift in a land rover from Zagreb, driving through this beautiful countryside of rolling hills, meadows and fast-running grey rivers, where each village we drove through was either completely destroyed or half destroyed – the houses standing being lived in by the perpetrators of the destruction.

And then in late 1995, just after the Dayton peace agreement was signed, I joined a convoy of buses organized by the Helsinki Citizen's Association to travel from Split in Croatia to Tuzla in Bosnia. HCA's goal was to integrate Europe from below, to establish a pan-European civil society. A conference was planned in Tuzla, to support the social-democratic mayor and Tuzla as a model of local democracy in Bosnia-Herzegovina. Around six hundred people gathered in Tuzla from ex-Yugoslavia as well as from the rest of Europe and beyond.

Our group consisted of eight buses filled with journalists, film makers, lawyers, academics, human rights activists from Bosnia, Serbia, Britain, America. We set off early in the morning from our rather grim hotel in Split, crossed the border from Croatia into Bosnia and drove in convoy through the scorched landscape and shattered villages, stopping for lunch at a café where a lamb was roasted for us on a spit – I've never tasted such fresh lamb. As we wandered briefly down a country lane two women came to ask us if we would post letters for them to their relatives; all postal services had stopped and they had no way of contacting their families to tell them where or how they were – normal life had disappeared.

And on through Mostar, where the famous old bridge had been blown up and as we looked across the river, we saw the Eastern part where the Bosniaks were based had been demolished while in the western Croatian part the roofs and houses were more or less in place.

The drive to Tuzla took twelve hours. We stopped to pee every now and then – women only and then men only – on the tarmacked road, because the sides of the roads were still mined. What we saw in this beautiful and tragic landscape was what Andrić described – the results of a pathological civil war where the 'others' whom propaganda hate speech had indicated as the legitimate object of your fears and fantasies, people you must drive away, slaughter, eliminate are people known to you – your neighbours, even kin by marriage – now made alien and terrifying by the unreason you have been infected with. The houses, streets, villages from which Muslims, Serbs or Croats were driven were not simply ruined by arson and looting; after the fighting they were systematically crushed and destroyed with bulldozers and dynamite. So hate speech resulted in one of the ultimate forms of censorship; the obliteration of the memory of a place as if those lives and communities had never been.

We arrived in Tuzla late at night, exhausted. The bar at the tower block hotel was open and sitting there surrounded by papers and bags and queen of all she surveyed was Susan Sontag, who had come to the conference by a different route.

The conference was extraordinary, gripping: speakers giving their accounts of the war - Bosniaks, Serbs, Peter Galbraith representing US policy - were graphic and forthright. They listened to each other attentively and represented all perspectives of the war; workshops on women, nationalism, fundamentalism, peace-keeping, humanitarian intervention, conflict resolution, the Roma, the role of the media, refugee rights in Europe. There was a moment of outrage when Susan Sontag, feeling she was not being listened to, said she was not just there for decoration, 'unlike Julie Christie.' The evening was spent in Café Bloom, where Michael Ignatieff and Ferenc Miszlivetz hosted an evening with writers Adam Michnik, Susan Sontag, Pierre Hasner, Timothy Garton Ash.

The next day local visits were arranged - to industries, regeneration projects, schools, hospitals. And a poignant visit to the graveyard to pay homage to the scores of students who'd been killed by a bomb in a local restaurant weeks earlier. After the closing speeches and rally on the third day, we climbed back into our buses. Some scuffling to try and sit next to Julie Christie and off we went. It had been a moving and hugely enlightening conference and I was trying to order my thoughts about what I'd heard.

We reached the border between Bosnia and Croatia, a small café by the side of the road and several fierce-looking Croatian guards coming out from the checkpoint. We were the last of the eight buses to go through. Our bus carried Britons, Americans and Serbians. Immediately the border guards demanded the passports of six of the Serbian journalists. They insisted they had to be sent to Dubrovnik to be checked. The Serbs refused to hand them over. What quickly became clear is that no one was in charge, no one had any authority or directions, not even a phone number of the organisers of the conference. There was much discussion and argument as to what should be done, tempers rose and suddenly there was chaos. During the impasse, when the passports were not handed over and the Croatian guards refused to let the bus go, people reacted in their own particular ways – some went to sleep, some drank a lot, some gathered outside to talk and argue and try and persuade the Croatians, some huddled together in their seats. This went on for some hours and then suddenly the chair of HCA, Mary Kaldor, appeared in a car. She had gone from Tuzla back to Split in a helicopter and clearly felt she had to do something to rescue the situation.

Eventually we set off, arriving back in Split well after dark, to be greeted by the news that a Serbian lawyer in our group had been arrested and taken off – he was held for a few weeks, it turned out and had probably been betrayed by the hotel staff. It was a horribly uncomfortable and frightening situation and many of us felt helpless and foolish about it all. We left early the next morning for the airport and England. I've never been back to Croatia.

32

FRANK AND THE WORLD
OF LITERATURE

I'D WANGLED MY way to a supper party with my friends the
Alvarez's, knowing Frank Kermode would be there, curious to
see him again after a brief introduction many years earlier, when
I'd found him attractive and quietly fascinating. That autumn
evening in 1997, Frank was wearing a brown double-breasted suit,
looking sombre, his face rather haggard. He was a tall man, well
built, benign-looking, spectacles. We talked, mostly about Stephen
Spender, a friend of his and the founder of *Index on Censorship*
which I was running at the time. He was charming and courteous.

We met again at a concert soon after – my invitation; he
started staying with me overnight and then I'd go to Cambridge
for weekends ('I'd like to lure you to Cambridge when the daffodils are out') and gradually we began a relationship which lasted
twelve years.

Frank Kermode, left, with friend and poet Al Alvarez, 2002

For me it began with very different expectations and desires from previous relationships. I was sixty. I worked in London and had a busy social life there, he was in Cambridge, retired but writing, always writing, connected to King's College. We both had children and I had grandchildren. He'd become accustomed to living alone, often quoting the advantage of 'being able to lie diagonally across my bed' (*Tristram Shandy*). I wanted a relationship in my life where we would have holidays and weekends together but not be together all the time. A love and a friendship where, as part of daily life, we would bear each other in mind. He was seventy-seven, I was sixty. I didn't find the age gap easy, but I realise, now that I'm past that age, how fit and energetic he was, how much he was prepared to do things, try things, without flagging.

And so in the late Nineties I entered his world – of literature and criticism, novelists and poets, of literary journalism which he hugely enjoyed, of academe which on the whole he didn't. I had never much loved academic communities myself; in my time with Frank in Cambridge this hardened into a more pronounced dislike – of the pettiness of the quarrels, the lack of generosity, the shrinking of the world into matters of Cambridge departmental matters – all things of which Frank was not guilty. And King's College, Frank's college, was unstuffy and dinner and feast days there were fun – especially when his friend Tony Tanner was alive. Frank was very good at including me in and I didn't feel overshadowed by his stardom.

I never learned to love Cambridge – it seemed to me cold in all senses of the word and very inward looking – not much interest shown in the world outside even by friends of Frank's who I liked. Frank didn't like it much either. He looked back with particular affection to his time as the Northcliffe Professor at University College London. So, I asked, why did he go to Cambridge. 'Vanity, probably. Terrible mistake.' 'Disastrous' was a common word he used when reminiscing about his life, about which he was often sardonic. Reticence was part of his make-up, but when we were alone together he would often open up and wanted to talk – about his professional life, about his marriages and his children, about whom he felt a strong sense of guilt, often explaining at length the circumstances which led him to make the decisions he had made. He didn't ask me a lot of questions, but listened attentively when I told him stories about my life.

He could be savage about pomposities and unpleasantnesses in academic colleagues, generous about people he admired even if he disagreed with them. There was a sweetness about him, but also a rod of iron and a kind of coldness, which, when I encountered it, I found very hard to negotiate and sometimes I caught trains rather than try and deal with it. He hated any hint of being criticised, or of my being cross – what he called being 'scolded'. He was unbelievably modest about his learning, his breadth of reading. He never stopped being interested in new ideas. But always behind them what mattered was the text, the writing on the page, the unique quality of every piece of writing he talked about. When he passed novels on to me that he'd been sent for review, all I saw was faint pencil lines throughout, rarely with comments. I asked him once how these minimal marks ended up as such extraordinary, coherent, original reviews. He rather pooh-poohed the notion that there was anything special, magical about the transformation. And when I once suggested that his reading of so many novels over his lifetime must have given him a deep understanding of how people relate to each other and to the world, he said 'Oh, I never thought of that'. His wry melancholy was always lurking, as was his sense that his life was a series of failures and that his often-gloomy expectations would be fulfilled.

Frank thought we couldn't entirely make sense of our lives but that literature could attempt 'the lesser feat of making sense of the ways we try to make sense of our lives. Fictions, unlike myths, are for finding things out and they change as the needs of sense-making change.' He was drawn to whatever opened up the literary work to the richest possible reading experience, hostile to anything that blocked that response in the name of non-literary concerns. He taught me a lot about how to read and I fell in love with his writing.

His range was impressive, his most constant scholarly interests the literature of the sixteenth and seventeenth centuries, especially Shakespeare, the Metaphysical Poets and Milton. Always open to new ideas, at University College he set up a famous graduate seminar and invited speakers on the new, often French theoretical developments, though later he became more critical of these ideas.

In the 1980s he fought a very public losing battle over 'theory', which he didn't himself support particularly but objected to the resistance to all intellectual change in the Cambridge English Faculty, a place 'exceptionally hostile to any kind of thought at all' I remember him saying. One morning, he told me, dispirited by the constant feuds, he woke up and thought 'I don't have to do this any more.' So he took early retirement from Cambridge in 1982, holding visiting posts in America and becoming a regular contributor to literary journalism in the United States and in Britain.

The pace at which he worked was astonishing. I arrived in his life when he was writing *Shakespeare's Language*, which became a commercial as well as critical success. He was unwell at that time, with recurrently bad bouts of asthma. One night he woke at 3.00 a.m. and was breathing with great difficulty. I said I was going to ring the doctor. The idea surprised him – 'how can you do that at this time of night?' The doctor came with the nebuliser and the next morning Frank was back at his desk.

In his quiet way he took an interest in my world – at that time human rights and free expression – and always read my editorials on request – making careful, rather modest suggestions. I once showed him a sonnet written by my thirteen-year-old granddaughter. He said quietly – 'I'd be proud of my granddaughter if she wrote that – but it's not a sonnet!'

Since his divorce from his second wife, Frank had lived in a light, airy modern apartment, filled with books, pictures and prints, a short walk from his college. The block was inhabited by quite a few elderly people and visiting dons. He called it 'the hospice', but despite the carpet that lined the walls of the lift and a certain stiffness in the decoration and atmosphere, he liked it.

Our weekends followed a certain pattern. He was usually leaning nonchalantly against a pillar when I arrived at the station; and then off we went shopping to Waitrose, Frank picking up each item I chose from the trolley, asking 'what's this?' (His own eating habits were deeply ingrained). In the evening it was the opera from New York, while I cooked the evening meal, then at 10.30 p.m, *Match of the Day*, with its tribalism and rituals – which Frank denied he liked but always watched. (He was an Arsenal fan and on his eightieth birthday 'Happy Birthday' Frank Kermode came up for him on the enormous screen beside the pitch, organized by his friend Tony Holden, a passionate Arsenal fan.)

On Sundays we walked in the flat, rather dull Cambridgeshire countryside, sometimes driving deeper into the Fens, with lunch at a pub or with friends. His children came from time to time, Frank might make bread in the afternoon, something he'd learned after his divorce. A good TV play in the evening, or reading. It was a quiet, orderly life and in many ways it suited me, though I did sometimes get restless. We travelled together, but for Frank travel was not for its own sake but always for a work project or to pick up an honorary degree or to visit friends and colleagues.

My mother never met Frank. She died in 1998. I think she felt somehow a bit vindicated, having been so unwell for so long, that she had survived longer than my father. She had been unwell and rather agitated for some months and by now she had a young woman living in her flat to take care of her. It was difficult to find such a person and though she was perfectly pleasant I always felt badly that we didn't manage to find someone warmer and a better companion for my mother. We were beginning to think we should consider a home for her. We said nothing to her about it at all. A week later she woke up, sat on her commode and died.

It was spring and I was on a trip to Italy with my friends Alexandra and Rick to a surprise birthday party for one of Alexandra's authors. We were on a small local train in the middle of Italy, chugging along when the phone rang. It was my daughter, sobbing, to tell me my mother had died. My first thought was to get off at the next stop of this local train and go back to Rome and England. But Alexandra and Rick persuaded me that her death was being attended to by my brother and sister and that they would look after me for the few days in Italy. It was a strange time, but they looked after me brilliantly, though the birthday party didn't work out well and there was a lot of emotional drama.

When I got back to England I saw my mother's body; she was cremated in Oxford Crematorium with a service conducted by her beloved vicar and quite a number of friends present. The crematorium scattered her ashes though they were asked not to. So I'm not sure where either my father's or mother's remains are buried.

The same year my mother died, Frank and I went on our first trip together, to the Yeats Summer School in Sligo, where he was giving a paper. Characteristically, when he opened his folder in the plane, he found he'd put the wrong lecture in. Equally characteristically, he simply set about reconstructing it as soon as we got to the hotel and did it in the quickest time.

After Sligo we drove down to Coole Park and the Tower at Ballylee, where, surprisingly, he'd never been. It was a soft, grey Irish afternoon. We walked in Coole Park, which Yeats called 'the most beautiful place on earth' and then stood and counted the swans. We could only see nine.

In 2001, I was diagnosed with breast cancer. Frank was, according to his friends, very distressed but concealed this from me fairly successfully. I was due to have a mastectomy; one night in London I had a dream that my breast had been cut off, woke in a panic, clutching my breast and thought 'I can't bear to lose it.' In the morning I rang Frank to tell him about it and to my surprise he said: 'Go with the dream'. So I did, and postponed the total mastectomy, though in the end I couldn't avoid it. He was wonderfully unsqueamish about the whole business.

In 2003, I wanted to show Frank Berlin. We'd been together for six years. Simon Rattle had given us tickets for his concert with the Berlin Philharmonic – Haydn's *The Seasons* – and afterwards we had supper, Simon buzzing with adrenalin, in a small restaurant in Berlin Mitte. The next day, the Iraq war started.

As ever, I felt this huge attachment to Berlin, which never

failed to make my heart beat faster and to excite new thoughts. We walked round the city, under the monumental Brandenburg Gate, just south of the rebuilt Reichstag Building, the entry to the long avenue of linden trees Unter den Linden and I was conscious of the resonances this place must have for Frank, who, as a conscientious objector nevertheless fought in the Second World War, believing he had to fight the Nazis, hating it. As it turned out, I'm not sure how much Berlin did resonate with him. Perhaps he wanted to keep it to himself, or perhaps he didn't feel much – who knows? I didn't ask him and he said very little. The war – he was in the navy – had been a traumatic time for him. And yet it also opened up the world for him – he travelled extensively, to Australia, Algeria, America, meeting writers and poets and musicians.

In between sightseeing in Berlin – the Jewish Museum, the Gemäldegalerie – we watched TV in our hotel, gripped and horrified as the US began the invasion of Iraq, operation 'shock and awe', co-ordinating a satellite-guided tomahawk cruise missile strike, with British, Australian, Polish and Danish military support – so strange to be watching this spectacle of war on TV with this convinced pacifist.

Sport on TV was a big part of our lives. We watched it for hours – golf, snooker, tennis, cricket, football. He was immensely fit himself. He walked very fast. He played squash until he was eighty. His friend Wynne Godley wrote: 'How did I know that Frank wanted to beat me so desperately, seeing that he never revealed his feelings? Because his stride became maddeningly jaunty if he won more than two points in succession; because of his firm insistence, so gentle sounding, on the replay of dubious points; because of the way he ruthlessly and unerringly killed the loose ball.'

Frank patiently tried to teach me to play the game, but I knew, from his polite exasperation when he pointed out that I was using tennis instead of squash strokes, that he was longing for a real competitor. He bounded up the steep, rocky hill opposite my house in Languedoc until he was well into his 8os, furious when he had to slow down. And he meticulously did his exercises every morning. He loved dancing, especially with Anne Alvarez. He saw himself as clumsy and inept, when he was the most graceful of men, with the heart of an athlete.

33

BERLIN AND FULL CIRCLE

B ERLIN JULY 2015: we are walking round an exhibition in the Historisches Museum, called '1945', revealing the condition of eight European countries at the end of the Second World War. For my friends Mary Chamberlain, our first Virago author, and Sally Alexander, the distinguished historian and myself it's our fifth visit to this city together. We're tired; we've already spent two hours looking at the photographic and documentary evidence in a crowded room, reeling from the numbers – 50,000 dead, 27 million dead, 60 million dead.

The exhibition leaves me wondering again about the accidents of history, about being Jewish and German, about how it would have been to be an eight-year-old living among the ruins of Berlin instead of learning how to belong in suburban Putney.

And next day, a day of dark clouds and driving rain, we travel for an hour on a crowded train to Ravensbrück, the women's concentration camp. It's pelting with rain when we arrive and we take a taxi through the forest to the camp. We shouldn't have taken the taxi, it betrayed the women who had to walk to this grim place. It is so silent everywhere and we walk through grounds where we could see the remains of buildings that have been demolished, to the museum itself.

Bleak and chilling though it is, the curated rooms are profoundly moving about the women who were sent here, many of them unbelievably brave in standing up to the Nazis – the largest numbers from Poland and Hungary, and SoE women, prostitutes, Jehovah's Witnesses, Jewish women from all over Europe. About 50,000 women died there from disease, starvation, overwork, despair. Over 2,000 were killed in the gas chambers. Only 15,000 of the total 130,000 survived until liberation.

As we drive back through the forest to the station, I apprehensively ask the taxi driver what he feels about living near to this place. His answer is humane enough, he says times have changed, but terrible things happened here and he doesn't really understand how people can do these things.

✺

On our last day in Berlin after the usual prolonged and argumentative breakfast, Sally leaves early and Mary and I tramp from the S-Bahn stop Greifswalder Straße, along Mahlerstraße, Sibeliusstrasse, Smetanastraße to the enormous Jewish cemetery at Weissensee – more than 110,000 Jewish graves – and finally, on our third attempt and with the help of a sympathetic official and his maps, find our respective family's graves. Mine is a monumental stone structure for my great grandparents Elias and Flora Sachs, the coal king and his wife, a star of David at the head, some Hebrew writing and an elegantly carved fern leaf at the base. I weep – partly tears of relief at finally having found it, partly for my family that they should be part of this huge memorial to Jewish lives in the city. Mary Chamberlain's family gravestone is black marble, inscribed with the name, Arthur Peiser, her daughter's grandfather, married to Lilli Palmer the famous film star.

Berlin is back in my blood, alive in my head, as it has been every time I go back.

After our trip in 1981 to find my parent's flat in Dahlem, I had gone with Bill Webb to Berlin for a second time in 1983 and this time we cross over to East Berlin, via Checkpoint Charlie. We take the S-Bahn to Friedrichstraße. The lighting is subdued as we shuffle with many others down the stairs and into one of the channels – narrow, makeshift passageways. We wait; it's dark. Being held in these dank passageways is a grim experience (my father said his encounters with the checkpoint guards were worse than his dealings with the Gestapo); but it's hard not to feel for the unsmiling guards, who can't leave their country to go anywhere. There is an official ahead and we slowly move towards him, eventually handing over our documents and our money for the one-day visa for which we're given a piece of paper. We change some money, and suddenly we're on the other side and there are the people, East Berliners and the trams and the Trabant cars.

We walk past the ruined Adlon Hotel; it's snowing and there are rabbits running in and out of the remains of the place that was once so grand (and, though uninspiring, is again now). We search the Jüdischer Friedhof for family graves, but it's hard to read the names with snow covering the gravestones. We go to the Historisches Museum, where Bill is told by an official that he can't carry his jacket over his shoulder – '*Das is nicht gestatet*'. '*Warum?*' enquires Bill. The answer is instant '*Weil es nicht gestatet ist!*' On to a hotel on Unter den Linden for tea. I fall asleep in the armchair and am woken up by a waiter who tells me that if I'm tired I must rent a room to sleep. In the evening we walk to the Komische Oper to hear Kurt Weill's *Mahagonny*. In the interval, the corridors and outer rooms of the opera house are filled with stern unbending-looking East German officials, their wives wearing long dresses in brown and beige slipper satin. The opera is long and we have to run hard to get to the checkpoint in time for midnight, when the crossing closes. I'm frightened at the prospect of not making it – where would we go, what would happen?

In February 1985, I go to Berlin with Hugh Brody, who is showing his haunting feature film, 1919, at the Film Festival. One of its themes, using brilliant archive material, concerns the intriguing question about the extent to which it is someone's psyche or the history they live through that defines their life. It's a question he and I have often talked about. Hugh, also a Jewish refugee child growing up in England, is the person I've confided in most about assimilating, about trying to belong; we understand each other in particular ways. Paul Schofield and Maria Schell star in the film and come to the Festival. The four of us have supper together, a delightful occasion. Next day Hugh and I cross to the East and confess to each other that in some ways we feel at home in this dour, austere, unglamorous place. We are both war babies. He is wearing an elegant suede jacket; the look on the young waitress's face in the café where we have our sausages and sauerkraut for lunch is a mixture of envy, anger and admiration.

In 2011, visiting Berlin with a group of friends, I walk around Prenzlauer Berg, in old East Berlin, near the Weissensee Jewish cemetery. The art deco apartment blocks, with their elegantly rounded balconies and Jugendstil decorations have been beautifully renovated. I have for the past few years been intensely involved in founding and setting up, with the help of the visionary Erik Rudeng, Free Word, the centre for literature, literacy and free expression in London and I feel like a break. I have a sudden wish to rent somewhere for a few months in this neighbourhood, to recover more of my Berlin past. At the end of the next street is a handsome round water tower, about eight stories high, converted into flats. I look it up in the guide book and read that the Nazis used the ground floor as a place of torture. I can't face living in a street where I can see this building. I wonder whether I can manage to live in the area at all, where memories of the Nazis are so inescapable. But then Berlin is heavy with such memories.

On a rushed visit to the newly renovated Neues Museum on my way to the airport, I hurry to the gallery with the head of Queen Nefertiti of Egypt, joined only by a modest bust of my great, great uncle James Simon. It was he who had donated the head to the museum. He had sponsored the excavations in Armana and when the finds were divided up in 1913, acquired the head.

Her gaze goes through the rooms of the renovated museum to the south dome, where it meets the statue of the sun-dog Helios from Alexandria. I think of the photo I have of her head on my staircase at home, which always stirs me. And how lucky I am to be able to come here whenever I like and bring my grandchildren to see this head, which James Simon so loved.

⚜

A cotton magnate who had wanted to be a philologist, James Simon was in 1911 the sixth richest man in Germany. An assimilated Jew, he founded the Aid Association of German Jews in 1881 and supported a range of Jewish causes. He collected art though not Judaica. He bought Christian art – Venetian Renaissance paintings and medieval sculpture. His taste was broad; Luca della Robbia, Andrea Mantegna, Luca Giordano amongst many others. He funded archaeological digs in Egypt and Mesopotamia. The only collector who brought out more objects from Egypt than he was Napoleon. Unlike Napoleon, James Simon paid for the objects (though there has been regular pressure from Egypt for some of them to be returned).

His fortune and political connections made him a central member of the Kaiser Wilhelm Society, which acquired art and antiquities for state museums. He was a prodigious collector but more benefactor than hoarder. In 1920 he gave his entire Egyptian collection to the Berlin museum. Simon Brothers, the family cotton business, suffered badly when it was cut off from the American market in 1914 and it finally failed after the crash of 1929.

James Simon Gallery. © *Nicola Lacey*

His brother and business partner Edward, also a collector, sold all his art before shooting himself in 1930. It's not clear whether this was triggered by financial ruin or despair at the prospect of the Nazis. James Simon died in 1932, just before Hitler came to power, having donated all his art, 20,000 art objects, to Berlin museums before the Nazis had the power to steal it. His villa was burned when Hitler became Chancellor. The Kaiser put a wreath on his grave. Few remembered his legacy until, after reunification, his role in building Berlin's museums re-emerged. As I write this they are completing a wonderful new gallery, designed by David Chipperfield, dedicated to James Simon on the Museum Insel in Berlin.

At the end of the trip in 2015 we go to see Käthe Kollwitz's bold and heartbreaking drawings, of war, of friendship, of motherhood, in a small museum near the Literaturhaus. Its posh café is filled with writers, the women in stylish frocks, the men in black hats, smoking cigars. We find a table and drink tea and I'm trying to imagine myself as my parents, as part of an assimilated, acculturated Jewish family, who probably gave money to Jewish charities, who certainly felt Jewish as well as German but were secular and not interested in Zionism. I know nothing about the synagogues in Berlin; they never went. I had no education in the Jewish religion at all and the first Seder I attended was with my ten-year-old granddaughter in 2003, at the house of friends in London. I wish now I'd made an effort to learn more.

⚘

Old age has turned out to be surprisingly intense; decisions, sometimes quite momentous ones, always having to be made, about how to live, about health and illness, about going out or staying in, about travel, about children and grandchildren, about friends and how we're all adjusting to frailer bodies and failing memory. And it's busy – I know I choose it to be so, I always have I suppose, partly because I have a lot of energy and get easily engaged with things. And partly because I always keep an eye on warding off blackish holes, which I still fear. I've been a trustee of the South Bank, of Free Word, the Centre for literature and free expression I founded, of Reprieve, the fearless organization working to end the use of the death penalty and extreme human rights abuses, of English Touring Opera, which in the hands of the brilliant James Conway perform all over England, somehow managing the most wonderful performances on the smell of an oil rag. I begin to read poetry much more and as a trustee of the Ledbury Poetry Festival force myself to learn reasonably competently how to interview poets like Sinéad Morrissey and Margaret Atwood.

There are new friendships. And then, more surprisingly, there's love, new versions of love. I find myself in a relationship, hard to describe – an intense trusting friendship. I feel extraordinarily understood. It's complicated and sometimes hard and hard to work out, but deeply satisfying. In the course of it I seem to start dealing better with silences and absences, to feel safer and to trust more.

At the launch of Stuart Hall's memoirs in the spring of 2017, I look at the faces in the room – people I've known since the 1970s – and feel our political bonds and connections and disagreements, the echoes of our struggles with doubt, our optimisms and pessimisms, our confusions and passions, our attempts to make sense of the world and how to live in it. I think of my friend Grace Paley, the poet and short story writer: she tells of her lifelong friend Sybil, who is dying, with Grace sitting next to her holding her hand. Sybil turns to Grace and says 'Grace, there is only one question: How is life to be lived?'

At my eightieth birthday party the same year, surrounded by friends and family (including great granddaughter Maya) on a boat on the Thames hosted by Alexandra, my beloved friend from Virago, my daughter and all four of my granddaughters make speeches, read a poem by Maya Angelou, give me pictures they've painted. I'm deeply touched and particularly so since they seem to recognize who I am, even though I live a very different life from theirs.

I grew up in a German Jewish family whose history was profoundly altered by anti-Semitism, war and migration. I grew up with a mother who struggled with madness; I was a girl anxious to please, compliant, conformist, passionately wanting to belong, to be part of what I thought was Englishness. I lived through extraordinary times, in England and other countries. I learned something about resilience and fighting my corner. Becoming a woman in these times, I slowly discovered that I was in some ways inevitably an outsider. And that being an outsider has its advantages.

Sitting in that Berlin café with those close companions, I had a sense of full circle. I started my life in Berlin; now I visit it at least once a year. Strangely, in some ways Berlin feels the closest place to home.

ACKNOWLEDGEMENTS

THIS BOOK STARTED as a long essay, which Andrew Motion encouraged me to publish in the volume of New Writing he was editing many years ago. I had been an editor myself for many years, and never thought of myself as a writer. But the business of assimilation and belonging had interested me for a long time, and I decided I wanted to expand that essay into this memoir.

I have been supported and encouraged in so many ways by family and friends. They have read drafts, asked probing questions, given me invaluable feedback, had inspiring ideas, and talked with me for hours about the memoir and about life.

Over many lunches I talked with my brother Peter Sachs and sister Ruth Cecil, comparing notes about our family and our childhoods. Peter has done a lot of wonderful work on family portraits which he's published privately. I'm indebted to my cousin

John Cooke for his illuminating writings on my paternal grand-parents. My cousin Nina Grunfeld came back with razor-sharp comments on an early draft, which led me to much rewriting and for which I'm forever grateful. My daughter Kate was always upbeat, kept dipping in and assuring me that it was worth doing. My ex-husband Roger liked the writing, which meant a lot to me.

Clare Algar, Margot Badran, Mary Chamberlain, Esther Freud, Kate Gavron, Antonella Mancini, Marianne Mays, Jane Miller, Veronica Plowden, Leina Schiffrin, Natalia Schiffrin and Antonia Till all offered hugely useful comments and much encouragement. Chris Gayford and I read our books to each other over months. Gillian Stern asked probing questions and reminded me of my potential readers. I am deeply grateful to them all.

Long conversations with Sally Alexander, Hugh Brody, Liz Claridge, Adam Munthe and Alexandra Pringle over long periods revealed, amongst other things, difficult territories that I knew I had to face. I owe them a great debt for the loving attention they gave to my writing.

Thanks to Susan Greenhill and Niki Lacey for letting me use their photographs.

Thank you to my agent David Godwin, ever supportive and optimistic. And to my publisher, Christopher Hamilton-Emery at Salt, for taking the book on with so much enthusiasm and sensitivity, and for his warm and patient responses to my worries whatever time of day or night I was expressing them.

This book has been typeset by
SALT PUBLISHING LIMITED
using Neacademia, a font designed by Sergei Egorov
for the Rosetta Type Foundry in the Czech Republic.
It is manufactured using Holmen Book Cream 65gsm, a
Forest Stewardship Council™ certified paper from the
Hallsta Paper Mill in Sweden. It was printed and bound
by Clays Limited in Bungay, Suffolk, Great Britain.

CROMER
GREAT BRITAIN
MMXIX